THE LEGEND OF
Cornelius Vanderbilt Whitney

Cady Hill House
40 Geyser Road
Saratoga Springs, New York 12866
Telephone # (518) 584-2166
Fax # (518) 584-5897

My late husband, Cornelius Vanderbilt Whitney, was a wonderful man who did incredible things. I was fortunate to have been married to this man for 34 years. We had a great life together.

C.V. (or Sonny to his friends and family) used to tell me to never look back, always look forward. That was a philosophy Sonny believed, and the reason he kept innovating until the day he died. Because Sonny lived in the present and for the future, he was a success in so many ventures. He never sought credit, nor stayed idle looking back at the past. He asked me to do the same.

In 1997, I married John Hendrickson who had such respect and admiration for Sonny's accomplishments that he wanted to commission a book to be written about his life. At first I said 'no,' as Sonny did not want me to live in the past. But John insisted, saying that he felt a need to honor such a man, whether he was my late husband or not. In addition to paying for this book, John has spent hundreds of hours aiding this book to a wonderful conclusion.

The Legend of Cornelius Vanderbilt Whitney, by Jeffrey Rodengen, recounts the fascinating life of this Renaissance man. John and I are very proud of this project, and we hope you enjoy the quality of this book--and the quality in which Sonny led his life.

Best regards,

Marylou Whitney

THE LEGEND OF
Cornelius Vanderbilt Whitney

JEFFREY L. RODENGEN

Edited by Melody Maysonet
Design and layout by Jill Apolinario, Rachelle Donley, and Dennis Shockley

With love for Eric, Sabina and Zoe,
another family of great distinction.

Also by Jeff Rodengen

The Legend of Chris-Craft

IRON FIST: The Lives
of Carl Kiekhaefer

Evinrude-Johnson and
The Legend of OMC

Serving the Silent Service:
The Legend of Electric Boat

The Legend of Dr Pepper/Seven-Up

The Legend of Honeywell

The Legend of Briggs & Stratton

The Legend of Ingersoll-Rand

The MicroAge Way

The Legend of Halliburton

The Legend of Stanley:
150 Years of The Stanley Works

The Legend of
York International

The Legend of Nucor Corporation

The Legend of Goodyear:
The First 100 Years

The Legend of AMP

The Legend of Cessna

The Legend of VF Corporation

The Spirit of AMD

New Horizons:
The Story of Ashland Inc

The Legend of Rowan

The History of
American Standard

The Legend of Mercury Marine

The Legend of Federal-Mogul

Against the Odds:
Inter-Tel—The First 30 Years

The Legend of Pfizer

State of the Heart: The Practical Guide
to Your Heart and Heart Surgery
with Larry W. Stephenson, M.D.

The Legend of Worthington Industries

The Legend of Trinity Industries

The Legend of IBP

Publisher's Cataloging in Publication

Rodengen, Jeffrey L.
     The legend of Cornelius Vanderbilt Whitney/
Jeffrey L. Rodengen.
     p. cm.
     Includes bibliographical references and index.
     ISBN 0-945903-60-X

     1. Whitney, C.V. (Cornelius Vanderbilt), 1899-1992
2. Philanthropists — United States — Biography.
3. Millionaires — United States — Biography. 4. United
States – Biography. I. Title.

CT275.W5539R64 2000   361.74'092 [B]
                             QBI99-1349

Write Stuff Enterprises, Inc.
1001 South Andrews Avenue, Second Floor • Fort Lauderdale, FL 33316
1-800-900-Book (1-800-900-2665) • (954) 462-6657
www.writestuffbooks.com

Library of Congress Catalog Card Number 99-96784
ISBN 0-945903-60-X

Completely produced in the United States of America
10 9 8 7 6 5 4 3 2 1

TABLE OF CONTENTS

FOREWORD

by
Marylou Whitney

MY LATE HUSBAND, CORNELIUS Vanderbilt Whitney (Sonny to his friends), was said to be born with two proverbial spoons in his mouth. His mother was Gertrude Vanderbilt, and his father was Harry Payne Whitney. When Sonny was born, the Whitneys and the Vanderbilts were two of the most well-known and wealthiest families in the world. Sonny could have easily lived a life known only by his fortune. He did not. He lived a full, prosperous, and adventurous life. He didn't have to do anything, yet he did everything.

He was also very modest about who he was and what he accomplished. He never sought fame or glory. He didn't dwell on the past; instead, he lived for the future. Quite honestly, he probably would be embarrassed that we were doing this book on his life and accomplishments. However, many things about Sonny's character and extraordinary life set him apart from others in his position. And for that reason, we decided to honor his life in detail in this wonderful book.

Sonny was driven from the time he was born. He knew at an early age that he was fortunate, but he was determined not to let his good fortune ruin him. He never had a wealthy, idle mentality. In the early 1900s, long before he inherited any money from his family, he made his first million on his own. Sonny always wanted his accomplishments to define him — and not be defined by

who his parents were or how much money they had.

Because of who he was and what he did with his life, Sonny did, indeed, live a charmed life. He entertained and socialized with royalty, presidents, and celebrities alike. But that is not what he lived for. Sonny was a man who lived for new innovations and projects. His life spanned nearly a hundred years (1899–1992), and so many of his endeavors helped shape the twentieth century.

Sonny was known as a gentleman to everyone, despite his stature. He was a patriotic war volunteer at a time when people avoided serving their country; a conservationist before it became fashionable; a pioneer in motion pictures, aviation, oceanariums, and mining businesses; a successful horseman; twice U.S. Open polo champion; an assistant secretary of the Air Force and undersecretary of commerce for President Truman; and a philanthropist in times of greed.

His dossier reads like fiction, but it is all true. Sonny was one of the largest landowners in New York state, owning over 80,000 acres in the Adirondacks. He produced La Cucaracha, the first Technicolor film, and the highly acclaimed motion picture The Searchers, and coproduced Gone With the Wind, Rebecca and A Star Is Born. He also cofounded Pan American Airways; flew as copilot for Charles Lindbergh; bred more stakes winners in the thoroughbred business than anyone else in the world for many years; founded Hudson Bay Mining & Smelting of Canada; and created Marineland in Florida, which was the first ocean aquarium in the world ... just to name a few of his achievements.

One of the most remarkable aspects of Sonny's life was how patriotic he was to his country. He loved America so much that as a young man, he insisted he serve his country in the First World War, even after he was told he was too young and after he failed the eye exam. And later in his life, he volunteered to serve in World War II, even when he was past the age of recruitment. But what touched me the most was when he was in his nineties, he asked me to tell General Schwarzkopf he was ready to serve his country again — this time in Desert Storm.

Despite everything in his life, Sonny Whitney was a simple man. Most men in his position would probably eat lunch at one of their men's clubs, but not Sonny. If he could not make it home from the office, he would eat alone in the Roosevelt Hotel, where he always ordered exactly the same lunch: fillet of sole, broiled, and boiled potatoes. Or he would dine at a Cajun restaurant near his office called Crawdaddy. No one would ever expect to see him at either place. He wished to have it that way.

When we were in the country, whether it be in Kentucky or Saratoga Springs, New York, he loved to explore the countryside. We had maps galore, and after we were in the car, he would surprise me by telling me where we were headed. He preferred finding a new stream or lake, but he also loved to be in the mountains. His favorite quotation was from David in Psalm 121: "I will lift mine eyes unto the hills whence cometh my help."

Sonny was a loving man who loved God. Every day he visited one of our chapels to thank God for his blessings, and he used to say to me, "Do not ask the Lord for anything — thank Him for what you have in life. Then He will bless you."

Sonny had a little-boy quality about him. We would often stop somewhere for ice cream, for he seemed to never have enough. It was a very special treat to him as a child, and he always considered it a reward. He loved to watch me in the kitchen while I was cooking. He would open his mouth like a little bird, and I would slip warm croissants or cookies straight from the oven into that darling, child-like mouth. He was very affectionate, and we all shared many hugs — all of the children and me.

For someone who I was told before we got married didn't really care much for children, he was the best father any child could ever have. He loved the cozy home life that I gave him — something entirely different from his elegant upbringing. His tastes were simple, but his life was plentiful.

Sonny always treated the people who worked for him as his equals. He was the least snobbish person I have ever known. The loyalty of his staff was unbelievable. Many of the same people who were at our house on the farm when he took me there as a bride forty-two years ago are still working there. Some of the older ones have passed on, but their children and grandchildren are still with us. There was never any discrimination in his feelings for people. We all lived together, laughed together, and cried together. These were his friends, and that is why he sparked such loyalty among his employees. The same thing was true wherever he lived. We were all so closely knit — Sonny, the children, the employees, and me. Everyone on the staff at all our homes still misses my late husband, and we reminisce often about all of the VIPs and royalty they helped entertain over the years. But most of all, they remember the friendship.

Sonny loved the outdoors and enjoyed sharing his love of nature with others. His friends always considered it an honor to be included in fishing trips and hunting expeditions at our Adirondacks camp, on the many trips to far-off places, and even the day trips to small towns in the mountains of Kentucky.

One time when we were supposed to be at a ball in Kentucky, Sonny, with a mischievous smile, said, "Let's skip this ball. Let's go off alone to the mountains in our jeans and go fishing." So the tuxedo and ball gown were hung up for another time, and we drove off to Natural Bridge, Kentucky, and stayed in the park for the night. It was high in the hilltops, and we went square dancing with the locals under the light of a full moon. It was one of the best times we ever had. We felt like two teenagers playing hooky.

Sonny was full of surprises, and it kept him young and alert, thinking of new projects and new things to do. The children and I loved his adventurous and spontaneous spirit. I can remember when the children all came home for Christmas one year. They no sooner had arrived on a snowy day than Sonny announced, "Anyone want to go on a picnic?" "Yes," we all said. So off to the kitchen the girls and I went to pack up a picnic lunch and to put on our heaviest parkas and snow boots. We then went into the hills and had our picnic lunch by a lovely frozen waterfall.

In the Adirondacks, I never knew where we might spend the night. Sonny had lean-tos built on his favorite lakes, and he would announce, "Get some food ready for breakfast. We are spending the night in our sleeping bags under the stars."

We spent a great deal of time at Flin Flon, Manitoba, while Sonny ran the Hudson Bay Mining & Smelting Company. He would say to me, "How would you like to fly out in the bush and go with me and the exploration team to look for new ore?" Of course, I always said yes. So off we would fly with canoes tied to the pontoons of the tiny float plane and land in the unexplored Northwest Territory. The only living things were bears and moose. What adventures we had! I learned how to skin a bear and cook it, and we lived off that bear for a whole week.

I was lucky to have been married to this terrific man for thirty-four years. We had a wonderful life together. He introduced me to a lot of new and exciting things, and I believe I gave him a home life that he hadn't experienced before.

I do miss him, but I know he is looking down on me from heaven with those bright blue eyes and saying, "Don't look back. Life is to be lived for today and tomorrow."

Marylou Whitney is an actress, artist, wife, and mother of five children. She has starred in the motion picture *The Missouri Traveler*, as well as her own cooking show, and has authored four books. She has also served on the boards of several companies, and her fundraising efforts and generous donations have earned her honors from communities and public officials alike.

ACKNOWLEDGMENTS

RESEARCHING, WRITING and publishing *The Legend of Cornelius Vanderbilt Whitney* would not have been possible without the effort and guidance of a great many people and organizations.

First, I would like to thank my research assistant Sharon Peters, who did an exemplary job of conducting the initial research and developing the original timelines for the book. Without her talents, this book would not have been possible.

Marylou Whitney and John Hendrickson also deserve a special word of thanks for their insight, support, and timely review of the work.

The candid insights of those who knew C.V. Whitney were crucial to this book. Special thanks go to Ivor Balding, Ted Bassett, Flora Biddle, Budd Calisch, Robert Mason Combs, Gerta Conner, Joe Hirsch, Hank Hosford, Hobbs Hosford, Jeannette Jordan, Pamela LeBoutillier, Ed Lewi, Maureen Lewi, M'lou Llewellyn, Heather Mabee, Leverett Miller, Louie Nunn, Jouett Redmon, Ben Roach, Cornelia Vanderbilt Whitney Tobey, Linda Toohey, Gloria Vanderbilt, and Sue Wylie.

I would also like to thank those individuals and organizations that contributed photos and images. They include Flora Biddle, the Buffalo Bill Historical Center, Anderson Cooper, the C.V. Whitney Convention Center, the Headley-Whitney Museum, Marineland, the National Museum of Racing and Hall of Fame, the Pan Am Historical Foundation, and, of course, Marylou Whitney.

And finally, a very special thanks to the dedicated staff at Write Stuff Enterprises: Melody Maysonet, principal editor; Alex Lieber, executive editor; Jon VanZile, associate editor; Sandy Cruz, senior art director; Jill Apolinario, Rachelle Donley, Wendy Iverson, Joey Henderson, and Dennis Shockley, graphic artists; Bonnie Freeman, proofreader; Mary Aaron, transcriptionist; Erica Orloff, indexer; Fred Moll, production manager; Marianne Roberts, office manager; David Patten and Tony Wall, executive authors; Serina Diaz, administrative assistant; Amanda Fowler, executive assistant; Bonnie Bratton, director of marketing; Rafael Santiago, logistics specialist; and Karine Rodengen, project coordinator.

Cornelius Vanderbilt Whitney, shown here in his eighties, was deeply involved in a variety of business and charitable endeavors. Yet he still found time to relax and enjoy life.

CHAPTER ONE

INTRODUCTION

CORNELIUS VANDERBILT WHITNEY. Even the name proclaimed a rich and rare heritage. Tall and lean, with the patrician good looks and aristocratic carriage that only good lineage and great wealth bestow, he was a man quite unlike most others.

He was born into two of the wealthiest families in America — the Vanderbilts and the Whitneys — in the final days of the 1800s, when enormous fortunes meant enormous mansions and plentiful servants, weekends at one of the country houses, boarding schools, polo and tennis instruction, Ivy League educations, and summers in Newport or Europe. And he lived his life in unapologetic exemplification of an era gone by.

His life was punctuated by associations with people of power and fame. He flew with Charles Lindbergh and Eddie Rickenbacker, served with General Douglas MacArthur, and socialized with the likes of John Wayne, Fred Astaire, Ronald Reagan, and Clark Gable. He hosted British royalty, lunched with governors and congressmen, and traveled with a virtual who's who of twentieth-century movers and shakers. He was a fixture in the New York and Palm Beach social and cultural scenes, his name and face appearing with regularity in the columns, his money behind many top-drawer arts events, institutions, and philanthropies. He also found time to lead his polo team to two U.S. Open championships, write four

books, and become a competent artist whose works commanded recognition at various charity auctions.

He propelled his way through the twentieth century applying old money to leading-edge enterprises and ideas, breaking new ground, and journeying far from the family patterns. Yet his elite origins were unmistakable.

And then there was the voice, cultured, deliberate but not loud, the voice of a man accustomed to being listened to and therefore disinclined to raise or hurry it. Aware of its power, he would often gather his guests after dinner and read poetry.

If there was great style, there was an equal measure of substance. He leveraged his name and his birthright into decades of adventure, accomplishment, and approbation while others of similar circumstances lived rather more idle lives. In fact, as *Quest* magazine pointed out in a 1984 article, his résumé read like that of "a national folk hero."[1]

He inherited millions while still in his thirties, but long before then he had proven himself a man of uncommon entrepreneurial acumen, earning his first half million with a crafty land deal in Mexico when he was only twenty-six. He also, when barely

Although he was an intensely private man who cherished his time alone, Whitney was a skilled communicator who others always said was an easy man to talk to.

out of his twenties, got in on the ground floor of the infant airline industry, cofounding an enterprise that would ultimately become Pan American Airways. In subsequent years he finessed his golden touch, making his mark in the film industry with such landmark films as *Gone With the Wind, A Star Is Born*, and *The Searchers*, and also in the horse industry, where he was to breed an astonishing 141 stakes winners during the fifty-four years he was actively involved. He also started the Hudson Bay Mining & Smelting Company and the first ocean aquarium in the world — Marineland of Florida. His philanthropic contributions included involvement in the Whitney Gallery of Western Art in Cody, Wyoming, the National Museum of Racing (which he cofounded with Walter Jeffords), the Saratoga Springs Performing Arts Center, and the National Museum of Dance.

And when he died at age ninety-three — quietly and gracefully in his sleep only hours after he and his wife had shared a late-night dessert of chocolates — the press heralded a life well lived.

He was called "a legend" by the *Saratogian* of New York, a "multibusiness magnate" by the

Palm Beach Post, a "pillar of the turf," by the *Daily Racing Form*, and "a man for all seasons" by the *Lexington Herald-Leader.*[2]

In death, as in life, the many accomplishments, contributions, and successes of Whitney were chronicled by the press. There were copious references to the ever-shifting inventory of estates and mansions, which almost always totaled seven or eight at any given time; the guest lists that mirrored changing administrations and fleeting

Above: Whitney grew up around polo fields and regarded the game as a diversion — until the late 1930s, when he decided to make a serious bid for polo's U.S. Open Championship.

Left: In his filmmaking days during the the 1950s, Whitney was involved with every aspect of production.

celebrity; the platoons of servants and secretaries and personal assistants; and the countless other accoutrements of high society.

But removed from public view, there were crevices and crannies of his character and soul known to only a few, paradoxes and quirks that make him far more interesting than mere wealth and stature.

Cornelius Vanderbilt "Sonny" Whitney — magnate, sportsman, and adventurer — was described

by *Quest* magazine as "by far the most fascinating, complex, confusing, and controversial Whitney."[3]

Indeed, much of what he did defied not only stereotype, but any fixed linear pattern. With all his great wealth, many travels, and constantly shifting interests, he structured his life with an orderliness not unlike that of a blue collar worker who takes comfort in the predictability of the schedules and rules he lives by. Whitney had rules and principles for everything from meal taking (large breakfast, medium-sized lunch, and small dinner, at precisely the same time every day) to keeping young in old age (always innovating, never looking back). And he

Above: President Nixon and his wife, Pat, and then-Governor Ronald Reagan and his wife, Nancy, were guests of C.V. and Marylou Whitney (far right and left) at Churchill Downs in 1969.

Below: C.V. and Marylou Whitney, who many said were a match made in heaven, enjoy a party in Palm Beach in the late 1960s.

was quite inflexible about abridging them, particularly as he grew older. He despised facial hair on men and could not abide spoiled rich kids.

And he was profoundly patriotic, flying the American flag every day at each one of his homes and diligently paying every cent of taxes he owed. "I resent some of my very good friends who are very rich and have found ways to avoid paying income taxes," he would declare. "I will never find a short-cut. I am proud to pay my income taxes because I'm proud to be an American."[4]

Whitney was accustomed to the finest cuisine served in the finest establishments all over the world, yet he took almost childlike pleasure in Long John Silver's fried fish dinners, cheerfully consuming lunch off a plastic tray at a formica table. He and his fourth wife, Marylou, were also late-night regulars at White Castle drive-throughs, to which, upon leaving some fancy function or another, they would often direct their driver to pilot the Lincoln Town Car.

"The first really vivid memory that I have of Sonny was in Old Westbury in my Aunt Gertrude's house," remembered his cousin Gloria Vanderbilt. "I must have been about eleven, and he was in his thirties. He had come over for lunch, and there were hors d'oeuvres and drinks that were passed around. He took a bite out of one of the hors d'oeuvres and didn't like the way it tasted, but he didn't want to appear rude, so he took the uneaten part and surreptitiously hid it underneath a box of matches lying in an ashtray. I saw him do it, and he caught my eye, and we both went into gales of laughter. It was such a human thing to do."[5]

If his was largely a life of lavish excess, much of the prodigious sums of money he spent seemed devoted to seeking out little wedges of life where he could immerse himself in the simpler things. He had chapels built at most of his properties, and on Sunday mornings he would gather together the staff and family and whatever guests happened to be about the grounds. Sometimes a local preacher would arrive to conduct services before

As an officer in World War II, Whitney cut a dashing figure, but he took his military obligation very seriously and won two distinguished service medals.

making his way to his own church to speak to his assembled flock. More often, Whitney would conduct services himself, reading from the Bible in his rich, cultured voice.

His passion for plunging himself into the rustic is legendary. For years he made an annual exodus to the Wyoming mountains to fish. He would be dropped off deep in the wilderness, where he would fish the icy streams, then hike for miles in search of a cabin or farmhouse where someone would put him up for the night. When he vacationed in his wilderness in the Adirondacks, he would often sleep in lean-tos and eat fish cooked over an open fire, even though he maintained a spectacular family lodge that was always just a lake or a mountain away. And when he married his fourth wife, Marylou, during the month of January, the honeymoon he arranged consisted of a wilderness outing to Manitoba, Canada, where they stayed in a virtually unfurnished cabin and ate moose and bear meat.

He was a man of many contradictions. Socially adept and always gracious, he was, nonetheless, emotionally reserved. His closest friends, the only men he permitted to penetrate his polished veneer, were three men who worked for him throughout his life — and theirs: Ivor Balding, his polo friend and horse farm manager; David Short, his fishing guide and, later, manager of Whitney Industries; and Jouett Redmon, his fishing pal and horse farm manager in later years.

And like many millionaires, he was highly skilled at assessing the financial aspects of every deal but woefully unprepared to deal with the routines of daily-life commerce. He rarely carried cash and seemed hopelessly unaware that it was sometimes necessary. He and Jouett Redmon were stuck in a parking lot in Lexington for quite some time once because, between them, they did not have the three dollars required to exit.

He was a hunter, a man who had no reservations about sighting a creature and pulling the trigger. This was sport, man against nature, and as he saw it, to the victor go the spoils. But he had no stomach for cruelty or unsportsmanlike behavior. One time in the 1960s, Whitney and Redmon were up in the hills near Natural Bridge, Kentucky, a wild and primitive place where the woods are dense and the waters meander as sluggishly as molasses

Whitney married his fourth and final wife Marylou — whom he always called, for reasons even he couldn't explain, Mary — in a small, quiet ceremony in Reno in 1958.

through the dusky glens. The two men happened upon a couple of wildcats cavorting in the distance — a rare and wonderful sight and one that both men were happy to have witnessed. A short time later, traveling through the backroads, they saw a sign offering a live wildcat for sale. Whitney asked Redmon to stop, paid the asking price of $150, and became the owner of a wildcat. The two men loaded the caged cat into the back of the van as Redmon pondered a life devoted to the care and feeding of a bored and hostile bobcat. "Let's go back as close as we can to those wildcats up in the hills," Whitney said as he settled happily into the passenger seat, "and let this one join them."[6]

Whitney understood well his position as an aristocrat in American society, and it was something he accepted with utter unselfconscious-

ness. Yet he had an intense interest in people of all walks of life and relished his relationships with ordinary people.

"Many people would think that because of his background, maybe he thought he was better than other people," said his daughter, Cornelia Vanderbilt Whitney Tobey. "But he always taught me that doesn't matter. If you're talking to the queen of England or somebody from the hills of Kentucky, people are the same and you should treat them with respect. Everybody has something interesting to say, and you should listen to everyone."[7]

Generous with those he cared about and gentle with the same, he had, however, an essential

---

Above: Dave Short, manager of Whitney Park and one of Sonny's best friends, often went fishing with Sonny in the Adirondacks.

Inset: Sonny and Marylou pose with smallmouth bass they caught in the spring of 1964 at Whitney Park.

grit to his soul that few who knew him only socially suspected, but the handful who knew him very well understood with solid certainty.

Whitney's longtime friend Ivor Balding, who worked for him for decades and knew him better than most, shared his insight with Whitney's niece, Pam LeBoutillier. "He said to me, 'You know, I've met a great many rich men through your Uncle Sonny. I wouldn't have known them otherwise, of course, but I know them now, having been on fishing and shooting trips and all of that with them. And I have to say that if all of them were set afloat with no money at all, there would be only one survivor who would be exactly where he is today — and that is your Uncle Sonny.'"[8]

That he did not ever have to prove the accuracy of Balding's observation was something Whitney was wholly and disarmingly grateful for. His favorite hymn, which he sang without a whit of smugness, was "Count Your Blessings."

"He was just your basic good man," said Linda Toohey, who met him in the 1970s when

she became publisher of the *Saratogian* and was
a regular in the Whitney orbit. "He really lived the
life of a religious, spiritual, ethical, well-meaning
human.... For a man who had seen virtually all
the wonders of the world, he was always happiest
in simple places and smaller groups."[9]

"He was a great believer in Christ but also
read the Old Testament," said Marylou. "He said
his prayers every night, and each night we used
to take turns reading to each other from the Bible
before turning off the lights."[10]

Right: Even in his later years, he was always up for some
frivolity. Here, friend Ruth Roach watches him ride a merry-go-
round horse at the Casino Carousel party in Saratoga Springs.

Below: Whitney maintained very little contact with his
children from his first three marriages but was very close to
the children from Marylou's first marriage and the daughter
they had together, Cornelia. Here, Cornelia, Sonny, Marylou,
and one of his stepdaughters, Heather, pose in the gardens
at Saratoga in the 1970s.

As a young boy, C.V. Whitney was often photographed with a very serious expression.

CHAPTER TWO

RARE HERITAGE

CORNELIUS VANDERBILT WHITNEY was well into boyhood, approaching adolescence, before he experienced that seminal moment that conveyed to him in no uncertain terms that he was not like other boys.

He had taken the Fifth Avenue bus home from school, and as he arose to get off at his stop, he was stunned when the bus driver, an unusually garrulous sort, announced to the passengers, "The mansion you see in front of you belongs to the Whitney family. They're millionaires. They have ice cream for lunch every Sunday."[1]

The boy disembarked and stood on the curb, frozen, until the bus pulled away. "I didn't want anyone to associate me with the brownstone mansion," he wrote decades later in *High Peaks*, his collection of autobiographical stories. "It was not that I was ashamed. I just didn't like being singled out and made to feel all that different. And furthermore, the driver's information was inaccurate. We usually had tapioca or rice pudding on Sunday. It was only on birthdays, Christmas, and Easter that we got ice cream. I never rode the Fifth Avenue bus again."[2]

Though as a boy C.V. Whitney was unaware of the extraordinary life and circumstances into which he had been born, the rest of the world was not. From the moment of his birth, just as the nineteenth century was flowing into the twentieth, he and his exceedingly wealthy family were

observed, assessed, and commented upon — for everyone else knew that most families did not have four-story summer homes and stables and governesses and vacations to Europe and ballrooms the size of city blocks.

C.V. Whitney had been born February 20, 1899. His father was Harry Payne Whitney of the fabulous Whitney fortune. His mother was Gertrude Vanderbilt of the even more fabulous Vanderbilt fortune.

When Harry Payne married the girl from the mansion across the street on August 25, 1896, at The Breakers, the Vanderbilts' showy castle-like seventy-room summer place in Newport, Rhode Island, the press heralded it as the all-American union of the aristocrat and the heiress. The wedding orchestra, evidently caught up in the imagery, played "The Star-Spangled Banner."

The amazing wealth of Harry Payne and Gertrude, generations in the making, had been handed down by uncommonly industrious and savvy ancestors who had arrived early — and not especially rich — to America and made the most of what they found. Each of the two families distinguished itself as much by hard work as by its uncanny ability to sight and focus

---

Sonny was the model for one of his mother's earliest sculptures.

Above: C.V.'s parents were married at The Breakers in Newport, Rhode Island, where, as a child, Sonny experienced many happy summers.

Left: Harry and Gertrude, shown here on their honeymoon in Japan in 1896, were married for thirty-four years, though their marriage was often less than happy.
(Photo courtesy Flora Biddle.)

Opposite: When C.V. was a young teen, in 1913, the Whitney Stables' famed horse Pennant won the Futurity.

upon winning propositions. With each successive generation, their holdings grew until, by the time Harry Payne and Gertrude were young adults embarking on marriage, the names Whitney and Vanderbilt conveyed great wealth and great stature.

Harry, age twenty-four at the time of his marriage, was understandably a bit "spoiled," according to Whitney family biographer Edwin P. Hoyt. His father, William C., a successful lawyer and political manipulator tapped by the Cleveland administration to serve as Secretary of the Navy, had developed into a cagey businessman. By the time Harry was in his teens, William C. had amassed a small but impressive fortune through

developing New York's cable car system and investing in such phenomenal performers as Standard Oil (where his brother-in-law, Oliver Payne, was a chief officer and was for years regarded as the richest man in America). The family owned homes up and down the Eastern seaboard and other accoutrements of growing wealth.

Upon graduating from Yale, Harry had, at his father's insistence, entered Columbia University Law School to become, as his father had started out, a corporation lawyer. But Harry found law school tedious and left, just as his father had, to enter law tutelage at a prestigious firm. Unlike his father, however, Harry was unable to make a go of it, perhaps, as biographer Hoyt concluded, because "he had no driving economic push to make him seek his living — he had millions at his disposal and every facility and toy a grown man could want."[3]

Harry's attention was absorbed by his polo ponies and fleet of yachts. And in his spare time he hunted tigers in India and lions in Africa and frequented the many clubs to which he had been warmly welcomed — clubs that centered on such avocations as tennis, polo, horse racing, and yachting, and social clubs which existed entirely so "people of quality would not have to eat in common restaurants or entertain their friends in saloons."[4] Harry was not without some awareness of his life-of-leisure existence. After he was arrested for speeding in Central Park when he was thirty-one and the officer asked his occupation, Harry replied, "I don't know what name to give that."[5]

Still, if as a young man he did not seem to seriously apply himself to the business world, he did seriously apply himself to those arenas in which he was interested. He turned polo from a gentleman's weekend fancy to a cutthroat sport, heading the team that brought the International Cup from Europe in 1909. He bred hunting dogs that were revered the world over.

Although he eventually involved himself in his father's many businesses, including mining, railways, various banks, insurance companies,

and loan and trust companies, his heart was never really filled with joy at the prospect. His true passion became horses — breeding and racing them — a sideline pursuit of his father's for which Harry developed enormous interest and success, winning the Kentucky Derby twice.

Gertrude, too, entered marriage with something other than conventional background and ideas. An introspective and searching young woman with a sensitive nature, vivid imagination, and rich fantasy life, she had from early childhood, expressed in page after page of the scores of journals she kept throughout her life, a fervent desire to be a boy rather than a girl. This seemed, in large measure, because she understood males had all the power, and also, in some measure never quite known, because of some gender-identification confusion. As she approached womanhood, she became fiercely independent, searching, restless, and sensuous — qualities that were rare for her time and station. She was anything but a soft, gilded heiress content to live out her days in listless pursuit of the latest couturier headgear. When she quickly realized she would find little of what she'd hoped for in marriage, she set about crafting her own happiness, becoming a sculptor of impressive note and a fervent patroness of the arts, championing fresh young American talent over the much-favored Europeans, eventually providing them with not only long-denied acclaim, but also a home — the Whitney Museum of American Art.

Harry Payne and Gertrude were not, in any way other than pedigree, a perfect match. Although they were married for thirty-four years and reared three children, it was not an altogether happy union. There were disappointments, despair, and, biographers agree, infidelities on both sides.

It was into this highly privileged if often conflicted arrangement that Cornelius Vanderbilt Whitney, second-born child and only son of Harry Payne and Gertrude, arrived.

C.V. Whitney — soon called Sonny, a name he originally despised but one that he grew comfortable with in old age — was not the most robust of babies, but he grew to be a vigorous young boy with vivid, sky-blue eyes that were at times wistful and almost always direct and probing.

Sonny's parents had a city house and access to several other family homes scattered about New York and New England, but it was the country place in Old Westbury, Long Island, that he regarded as his boyhood home. In *High Peaks*, he described it as a "glorious country estate of some thousand acres ... a big red brick house situated on top of a hill with rolling green pastures to the south and a wild forest to the north."[6] It boasted a "stable full of horses, a good-sized kennel, an outdoor tennis court and swimming pool and an indoor gymnasium replete with bowling alley and squash court."[7] There were also servants and groundskeepers and governesses and tutors.

Being a boy who could visit unimaginable mischief upon his two sisters, he was, as was common for the time, assigned to "Spartan quarters in the attic," where he was provided with a cot, a small bathroom and an empty storeroom beyond, an arrangement he always claimed he cherished because "I prized my privacy."[8]

Though Sonny enjoyed the privacy of the attic, his tutor, who was actually a sort of male governess, was often cruel to him, sometimes

Opposite: Gertrude Vanderbilt Whitney was a rather unconventional woman for her time. She became a nationally known sculptor and patron of the arts. Here, she works on her sculpture *On the Top* in 1919. *(Photo courtesy Flora Biddle.)*

Above: In the early 1900s, the very rich had a penchant for dressing their boy children like girls. C.V. Whitney grew to hate this portrait of himself, painted when he was four years old.

primitive eighty-five thousand acres of land and forty lakes, where he was taught to fish and canoe and build lean-tos for sleeping out-of-doors.

It was all very exciting and grand, he acknowledged in later years. But since his chums all inhabited neighboring estates and mansions and lived lives quite similar to his own, and since the rich lived rather cloistered existences that rarely brought them in contact with those of lesser circumstances, he had no way of knowing as a boy that this was all quite phenomenal. Life seemed an endless succession of new and greater adventures.

"We had such great fun growing up," Sonny's sister, Flora Payne Whitney Miller, told a writer for *Town & Country* in the 1980s.[10]

Undoubtedly so, but they had little in the way of conventional family life. Family outings and activities that united the Whitney children with their parents were quite rare and compressed into tight pockets of time that punctuated an otherwise rather detached relationship.

Both Whitney parents were otherwise engaged — he with his various adventures and she, as the years went on, with her sculpture and art patronage. So the occasional moments of clannish endeavor were etched in memory with the permanence of letters chiseled in granite.

"My mother was a very busy person, ... but she did marvelous things with us," Flora Miller said. "Sometimes she would invite us down to her studio on McDougal Alley in Greenwich Village. There would be a hot lunch in the automobile that she had sent for us. Or we would all lunch in her studio."[11]

The brightest of the vignettes were the sparkling summer days when many Whitney and Vanderbilt aunts and uncles and cousins would converge on the mountain property. "Many of our summers were spent in the Adirondacks, and they were wonderful," Miller recalled. "My grand-

locking him in the attic with only bread and water. "It was at times like this that his sisters' mademoiselle would comfort him," said his fourth wife, Marylou. "Sonny rarely saw his parents to tell them how badly he was treated. And, as he was used to being treated badly by his father, he really lived in a world of his own, planning how he would make people respect him one day."[9]

During the school year, the family generally spent the week in the massive Manhattan brownstone built by his grandfather William C. at 68th Street and Fifth Avenue, an elegantly appointed mansion with a sweeping marble staircase and what was for many years the city's largest ballroom. Young Sonny usually roller-skated the two miles from the mansion to the private school he attended on East 49th, and after-school hours were passed chasing squirrels and rabbits in Central Park. Summers were whiled away in Old Westbury; in Newport, where his parents had built a summer cottage almost immediately after marrying; and in the Adirondacks, on his grandfather's

Above: Sonny and his sister Flora at a wedding of family friends in 1905. *(Photo courtesy Flora Biddle.)*

Opposite: The Whitney children summered in all the best places, including Rhode Island and Europe, and attended private schools. Here Sonny, at age six, poses with his two sisters, Flora (left) and Barbara.

Gertrude with her beloved dog, Loup, in Paris, 1914.
(*Photo courtesy Flora Biddle.*)

father Whitney had acres and acres there, and it's always been a family place."[12]

Sonny became the anointed leader of the summertime activities. His cousin John Hay "Jock" Whitney, five years Sonny's junior and in later years often a rival, recalled sitting "entranced while [Sonny] read stories to the other children," according to Jock Whitney biographer E.J. Kahn, Jr. And Jock often recalled his admiration at the "skill and assurance with which Sonny conducted sailing classes for the rest of the Whitney flock."[13]

When Sonny was approaching age five and his father was not quite thirty-two, Whitney patriarch William C. Whitney died, leaving homes in New York, Maine, Massachusetts, and South Carolina; La Belle horse farm in Lexington, Kentucky, which later became the Headley-Whitney Museum; a bulging portfolio; and business interests in everything from exploration and mining to steamships and railroads and to banks and insurance companies.

Harry inherited more than $10 million and grew more serious about preserving the family wealth. A few years prior to his death, William C. had dedicated himself to bringing to Harry's consciousness "all the old Puritan virtues of thrift and hard work, and to a certain extent he had succeeded."[14] Henceforth, Harry was almost as involved in moneymaking as money spending, a proclivity that grew ever more obvious with passing time and caused him to spend even less time with his family. For he wasn't willing to allow business to supplant his quest for adventure; it was merely something that he added to his agenda. When he was thirty-seven, he decided he simply had to see polo's most prestigious trophy back on U.S. soil and became relentless in this pursuit, training and grilling and goading his team to championship quality, the culmination of which the children were able to witness.

"I remember when I was twelve my father went to England to win the America Challenge Cup back from the British, who had had it for years and years," recalled Miller. "My mother and

I, my brother, Sonny,... and my sister, Barbara, went over, too."[15]

During the two months the family spent in England — before Harry and his team did in fact win back the Cup — the family was unusually close and involved with one another. All five of them were received by the king and queen and other members of the aristocracy. Gertrude took the children on a day's outing to the Louvre. And Harry took Sonny on a shoot in Holwick for a few days.

What the children seemed to relish most was the mere fact of being in a house with many adults who were paying them great attention. "It was a lark because the polo players all lived in the house with us and we used to follow them around and play all kinds of games," said Miller.[16]

Once the matches were over and the horse racing season was about to begin, Harry and Gertrude moved into a smaller house near the track and the children were shuttled off to a hotel with the governess. In later years, Sonny confided to his wife Marylou that he loved his mother very much — although he didn't see her as often as he wished — but he rarely mentioned his father. Instead, he looked to other men to fill the void his father had left.

The family took other trips abroad. In 1912, Harry, Gertrude, Sonny, and Loup, the German shepherd, headed for London on board the *Mauritania,* the best steamer of the time. Once landed, Sonny was deposited with his uncle Payne, who took him on a tour of Scotland. Payne Whitney became something of a father figure to young Sonny. While Sonny was away at school, his parents rarely came to see him, but his uncle Payne did.

With much of the time spent traveling, socializing with their parents' acquaintances, or being assigned to one of the estates, the children grew up in a world mostly populated by rich adults and hired help.

Though Sonny acknowledged in later years that his best friend in the family was his sister Barbara, he had an agreeable relationship with his sister Flora as well. "Mostly it was Sonny I played with," she said. "We're only two years apart, and we were both full of mischief."[17]

Indeed Sonny, a mostly well-behaved boy, did have a streak of unpredictability coursing just under the mannerly surface. He had, for example, a collection of snakes that he stowed away in an

Sonny grew up in enormous wealth, but he spent very little time with his parents.

unused room in Old Westbury. There they stayed, year after year, secretly and lovingly tended to by the young boy. One Sunday, for reasons never clear to anyone, most particularly Whitney himself, he wrapped his beloved three-foot-long king snake around his neck and strode into the dining room, where a large group of family and friends were assembling for Sunday dinner. Stunned silence ensued. No one found it amusing.

When Sonny reached the age of twelve, he was sent to Groton School, a private school in Massachusetts, where his father had gone before him. "I was not a dedicated student," he granted, "but I devoted my energies to sports: football, crew and baseball."[18] And he also became quite proficient on the piano, studying under the celebrated Josef Hofmann, who was a friend of the family.

He also spent hours and hours in the library, not, he acknowledged in *High Peaks*, in scholarly pursuit, but rather pouring over adventure stories having to do with exploration in primitive areas. "I vowed that some day, somehow, I would explore those faraway places."[19]

Adventure stories, in fairness, were not the only books he found irresistible. Although he was not much interested in his assigned academics, he was at Groton, as he had been from early childhood, a voracious reader of all manner of tomes, some of them quite educational. As his sister recalled, "When I'd come home on vacations from Foxcroft and he was in from Groton, we would test each other with literary games."[20]

But such visits were quite infrequent and probably quite unfulfilling to the boy. As biogra-

pher Hoyt pointed out, "His family life consisted largely of reading about his parents in the society columns and going home to whichever of the family mansions they seemed to be frequenting at the moment, there to engage in whatever activities were being supervised either by other relatives or paid help. It was not recorded that Harry Payne ever stopped his whirlwind of activity long enough to have a man-to-man talk with his son."[21]

Sonny's cousin Douglas Burden, who was also one of his good friends, had Marylou in tears one night, telling her how badly Sonny had been treated by his father. "Douglas grew up with

Sonny, spending a great deal of time at Whitney Park in the Adirondacks and at Old Westbury," Marylou explained. "He told me that Harry Payne constantly belittled Sonny. If he won at tennis, Harry would say things like, 'Oh, does the pretty boy with blonde, curly hair really think he plays well?' Or when he entered a horse show and won ribbons, which he would proudly show his father, Harry would laugh and say something like, 'Oh, so you think you did a good job. You don't know how to ride a horse well. You can't do anything well.' I could not imagine a parent being so cruel. But it worked well in the long run, for it made Sonny work harder at all sports and to always try to excel in everything in life, whether it be sports or business ventures."[22]

Nor did Gertrude lavish attention on the young Sonny. By the time he was away at school, she had become a burgeoning sculptor with work studios in not only New York but also Paris. It seemed as much a defense mechanism as any-

Many of Whitney's happiest memories sprang from his grandfather's place in Old Westbury.

thing. She and Harry were leading entirely separate lives, a reality that filled her with despair. In the spring of 1913, she wrote Harry a poignant letter, found later by biographer B.H. Friedman: "It seems very obvious that we are drifting further and further apart and that the chances of our coming together are growing remote.... Our mutual indifference to the pursuits and pleasures of the other is leading us constantly to have even less to talk of and forms no bond on which we might rely to bridge our difficult moments."[23] It was a several-page letter over-

Left: Though C.V. did not have a particularly close relationship with his mother, she still had a profound influence on him.

Above: Upon graduating form Groton, Whitney immediately joined the Signal Corps. Shown here with his Groton graduating class, he is in the third row, the last young man on the right.

flowing with pain and resolve. When it was completed, she did what she had always done with her most heartfelt writing. She tucked it into her journal.

The children, attending school away and in any event accustomed to a high level of detachment in their family, may not have particularly noticed the widening gulf between their parents. On some level, however, given the subsequent and repeated difficulties each of the children had with marriage, Harry and Gertrude's disengagement must have had an impact.

Upon completing his education at Groton in 1917, Sonny went home to Old Westbury. "I was greeted with warmth and affection," he wrote in *High Peaks*. "After all, in graduating from Groton I had done what was expected of me."[24]

NOTABLE RELATIONS

FROM BOYHOOD ON, C.V. WHITNEY watched with the rest of the world as his family periodically captivated the nation. The various branches of the Whitney and Vanderbilt trees were perhaps unparalleled in terms of their accomplishments, their controversies, and their ability to grab and hold headlines. Sonny's uncle, Payne Whitney, married the daughter of the secretary of state in a wedding attended by President Roosevelt and his entire cabinet. Upon Payne's death in 1927, he left the largest estate that had ever been appraised in the United States.

Payne's son and Sonny's cousin John Hay "Jock" Whitney, with whom Sonny had an almost lifelong love-hate relationship steeped in and fueled by childhood and adult competition, was a noted sportsman, horse breeder, polo player, war hero, ambassador to Great Britain, and owner of several communications properties, including the *New York Herald-Tribune, Parade,* and *Interior Design.* Some of the headlines Jock made were on his own; some were in partnership with Sonny, as when the two were involved in the development of Pan American Airways and also with the production of such movies as *Gone With the Wind.*

Sonny's second cousin Consuelo Vanderbilt had married in 1896 the ninth Duke of Marlborough (an impoverished, if titled, man) in a union orchestrated and forced by the young woman's mother. Consuelo made an enormous name for herself in England by restoring her husband's down-at-the-heels castle, Blenheim Palace, to magnificent splendor.

Sonny's cousin Gloria Vanderbilt became a famous fashion designer in adulthood. But prior to that, in the 1920s, she was the subject of months of newspaper headlines as Sonny's mother, Gertrude, fought a vicious yet successful battle in the courts for custody of the little girl, who Gertrude insisted was being abused and ruined by her mother's selfish and depraved lifestyle.

Among C.V. Whitney's many famous relatives was Consuelo Vanderbilt, who married the Duke of Marlborough, became a duchess, and devoted her life to restoring Blenheim Palace (below).

THE WHITNEY FAMILY TREE

THE AMERICAN WHITNEY-OCRACY HAD its beginning in 1635 when British merchant John Whitney, his wife Elinor, and their five children settled in Massachusetts after sailing across the Atlantic to escape the economic uncertainties of Mother England. John provided well for his family, and his offspring carried the Whitney name forward with singular purpose and diligence. Son Eli invented the cotton gin and developed the assembly-line technique that revolutionized industry; son Josiah was a geologist of such note that a mountain, Mount Whitney, was named after him. Son Asa was an inventor and president of the Philadelphia & Reading Railroad. And daughter Anne became a poet and sculptor with a significant following. When John died in 1673, he had increased his original land holdings of sixteen acres to three hundred acres.

Subsequent generations of Whitneys included State Senator Josiah Whitney — who, with his son Josiah Jr., helped defend Boston Harbor against the British — and Representative James Scollay Whitney, a successful industrialist.

The Whitney family wealth, which for nearly two centuries was decidedly modest, surged in the mid-1800s with William Collins Whitney, C.V. Whitney's grandfather. William C. Whitney deemed Manhattan a fallow land ripe for attention and left New England for New York after dropping out of Harvard Law School, declaring he would learn law by working at a law firm. This he did, and within months he was admitted to the bar, sans examination, largely on the avowals of his mentor, a powerful attorney who submitted that the young Whitney was an able jurist.[1] In fact, he became just that, and over time he developed an impressive clientele, including the imposingly rich Commodore Vanderbilt, whose great-granddaughter Gertrude would marry Whitney's grandson Harry Payne decades later.

William C. labored hard and married well, to Flora Payne, daughter of a wealthy political figure from Ohio who would soon become that state's Senator. William C. Whitney himself entered the political arena, becoming an active Boss Tweed opponent and Tammany Hall manipulator who rose in the Democratic Party ranks with great speed.

President Cleveland invited him to be secretary of the Navy, and although he was disinclined to accept, wishing instead to channel his energies into building a fortune of his own, his wife had social aspirations, and her wishes prevailed. She became the most talked-about hostess of Washington, while he set about returning the moribund Navy to some semblance of dignity and military readiness. Their marriage became a distant and often contentious one.

In a few years, they returned to New York, where he devoted all his energies to making money. He developed the Metropolitan Street Railway System, which was a virtual monopoly of the New York cable car system, the profits from which he invested wisely into such companies as Standard Oil. He became involved in scores of enterprises, from mining to automobiles.

Edwin P. Hoyt. William C., Hoyt wrote, "was so busy with politics and, later, with making money that he never thought about giving his boys some goals; instead, he gave them America on the halfshell."[2]

Still, although Harry Payne's interests ran more toward sports and polo and the race tracks, he did have success. He led his polo team to two U.S. Open championships, managed his inherited portfolio well, and ran a world-renowned stable that included Regret, a heart-of-gold filly that for more than five decades (until 1980) bore the distinction of being the only filly ever to win the Kentucky Derby, and his other Kentucky Derby winner, Whiskery. And when Harry Payne died, he was able to hand down to his children and grandchildren holdings worth $65 million — an inheritance far greater than that which he had received.

When he died at age sixty-three, he left ten huge homes and hundreds of thousands of acres of property, including an estate at Old Westbury on Long Island; eleven thousand acres of game preserve in the Berkshires; seventy thousand acres in the Adirondacks; a summer cottage in Bar Harbor; and a mansion on Fifth Avenue and 68th Street with the largest private ballroom in Manhattan. He had also amassed a huge art collection and built one of the largest and most successful thoroughbred racing stables in the country.

Much of this wound up with Harry Payne Whitney (born Henry), owing to a family dispute years earlier over William C.'s decision to remarry after Flora died, an action which left him estranged from two of his children. This type of estrangement, along with its root cause — a woman — was one that would reemerge often in subsequent generations of Whitneys.

Harry Payne Whitney did not possess the business drive that had motivated his father, a predictable deficiency under the circumstances according to Whitney biographer

Opposite: General James S. Whitney and Laurinda Collins Whitney were New Englanders and C.V.'s great-grandparents.

Above left: This portrait of Whitney's grandfather, W.C. Whitney, hangs in the National Museum of Racing.

Above: Harry Payne Whitney, C.V.'s father, was a noted horseman who not only bred and raced thoroughbreds but was an accomplished equestrian.

THE VANDERBILT FAMILY

JAN AETSEN VAN DER BILT ARRIVED ON American soil in the mid-1660s and died there in precisely the same condition as several generations before him and four generations after — as poor Dutch farmers. It was his great-great-great-grandson, Cornelius Van Derbilt, born in 1794 on a farm on Staten Island, New York, who radically changed the economic condition of his family for all posterity.

Cornelius left school at age eleven to help on his father's farm and to assist him with some boating activities on the water-front. By the time Cornelius was sixteen, he owned a boat and was ferrying passengers between Staten Island and New York; at eighteen he had several boats and a government contract to provision New York Harbor forts during the War of 1812.

His presence, acumen, and holdings along the waterfront grew to the point that as he settled comfortably into his forties, he owned several steamships, was worth millions, and was known to one and all as "Commodore." It was an appellation that denoted and demanded respect along the wharves but held little sway in society. As Vanderbilt family biographer B.H. Friedman pointed out, the Commodore may have been extraordinarily hard-working, forward-thinking and wise in the ways of making money, but he was also "loud," he "chewed tobacco," and he was coarse "in manners and speech,"[1] qualities that did not smooth the path to the drawing rooms of New York's upper crust.

As the years went by he added more steamers to his line, formed the American Atlantic and Pacific Ship Canal Company to provide shorter and cheaper East to West Coast ship passage through Nicaragua rather than Panama, and began investing heavily in railroads, ultimately acquiring and merging so many lines that he was in control of a virtual rail empire. When in his seventies, he built Grand Central Terminal in New York City, and the city's gratitude was immortalized in the form of a bronze statue of him that still stands at the Park Avenue ramp.

When Commodore died in 1877, he left about $100 million, some $90 million of it to son William H., the eldest of his thirteen children. As his only charitable bequest, he also left, for reasons lost to history, one million dollars to Central University in Nashville — a gesture so appreciated that the college promptly changed its name to Vanderbilt University.

William H., the new head of the Vanderbilt clan, had in earlier years disappointed his father mightily, first by being a rather sickly child and later by making what Commodore believed to be unwise decisions, including his choice of a bride. But in the final twenty years of Commodore's life, William H. had proven his mettle, angled his way back into his father's graces, and learned under Commodore's guiding hand. Within five years of Commodore's death, William H. had doubled the family fortune.

A careful businessman, he was also the first of the Vanderbilts to be a great philanthropist, contributing millions during his life to many churches, schools, and causes and bequesting millions after his death to many more. He was, however, most remembered for a single quote: "The public be damned." Despite the enduring quality of that line, Vanderbilt probably didn't say it, according to biographer Friedman. It seems that when a *Chicago Daily News* reporter was denied an interview with William H., the

Opposite: On the Vanderbilt side of the family, Cornelius Van Derbilt (1794–1877) was Sonny Whitney's great-great-grandfather and namesake.

Above: Three generations of the Vanderbilt women: Gertrude (center); her mother, Alice Gwynne; and Gertrude's daughter Flora.

Above right: Cornelius Vanderbilt, Gertrude's father, was a trustee of the American Museum of Natural History, among other philanthropies.

reporter protested by declaring, "Mr. Vanderbilt, your public demands an interview." To which, the Vanderbilt family has insisted ever since, William H. responded "My public be damned."[2]

William H., like his father, built a new home in Manhattan, a Fifth Avenue mansion filled with priceless artworks, but he was also rejected by society.

When William H. died in 1883, he left the bulk of his fortune to the two eldest of his nine offspring, Cornelius and William Kissam. Cornelius, the harder working of the two, became the chairman of New York Central as well as the accepted head of the family, and finally the Vanderbilts were accepted into society. Within a few years, his personal wealth was estimated at about a hundred million dollars. Cornelius continued his father's pattern of philanthropy and procreation. He and his wife, Alice, had seven children, including Gertrude, who would be the first of this particular dynasty to marry into another dynasty whose wealth approached their own.

Whitney as a young airman was gaining confidence in his capabilities, for the first time being absent of family connections.

CHAPTER THREE
GROWING PAINS

SONNY WHITNEY'S INTENT after graduating Groton was to begin college at Yale the following fall — a notion born of nothing more than the fact that this, too, was expected of him. His father had been a Yale man and his father before him.

But the war was raging overseas, and young Whitney had a powerful urge to become involved. His mother was already in France — a country for which she had a deep and abiding respect — serving as a nurse in the ambulance corps. His father was funneling thousands of his dollars into the war effort. And the son wanted to do something as well, not so much to continue the family pattern, but because he felt it was his patriotic duty.

Only eighteen years old, he was too young to join the Army. "The best I could do under the circumstances was to enlist in a training camp for lads under nineteen that was located on Plum Island at the eastern tip of Long Island Sound," he wrote years later in *High Peaks*.[1]

Once he completed training camp, he got work in the city as an apprentice to a surgeon. He disliked the work intensely but bore it because he hoped it would get him a job with the ambulance corps in France, a reasonably acceptable alternative, he thought, to serving in the Army.

Then he had a provocative thought. He was now approaching his nineteenth birthday, and there was

reason to believe that the newly formed Army Signal Corps, the air force branch of the regular Army, would accept him and provide training until he was old enough to become a fighter pilot.

"One day, without a word to my family I packed a bag and took a train to Washington, where the U.S. Army Signal Corps had its enlistment offices," he wrote in *High Peaks*.[2]

Everything seemed to be proceeding quite well until, during the physical exam, the doctor found fault with his adenoids (tissue growth in the back of the nose that when swollen could obstruct breathing). "Take them out," Whitney urged.

The doctor complied — immediately and without benefit of anesthetic. That done, he propelled the young man forward for the rest of his testing.

Dazed but determined, Whitney proceeded through the process, only to fail the color test.

Convinced that his dismal performance on this task was probably attributable to the impromptu surgery, the enlistment officers suggested he come back the next day and retake it. Certain he could pass the test the next day — an improbable eventuality given that he had been

---

Once in the Signal Corps, Whitney was quickly tapped as a pilot and received excellent ratings for both service and character.

slightly color blind since earliest memory —
Whitney made his way to the Western Union office
to wire his father for consent to join up, a governmental requirement because he was underage.

That evening Sonny had dinner with his
cousin Evie Wadsworth, who, in a remarkable turn
of good fortune, had a friend who was also color
weak, and this friend had a color chart that might
help in Whitney's endeavor. The chart, quickly
obtained and presented to Sonny, was, as it
turned out, identical to
the one the Army was
using. Late into the night,
Whitney and Evie huddled
together, she coaching him
so he could memorize the
colors and pass the test.

The next day the
elder Whitney's permission
telegram arrived, Whitney
passed the test and signed
the necessary papers, and in
October, he was bound for
Signal Corps ground school
training at Princeton.

This was, he wrote years
later, his first important and
independent decision, "one
that literally changed my life."[3]
Prior to this, he had "lived in a
very comfortable world but a
very small one shared with
friends who, like me, represent-
ed the so-called upper stratum of society.
Physically I was tough, but I knew little about life
outside my own limited area," he wrote.[4]

His introduction to the other side was fast
and relentless, evident from the journal he kept
from October 27, 1917, to January 1919, which
was discovered by his wife Marylou seven decades
later and published under the title *First Flight*.

After a few weeks at ground school, where, he
wrote, "the work was so hard there was very little
time for anything other than work,"[5] he was
shipped off to Love Field in Dallas. It was very
cold in Dallas that January, and there was no
coal to heat the vast, barnlike quarters occupied
by the young recruits, so they did whatever they
could to stay warm, including sleeping in their
helmets and organizing tackle
football games in their barracks every night. "Those
games," Whitney wrote, "always
broke up because someone
got badly hurt."[6]

Whitney's cot mates were
"a Greek who had been
dressed up as a woman in
Turkey as a spy for two

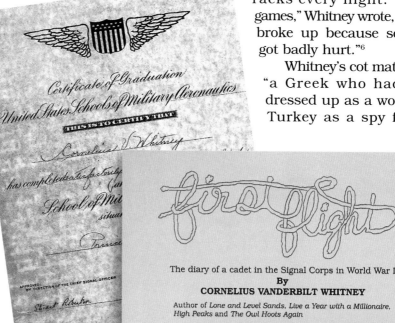

The diary of a cadet in the Signal Corps in World War I
By
CORNELIUS VANDERBILT WHITNEY

Author of *Lone and Level Sands, Live a Year with a Millionaire,
High Peaks* and *The Owl Hoots Again*

Center: Whitney's certificate of graduation from the School of
Military Aeronautics at Princeton University.

Right: Whitney's journal of his adventures in the Signal Corps
in World War I was published in the 1970s.

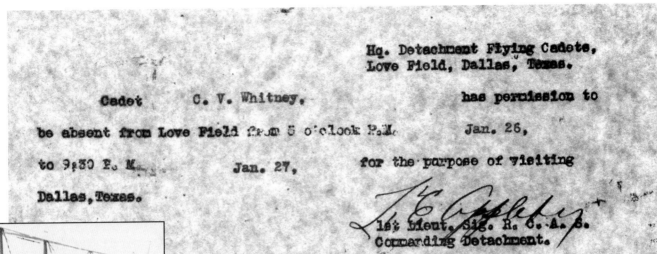

Cadet   C. V. Whitney,

be absent from Love Field from 5 o'clock P.M.

to 9:30 P. M.   Jan. 27,

Dallas, Texas.

Hq. Detachment Flying Cadets,
Love Field, Dallas, Texas.

has permission to

Jan. 26,

for the purpose of visiting

1st Lieut., Sig. R. C. A. S.
Commanding Detachment.

years" and an American called Carl Smith, "a lazy sort of a dreamer."[7]

None of this troubled Whitney. What did wrench at his sensibilities were the military rations, which he characterized as "the most disgusting food I have ever tasted,"[8] and also the utter disinterest with which he and his band of shiny-faced recruits had been met.

After three weeks there, Whitney was dour and blue. He had done nothing but shovel what little coal there was, take a few courses on filling out government paperwork, and unload airplane parts. He seemed not one whit closer to becoming a fighter pilot than when he had arrived. Indeed, he had not been near a plane.

Deep in the throes of frustration and disappointment, writing regularly of his disillusionment to friends and family, he was granted what to him was the ultimate bright spot. He received a pass to leave the base and made his way to a dance at the Adolphus Hotel in Dallas, where he spent some happy moments with a young woman named Miss Montgomery, a Texas rose whom Whitney described as "black haired, black eyed, [with] beautiful ankles and a strange wild dress, very Indian looking."[9] In a night, his perspective changed. "I remember thinking things weren't so bad after all."[10]

A couple of days later, he and his new-recruit buddies got orders to report to Benbrook Field in

Above: In *First Flight*, Whitney identified his pass from Love Field as "the only pass we were given during the entire four weeks."

Left: Whitney was considered one of the Signal Corps's top pilots — daring and inventive — and he trained dozens of other young men who were heading off to fight in the war.

Fort Worth, where they would serve under Canada's Royal Flying Corps.

There the boys learned fast or were drummed out. Whitney, with one hour and fifty minutes of flying instruction and five landings under his belt, was ordered to solo.

He took to the sky, nervous but determined, repeating like a mantra his instructor's final orders: to land as near him as possible. "I did," Whitney wrote. "He had to run like a rabbit, but I got away with it all right and after making two more landings I went in. And that night I think I felt happier than any night of my life."[11]

He had finally broken through the barriers that for weeks seemed to have been conspiring to keep him on the ground. Socially he began breaking out as well. Friends of the family invited him to the country club and to dinner parties, as would have been expected, but he also ventured into previously forbidden or at least unexplored territory — dances at the Elks Club. "In the social world of Fort Worth, the very 'best' didn't go to the Elks Club dances," he wrote.[12] But he did, and often.

A GIFT OF PROSE

THE JOURNAL WHITNEY KEPT AS AN eighteen-year-old was his first of many writings. Throughout his life, he recorded many of his experiences and impressions, some fact and some fiction, just as his mother had done, and much of it was published in some form or another in later years.

Even as a young college student, his skill with words and remarkable eye for detail were recognized. Three of his efforts were published in the *Yale Lit,* no small feat.

By the time he died, five catalog card numbers at the Library of Congress bore his name: *First Flight,* written in 1917 and published in 1977; *Lone and Level Sands,* an account of his World War II adventures published in 1951; *High Peaks,* a years-long attempt at an autobiography that he eventually overhauled into a collection of upbeat vignettes detailing various events in his life, published in 1977; *Live a Year with a Millionaire,* ruminations on his life presented as a 1981 Christmas gift to friends, which the *New York Times, Newsweek,* and other publications found interesting enough to merit mention in their pages; and *The Owl Hoots Again,* a collection of actual accounts and fictional short stories written between 1918 and 1937 and published in 1988.

Men of power and wealth regularly manage to get their works published, even in the absence of any real writing ability. Whitney, however, was a natural storyteller with an engaging style —

something that often caught the uninitiated off guard.

Lexington, Kentucky, newswoman Sue Wylie remembered the memorable debut of *High Peaks.* The book was released, as it turned out, during the same week Whitney and his wife were entertaining Princess Margaret at their Kentucky horse farm. The national press had been roaming about the farm for days, eager for any detail they could dredge up on what the visiting dignitary was eating, doing, or discussing. When Whitney announced one morning there would be an afternoon press conference, the media were delighted, convinced they would be fed something worthy of being included in that evening's royals coverage.

At the appointed hour, the newspeople gathered eagerly in Whitney's office, elbowing for space. Whitney addressed the throng: "I'd like to read you a chapter from my new book."

The assembled mass was at first stunned, then openly dismayed. There were a few audible groans. Feet shuffled. Eyes darted toward the exits.

"Then," Wylie recalled, "Mr. Whitney began reading. Soon these crusty newsmen were utterly transfixed. There was not another sound for as long as it took him to finish this chapter, which was not short."[1]

This advertisement for Whitney's book appeared in the *Sunday Times Book Review* section.

On base, he sped through several sequences of training, achieving advanced flying status, which meant he could fly in tight V formation, had developed precision accuracy for bombing and had mastered dives and spirals.

This was during the very early days of flight, an era of primitive airplanes, inconsistent fuels, and novice mechanics. Forced landings were common, and on many occasions, Whitney found it necessary to slide his plane onto a pasture, a field, or, one time, onto a baseball diamond.

During the time he was in training, seventeen would-be pilots died, a figure that Whitney, ever the pragmatist, insisted was quite low, considering the number of men who were going through training and the speed with which they were doing it.

With nearly six weeks of intensive training under his belt, he was transferred to Hicks Field to complete aerial gunnery school, an experience he hated for the classroom tedium and, just as importantly, because he was trapped, if only for a few weeks, on base without passes to town. The latter he addressed. He and a pal began forging passes, shoving them at the gate guards at dusk, when suspicious details were not likely to be detected. Then they would make their way to town to go to movies or Elks Club dances. Returning to base after a night on the town was a bit more difficult and often entailed crawling on their bellies across the airstrip out of sight of the sentries.

By the end of spring, he had finished the required courses and was awaiting his commission, after which, he hoped, he would be shipped off to the front to fight the Germans.

"I was nineteen years old," he wrote in a story that would be published decades later in a collection titled *The Owl Hoots Again,* "and fighting in the air seemed romantic for at that age you do not expect to be killed. The speed and novelty of this form of warfare was absorbing. We talked of nothing else."[13]

But the wheels of government turn at their own pace, and word was slow in coming. Without Washington-sanctioned wings upon his chest, he was not even permitted to help instruct the new recruits, who were arriving almost daily. So he killed time by practicing. He would check out a

Whitney noted in *First Flight* that this pass, which allowed him out of the School of Aerial Gunnery until midnight, was not valid because it had yet to be stamped.

plane at every opportunity and take to the skies over Texas, where he would do spirals and barrel rolls and then descend through the clouds for precision landings.

He developed uncommon skill, and when his commission and orders finally came through, he was assigned not to the front, but to train others. He was transferred to Carruthers Field, where he spent his days at the nerve-wracking task of instructing sometimes recalcitrant young men in the finer points of barrel rolls and other advanced acrobatic maneuvers that might help them in combat. He was the youngest instructor in the U.S. Army Air Corps and, in many people's reckoning, one of the very best.

The young recruits he instructed revered him. One of them, Edward Wells, was moved to write him a letter sixty years later after seeing Whitney on the *Today Show:* "I was reminded of Carruthers Field ... [and] that first flight when you explained how important it was to keep the rocker arms on the horizon, then thrilled me with your famous 'falling leaf' maneuver as the finale."[14] Wells also recalled that one day when Whitney was practicing landings with his students, Gertrude arrived by car and "sat on the ground beside the field watching as you patiently took your pupils, one by one, and let us endanger your survival with our awkward attempts at three-point landings.... When I was waiting my turn I enjoyed sitting with your mother, conversing with her, and I recall she was very kind to me and very proud of you."[15]

Just as it appeared that Whitney would finally be sent abroad, the armistice was signed. He was sorely disappointed at having lost his opportunity to join the air wars over Europe. But he had distinguished himself without regard to name, pedigree, or social standing.

He had been promoted to first lieutenant and had been chosen by Eddie Rickenbacker, a renowned and highly decorated combat pilot during World War I, as one of the top five fighter pilots in the country. He was not yet twenty years old.

"In one year I had become an adult," he wrote in *High Peaks*. "I had made friends from all parts of the country and all walks of life and I could hold my own with them. Now I felt really ready to step out on my own. And the time was ripe. It was a great time to be young."[16]

Off he went to Yale, a substantially different person with substantially different perspectives than would have been the case had he entered college immediately after private school. He had spent the previous year involved in arenas that most sons of millionaires did not venture into. He had developed a taste for living life close to the edge. And he was accustomed to making his own decisions. On top of that, he had all the money and contacts he might need to pave the way to whatever future he might choose.

Thus his Yale years served not as the protective transitional cocoon where young men of his station took small and gradual steps to the bigger world beyond, but rather as an opportune launch pad for experiencing all that the Roaring Twenties came to represent.

There was little in the way of scholarly pursuit. Indeed, his years at Yale were dismissed years later by his public relations man with

one deeply telling line: "... resigned [his commission] to enroll in Yale, where he rowed on the crew for two years."[17]

Whitney himself acknowledged that academics was not his forte at Yale. "I never stood any better in my class than third to last,"[18] he cheerfully told a magazine writer decades later. Interestingly, though, he developed a later-life affection for the school, or at least its mascot — the owl. He would often have the running cat symbols removed from his Jaguar automobiles

Whitney as a young man had an earnest, some-times almost wistful look that women found irresistible.

and replaced with custom-crafted owls, and he collected owl figurines.

He may have expended little energy in the classroom, but "socially I was very active.... I played the field — society girls, stage celebrities and, well, all sorts,"[19] he wrote in *High Peaks*. There were evenings at speakeasies (these being the years of Prohibition) and glamorous parties and balls hosted by haute society.

The gangliness of his youth had settled nicely into patrician good looks and an easy, natural charm that young women — and their mothers — found utterly irresistible. The fact that he had a hefty allowance and a direct line to a large fortune did not diminish his appeal. He cavorted with various young women, always just briefly, and seemed singularly devoted to making the most of his standing as man of the moment.

During the summers, he partook of various wilderness adventures, including one in which he sailed the south coast of Alaska with his cousin Douglas Burden. And on holiday breaks during the school year, he usually visited Old Westbury.

His parents began to worry about him. But Gertrude, by then an established sculptor who was working on her most massive and enduring work, a bronze of Buffalo Bill Cody, which stands in Cody, Wyoming, was too busy and, in any event, unwilling to intrude. Harry Payne viewed his son's behavior as yet another example of the unreliability of life.

About midway through his Yale years, Sonny took up with a woman who was variously described as a chorus girl, a Ziegfeld Follies girl, and a show girl. Whatever the precise definition of her previous vocation, Miss Fontaine quickly became known by one title: paramour of Sonny Whitney. The society columnists enthusiastically recorded the couple's every outing, but their early interest in the story was nothing compared with their frenzy when Miss Fontaine (who was actually a Mrs.) announced she was suing Cornelius Vanderbilt "Sonny" Whitney for breach of marital promise and, according to some accounts, paternity.

Top: Whitney was a member of the crew team at Yale, where he was more accomplished at athletics than academics.

Above right: C.V. Whitney (second from left, top row) with members of his Yale graduating class and their revered mascot, the owl.

Suddenly, C.V. "Sonny" Whitney, a name that had previously been known in only a few circles, resonated for both high society and blue-collar ranks alike, each eagerly awaiting the next installment of the Sonny saga.

The headlines and court maneuverings went on for months, but Harry Payne's wealth and battery of lawyers eventually prevailed in obtaining the truth. As it turned out, Miss Fontaine's breach of marital promise claim was thrown out because she was actually Mrs. Fontaine.

The Whitney family always insisted that Sonny knew the woman only socially, not intimately, but whatever the situation, Sonny acquired a reputation as a playboy, a fact that angered his father, embarrassed Yale (which did not tap him for the senior societies) and set the stage for something of a lifestyle turnabout for the twenty-three year old.

Just prior to the rain of lurid headlines, Sonny had stepped up his attentions toward Marie Norton, the daughter of a family that lived near the Whitneys in Old Westbury. Although she was a perfectly acceptable young woman, Harry Payne was displeased with the speed with which Sonny seemed committed to moving toward the altar. In a May 1922 letter to Gertrude, who was in France on holiday, Harry wrote, "Have had several séances with your son which is not pleasant. Have not been cross or disagreeable with him. But he has only one idea in his mind. Marriage in the early fall and love feasts between us and the Norton family."[20]

Harry's reluctance probably sprang from normal parental concern that a man not quite out of college may not know his mind well enough to make appropriate marital choices. And according to biographer Friedman, Harry perhaps harbored deeper doubts, based on what little he knew about the show-girl controversy that was about to break in a hideously public way.[21]

It was perhaps in the interest of removing his son from the various home-soil temptations and headlines that prompted Harry Payne to present an interesting proposition. On his first night home after graduating from Yale, Whitney wrote, "to my great surprise … my father said, 'Son, why don't you go to Europe for the summer? I'm sure your uncle would welcome you in Hungary. And you should visit France and Italy and have a good educational vacation.'"[22]

The younger Whitney was thrilled at the prospect but announced, quite accurately, "It sounds great but I don't have any money."[23]

His father offered up $2,000, and Whitney began making calls, arranging to pass some time in northern France with his good pal Tommy Hitchcock, who would be there playing polo; with a couple of Yale buddies who would be in Paris; and with his mother's sister Gladys, who had married a Hungarian and was proposing such diversions as a stag hunt in the mountains and several black-tie affairs in Budapest.

Whitney packed hunting clothes and tuxedos and boarded an ocean liner, arriving in France to embark, as usual, on an adventure that was "hardly the educational type my father had in mind."[24]

He and his friends prowled the casinos (where he lost virtually all the money his father had given him, only to have a last-minute change of luck and, afterwards, "sense enough to go straight to bed"[25]) and the art shops, where he bought his first oil painting, by Oudry, of two of King Louis XV's favorite hunting dogs — an artwork he said even fifty years later was still a favorite.

At night they explored the Montmartre district, with its cabarets, bistros, and bar girls. The French he had learned from his sisters' French governess served him well.

It was with some regret that he boarded the legendary Orient Express to go off to Hungary, where his uncle Count Lazlo Sczechenyl was at the top rung of Hungarian society. His hosts sought to keep him perpetually amused with hunting expeditions, society balls, and gypsy entertainment. On one particularly memorable night, he was taken by his uncle to a gathering of distinguished men and young, beautiful women. "Tonight we are out with our girl friends," his uncle announced. "Our wives know it, and I suspect they are glad to be rid of us for an evening."[26] His uncle presented him with a beautiful blond actress.

Although his plan was to stay in Europe for only a couple of months, the scandal headlines had broken back home, and he decided to stay in Paris until the furor died down. Marie Norton arrived in Paris at his urging, and soon they were planning a wedding. He sent a series of beseeching letters to his parents, expressing how much it would mean to him if they were to come to the wedding, and Gertrude and Harry finally acquiesced and made the ocean journey.

During his post-Yale European adventures, while he was staying with his aunt and uncle in Budapest, Whitney went on a stag hunt in the mountains.

Soon after arriving, Gertrude presented a cast of *The Spirit of the Red Cross* to the War Museum in the Invalides. It was her only son's face that she used as a model, and the papers, delighted at her presentation, proclaimed that "the face of young Cornelius Vanderbilt Whitney will be immortalized" as the aviator in the group.[27]

The wedding took place on the morning of March 5, 1923, a cold and bitter day as winter lingered resolutely over the city streets. It was small and simple; first, a civil marriage in Paris' City Hall of the first arrondissement, witnessed by Gertrude and Harry and Mrs. Norton and Marie's two sisters, then a religious ceremony at the Church of the Holy Trinity. Both took only a few minutes, and then the wedding party adjourned to the fashionable Hotel Brighton for a celebratory breakfast.

The couple embarked on a several-month honeymoon that took them most of the way around the world. It was Sonny's goal to stay away from New York until the lawsuit publicity had blown over and then return quietly to take up a place somewhere among his father's various enterprises.

By the time the couple returned home to New York, the headlines had indeed dissipated. But Sonny's father's anger had not. The prodigal son's arrival was met with something less than a welcoming paternal embrace.

Sonny would have to prove himself a man of some substance, not just a playboy, his father decreed. Harry gave the young couple an allowance of $20,000, then dispatched them to the West, where Sonny would take up work at his father's mines in Nevada.[28]

Whitney as a young man was always known to seek out good times, but that did not stop him from pursuing more serious endeavors.

CHAPTER FOUR

MAKING HIS FIRST FORTUNE

BANISHMENT TO THE MINES WAS regarded as unduly harsh treatment by friends and family alike. Comstock, Nevada, was a barren, rough-and-tumble mining town with no grace, no amenities, and relentless heat.

As it turned out, the Comstock penance was actually much worse than any of them imagined it might be. Whitney was assigned, not, as everyone had assumed, to some mid-level manager job, but to a mucker position, the worst of some very bad jobs in mining. Wearing steel helmets with a light attached, muckers worked the narrowest, most remote tunnels, using picks and shovels to dig deeper and deeper into the earth in pursuit of veins of silver and other ores.

The work was hard on a man's body. The half-crouch position required to navigate the tunnels and hack deeper into them transformed many strapping young men into stooped old ones long before their time. And the heat was intense. Every hour or so, muckers were hauled out of the stopes and laid out on a slab of ice for a few minutes to allow them to recover enough to return to the tunnels and finish their shifts.

The work was also hard on a man's spirit. Hour after hour in the black darkness broke many a man as he toiled hundreds of feet beneath the earth's surface with only the occasional jolt from a dynamite blast one tunnel over to intrude on the monotony.

It was to this environment that Harry Payne chose to arrange his only son's debut into the workaday world of the various Whitney enterprises.

If young Whitney was surprised, disappointed, or distressed, there is no evidence. "C.V. was used to hard knocks from the family, for he had been taking them for years," wrote Whitney family biographer Hoyt.[1] From early boyhood he had been told by his father that he wasn't smart enough or athletic enough or responsible enough, a refrain that was ultimately taken up by some of the relatives.

When Whitney wrote about the Nevada episode years later in *High Peaks,* there was no hint of anger or bitterness. He presented it as a high-drama adventure that, viewed in the proper way, could be seen as a stepping stone to opportunity.

And that may be exactly as he saw it, even then. Whitney, even in his twenties, had an uncommon ability to recast or reframe things he found painful or unpleasant. Wallowing in disappointment or anguish was not only unseemly but unproductive, and when certain unhappy realities threatened to become daunting or oppressive,

---

For nearly a year, Whitney worked as a miner in the little town of Comstock, Nevada. It was an unpleasant time in his life about which he rarely spoke.

he merely recast those realities into something more palatable. This was a skill he honed to fine precision as the years went on, along with the ability to simply ignore or refuse to revisit things he did not wish to relive. Indeed, in later years, many a dinner guest recalled seeing Whitney's finely chiseled face shift slightly when asked about a painful or awkward moment. "That is not at all interesting," he would respond, closing the matter entirely to all future discussion.

He was able to live in his own world," his daughter Nancy Whitney told a magazine writer years later. "Anything that displeased him he could simply cut out of that world and replace it with something [else]."[2]

Whitney's public presentation of the Nevada atonement period was undoubtedly an example of his ability to push aside disturbing aspects and focus on the upbeat. He also, when he wrote about this phase of his life, failed to make any mention of his wife Marie, who had gamely joined him there. The marriage disintegrated quickly, and he was divorced from her after only six years. It was a union he rarely talked of again.

But for at least the first few months of marriage, Sonny and Marie engaged in what appeared to be a normal if Spartan life among the miners. When he got off work every day at 4:30, they would often go horseback riding. In the evenings they often ate with the other miners and their wives or went to the movies. There was talk of starting a family.

When they married, Marie must have appeared to Sonny the perfect melding of two worlds. She possessed the social acceptability his family would have insisted upon, but she also had an earthy, salty quality that Sonny had come to like in women during his airman days.

"The daughter of a prominent Democratic lawyer and a wonderful old character of a mother who was part Jewish and part Irish, [Marie] had the mongrel's love of the unconventional,"[3] wrote Peter Duchin, son of famed 1930s bandleader Eddie Duchin. Peter was raised by Marie and her post-Sonny husband, Averell Harriman, after his mother died in childbirth and his father went on the road.

"She spoke out of one side of her mouth in a sort of drawl through clenched teeth," Duchin

Whitney and his mother, Gertrude, on a leisurely ride in New York during the 1920s.

wrote.[4] She also "chewed gum and smoked Viceroys in white plastic holders that were scattered everywhere in china and silver cups. She had a habit of emptying the contents of one ashtray in a larger ashtray and carrying the whole mess out to the kitchen. It was the only time I ever saw her go into that room."[5]

Direct, straightforward, and no-nonsense, she "swore like a trooper" and "loved talking about sex," Duchin wrote.[6]

The miners appreciated her. And they also appreciated her husband, who was nothing at all like what they expected of the Ivy League–educated son of the owner.

Sonny and Marie spent a year in Comstock, where Sonny worked his way up through a series of menial jobs until he was promoted to the company's main office in San Francisco to head an exploration department and to acquire other mining properties.

The following year he was back in New York. Having earned his father's grudging respect for his hard work and uncomplaining compliance, he had settled into a "small office on Wall Street … installed there by my father who had decided it was high time that his son and heir learned the ways of banking and high finance."[7]

By all accounts, the father-son association, though improved, was still strained. And when Sonny received word one afternoon that his father wished to see him in his office, he expected the worst. "This happened very seldom and usually meant that I had done something wrong," Whitney wrote.[8] The old man, however, was not feeling punitive that day. He declared that he was resigning from the boards of The Guaranty Trust Company, the Metropolitan Opera Company, the Museum of Natural History, and the Metals Exploration Company and wanted Sonny to take his place. The younger Whitney, caught completely off guard, was practically speechless. He was directed to visit his father's secretary, Mr. Regan, who would share with him all the pertinent details relating to the various duties and responsibilities that would follow.

In yet another turn of the fortuitous timing that seemed to regularly visit Sonny Whitney, the young man entered the secretary's office just as Regan was announcing over the telephone that Harry Whitney had decided that morning that he wanted to sell his one-third interest in the Richardson Construction Company in Mexico. Harry Whitney had put half a million dollars into it, had seen nothing in return, and wanted the shares sold on the over-the-counter market the next morning.

Sonny was very interested in this announcement. He knew something about that property — one million acres in the Yaqui Valley of Sonora, Mexico. He had spent some time in the vicinity several months earlier on one of his trips in search of new mine sites. While there he had met General Alvaro Obregon, the governor of Sonora, later to become the president of Mexico, who owned

several thousand adjacent acres and was very interested in and enthusiastic about the future of the valley, if properly developed. Whitney had passed a pleasant afternoon with the general, then continued on with his travels, never giving the man or the land another thought.

Until now. As Whitney later remembered it, he sat dutifully as Regan hung up the telephone and turned his attention to the matter at hand, rambling on about the various duties the young man would be taking over from his father. But Whitney heard little of it. All he could think of was the general's firm conviction that the land had limitless potential.

"I have about seven thousand dollars in my bank account," he thought to himself. "Will that be enough to buy the certificates of ownership my father wants to sell?"[9]

The next morning he bought the certificates for $3,150. He wired the general to request a

Whitney and his first wife, Marie, early in their marriage.

meeting and boarded a train the next morning for Tucson, where he hired a car and drove across the border for the meeting he fully expected would make him a fortune. "How big a fortune? I had no idea," he later wrote.[10]

In a cramped back room reeking of tequila and cigar smoke and jammed with Mexicans playing poker, Whitney laid out his proposal to the general. He had certificates he was willing to sell to the Mexican government, he wished to entertain whatever offer they might make, and he wanted it settled quickly. The next morning Whitney accepted a half million–dollar deal — $50,000 per month for the next ten months — then boarded the train and returned to New York.

Four years away from age thirty, he had made his first significant money. Harry Payne Whitney never knew that it was his son who bought the certificates he was so eager to be rid of.

It was this $3,000 investment, he always maintained, which led to his rapidly becoming a millionaire in his own right. "With this windfall I founded Pan American Airways and the following year, by selling some stock in Pan Am, I founded the Hudson Bay Mining & Smelting Company."[11]

During his exile to Nevada and points west, Whitney had learned well and was taken under the wing of Roscoe Channing, president of several of the Whitney mining operations and a mining engineer of some note.

In 1925 the two men became involved in a salvage operation established to extract additional gold and silver from the scrap ore that had been tossed aside during the mining boom years of the 1890s. An examination of some of the refuse piles had convinced Whitney and Channing that millions of dollars worth of ore was just lying about, waiting to be captured by anyone who would take the time to develop more refined extraction processes than those used before the turn of the century.

This 1936 illustration was prepared by the American Bank Note Company for the Hudson Bay Mining & Smelting Company.

They established a laboratory in Denver to experiment with various techniques and within a year had developed a flotation process by which they were ultimately able to rescue more than a million dollars worth of ore from properties Harry Payne owned in Utah, Mexico, and Arizona.

Having mastered the technique, Sonny and Channing set their sights on Manitoba, where they were certain they could make millions from an abandoned mine, called Guggenex, which they had optioned for a few thousand dollars.

Sonny sought and received financing from Harry Payne, some $600,000, to construct the flotation plant at Flin Flon, Manitoba.

Sonny and Channing set off for the northlands, traveling with provisions and equipment hundreds of miles by canoe and an additional seventy miles on foot.

It might have turned out to be a fool's errand, but as fate would have it, their mission was successful. The modest operation at Flin Flon became, in short order, the Hudson Bay Mining & Smelting Company, worth $30 million before the end of the next decade.

With equal measures of risk-taking, courage, and sweat equity, Sonny had pulled off another one, almost single-handedly.

"I made my life," Whitney declared with what was obvious enormous pride when he was approaching his eighties. "I always thank my father. He never gave me a damn cent."[12]

This was not technically true. When Harry Payne died in the 1930s, $20 million went to his son, most of which he could not claim until he turned thirty-five. But by then, C.V. "Sonny" Whitney, still barely into his thirties, had already started a handful of companies on his own and was worth a few million in his own right.

As his business acumen and success soared, his marriage soured. Marie, for all her strength and spunk, had begun to feel she was a woman abandoned. Her confidence and resilience were crumbling in huge chunks. Indeed, for the rest of her life, one of her defining characteristics was a deep channel of great vulnerability, Duchin maintained.[13]

In 1929 Sonny and Marie went their separate ways, Marie to wed Harriman. There were two young children. Harry Payne Whitney II was five years old when his parents divorced, and Nancy Marie was four.

Left: Whitney and Marie had two children, Nancy and Harry, shown here in a rare moment of closeness with their father.

Below: Flin Flon, the site of Whitney's mining company, is a small city in the Canadian province of Manitoba.

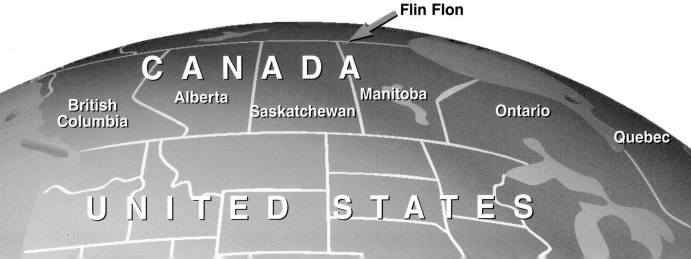

One of Whitney's early ventures was cofounding Pan American Airways, which grew to be the largest commercial airline in the world.

CHAPTER FIVE

ON WINGS OF GLORY

WHITNEY'S MEMORIES OF THE glory and the potential of flight were enduring ones, and while the Roaring Twenties were still roaring, his attention again turned to airplanes.

An old Yale acquaintance, Juan Trippe, approached Whitney with a bold plan involving planes and government contracts and a large measure of derring-do, and Whitney, reacting more on gut instinct than to any solid business plan — which, if it existed at all, existed only in the head of Trippe — promptly signed on.

Trippe, the son of a New York investment banker, had been besotted with flying since age ten, when his father had taken him to an air race over lower New York Bay. With single-minded determination, Trippe had mastered Morse code, learned what little there was to learn at that time about radio communication, and gone to flight school, all while still in his teens. In college, he absorbed everything he thought might be relevant to starting a business, ignored the rest, and within a few months after leaving Yale, he had bought up surplus Army planes and started his own business — plane rides along the New York coastline for joy-seekers. Soon he even had a contract in Central America with United Fruit Company to fly documents from the Honduran coast to the mountains. In a few short months, he also started several other flying ventures, but the one that seemed the most promising to him was winning the government's contract to fly mail from New York to Boston.

Air transport was regarded as a daring, even foolhardy venture in those days, an endeavor "as perilous and primitive as the Pony Express," wrote biographer Robert Daley in his book about Pan Am and Juan Trippe.[1] Airplanes in the mid-1920s were still unreliable, expenses were huge, and the notion of entrusting important items to air carriers was seen by many as fanciful and impractical, what with the solid growth and proven track record of rail systems. "People learned to send duplicate letters by train," Daley wrote.[2]

All of these circumstances coalesced to make Trippe's proposition irresistible to Whitney. Sonny's crafty land deal in Mexico provided the resources for him to embark on yet another pioneering effort, and he joined with Trippe and World War I pilot John Hambleton to unite with some investors from New England to organize Eastern Air Transport, which then merged with Colonial Airways. They hired pilots and secured the New York–Boston contract, which, as it turned out, was one of the busiest and most lucrative runs in the country.

In 1936, Pan Am's M-130 *China Clipper* flying boat seemed "as futuristic in design as a space capsule." *(Photo courtesy Pan Am Historical Foundation.)*

Bottom: For most of his life, Whitney was fascinated with planes and spent much of his business and leisure life around them.

Within a couple of years, Trippe, Sonny, and their moneyed young backers were so convinced of the wisdom of their decision and the potential of the fledgling business that when the majority of the Colonial board ousted Trippe for wanting to extend Colonial's routes into the Chicago–New York market (an expansion they saw as too daring since Colonial was losing money), they set up a new company called Aviation Corporation of America. This, they hoped, would ultimately not only expand into new territory but also transport passengers as well as mail. Whitney went to William Rockefeller; his cousin John Hay Whitney, known as Jock, whose fortune was far greater than his own; his cousin William Vanderbilt; and to Averell Harriman (who in a short time would become the husband of Sonny's wife Marie) to secure support for the venture.

There was a decided advantage to being a Whitney. The well-heeled set supported its own, and soon the financial commitments were pouring in. They set up a Florida-to-Havana segment in 1927 by merging with some investors in another proposed air service. And they named the operating company, in what probably seemed overzealous optimism to some, Pan American Airways. "I can remember going to bankers for financing of our first run, the 235 miles from Miami to Havana," Whitney told a magazine reporter years later. "They all said we were crazy. It was much too far for a commercial flight."[3]

But it wasn't too far, and the name was not an overstatement. In just a few months Pan American airplanes were flying to Puerto Rico and the Panama Canal Zone. And in a few years they were covering much of Latin America and the South Pacific as well as Asia. Sonny Whitney, who had put up $49,000, served as chairman of the board. Trippe, the man with limitless knowledge of airplanes and the proven ability to forge deals most people considered impossible, was named managing director.[4]

According to Whitney family biographer Edwin Hoyt, Whitney, already deeply involved in the Flin Flon operation and other enterprises turned over to him by his father, served primarily as a front man for Pan Am — at least in the early months of the venture. He had the name and cachet that could open doors and attract money, and he had the grace and style that could give an infant company the stature that potential customers, investors, and the public at large would find comforting. Lending his name, face, and money to the operation was his primary function as Pan Am's chairman of the board.

But Whitney was enamored of airplanes and intrigued with what he saw as Pan Am's almost boundless possibilities, and soon he was more involved in the overall operations. He helped scout new territory and pushed for expansions that would take Pan American into new countries and onto new continents.

He went to Mexico in 1928 and, after discussions with some businessmen there, recommended that Pan Am buy the Mexican Aviation Company, which it did. Aided by his pilot's background and what had evolved into an uncommonly keen eye for recognizing dormant opportunities, he zeroed in on promising new routes.

He spent months trudging about Latin America helping to locate the best areas for the company's next wave of expansion. Whitney had become increasingly taken with Latin America and was convinced that if air travel were available to these largely undiscovered regions, hordes of tourists who were then traveling to Europe would turn their eyes to the Caribbean and Latin America. As the years went on, he set his sights on crossing the Pacific as well.

As Whitney often said, when one is attempting to build the world's greatest airline, one must turn to the world's greatest pilot. Thus, when famed pilot Charles Lindbergh returned from overseas, Whitney met him at Roosevelt Field and asked him to join Pan Am as consultant and technical advisor to explore possible commercial air routes. Whitney and Lindbergh covered thousands of air miles together, with Lindbergh

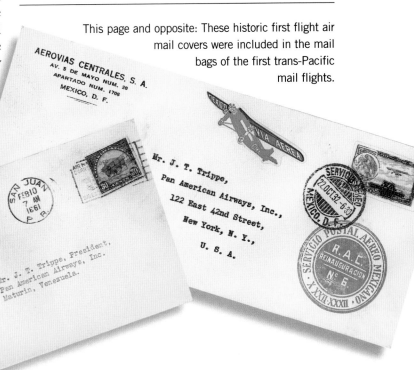

This page and opposite: These historic first flight air mail covers were included in the mail bags of the first trans-Pacific mail flights.

With Charles Lindbergh piloting, Pan American Airways' airliner *General New* made a run to Cuba in February 1928. Whitney often accompanied Lindbergh on his flights with Pan Am.

as pilot and Sonny as copilot. The fact that Lindbergh was a national hero also helped the company gain governmental and public support.

Less than a decade after Pan American Airways was founded, Whitney made the first passenger flight across the mid-Pacific to China, for which he received the Order of the Blue Jade, then that country's highest decoration. When the trip began, it was not at all clear to Pan American officials whether the journey would have to be halted before reaching China. It was billed merely as the official opening of the first trans-Pacific air route to passengers. The stated final destination was Manila, and the China leg of the journey was held in deep secrecy. The people aboard would be covering an island-hopping course that theretofore had been traversed only by Pan American pilots ferrying mail and other goods, an undertaking considered remarkable enough that the press showed up in droves.

Whitney recorded the journey, which began on October 14, 1936, in a story that was published years later in a collection of his stories titled *The Owl Hoots Again.*

"A small heterogeneous group of eight citizens of the United States stood in a rather foolish looking array before a battery of cameras.... A little later on they marched self-consciously down a long gangplank ... and silently disappeared one by one in the bowels of the *Philippine Clipper.* The neat row of immaculately white airline officials sprang into controlled movement — silent and organized — and the *Clipper* slid from her dock out into the bay.... Our fifty-two thousand pounds took to the air in fifty-five seconds. San Francisco below us ... men embarking for China — the first hop to be twenty-four hundred miles of open ocean separating San Francisco and

Honolulu.... Nine thousand miles from Hong Kong with stops at Honolulu, Midway, Wake, Guam and Manila. Will we get to Hong Kong? That is what we are wondering."[5]

The suspense flowed not just from the incalculable perils of crossing the Pacific Ocean but from the awareness that they had not yet received, and might not ever get, permission from the British to land in Hong Kong. No other airplane had made such a journey. None had been permitted to land on soil much west of Manila.

The intrepid travelers were met in Honolulu with great celebration, hula dancers, and a luau on the beach. Once those festivities ended, they continued on through storm winds to recently settled Midway. Next came Wake Island, where the rats were so huge and bold as to constitute a menace, Whitney wrote, and where man had settled only one year earlier, after Trippe had declared the island a crucial setdown point for Pan Am and built a hotel and other facilities there. From Wake Island, they were off to Guam, where the heat smothered them with hideous intensity and the locals were so joyful for the visit that they plied the travelers with copious amounts of liquor, rendering them practically unconscious for the trip to Manila the next day.

Once they arrived in Manila, Whitney wrote that the passengers were largely oblivious to the magnitude of the feat that had been accomplished. They were consumed with only one thought: "Our progress was being watched with an interest that would startle the layman.

We had a permit from the Portuguese to land at Macao, south of Hong Kong, but the question that statesmen and aviation executives want answered was would the British give Pan American Airways permission to fly into Hong Kong."[6]

The Hong Kong issue was crucial to the company's expansion plans. For unlike shipping, in which ships flying the flags of virtually any country could, in most circumstances, put into any port anywhere in the world, aircraft had to receive permission from the host country. The British and French had Europe completely sewn up, and Britain, with all its various holdings in South America and the Caribbean, at any moment could create great difficulties for Pan Am's South American routes. So the logical expansion was into the Far East. If Pan American could get a foothold in the Orient, it could provide a quicker route from the Orient to Europe via the United States than England would be able to provide via India.

On the second day in Manila the news came: permission granted. After a brief stopover in Macao, it was on to Hong Kong. The Pan American passengers, now weary from travel, ragged from the oppressive heat, and nauseous from excessive celebratory toasting the night before, compelled themselves through sheer force of will and the last adrenaline reserves still left in their bodies to approach Hong Kong with appropriate excitement and reverence. After all, this was the dreamed-of destination previously visited by very few Americans.

There they were warmly greeted and feted before continuing their journeys through a host

Whitney's scrapbook of the trans-Pacific passenger flight depicts history in the making. As Whitney noted, "The flight to Honolulu, and thence to Midway, Wake, Guam, Manila, and Macao, all duly reached on schedule, was preliminary to the establishment, the following week, of a regular trans-Pacific passenger service." In the background, the *Philippine Clipper* passes over the Golden Gate Bridge before heading out to sea. The inset above shows Juan Trippe (third from left), C.V. Whitney (fifth from left), and the six other passengers before they take off from Pan Am's Alameda base in San Francisco. Before reaching Macao (last inset, opposite page), the *Philippine Clipper* made several stops, where the passengers were greeted with unveiled enthusiasm.

Whenever Pan Am flights made their way to the Pacific islands, the natives offered warm welcomes and great festivities.

of Chinese cities. One night the mayor of Shanghai treated Whitney to a rare glimpse of the inner life of his city. He arranged for the American to be the honored guest at an evening with singsong girls — beautiful young women who play music, sing, or dance for men as part of the apprenticeship they must serve before they may become concubines.

Finally the travelers made their way to Peking. They were, Whitney wrote, "the first people to fly from New York to Peking every inch of the way, halfway around the world."[7] The trip had spanned eight days and scores of cultures, and it set the course for aviation's future for many years to come.

"We had linked China to the New World with a chain which took eight days in forging," Whitney wrote. "It was a small chain but it would bind together two important personages, and to paraphrase Kipling: 'East is East and West is West and sometimes the twain shall meet.'"[8]

Whitney was on another pioneer flight during that same decade when Pan Am decided to, in Whitney's words, "conquer the vastness of the South Pacific Islands."[9] While escorting a group of newsmen and dignitaries on the unspeakably long and arduous journey to New Zealand, Australia, Bali, Java, Borneo, and the Philippines,

Whitney also negotiated contracts with the various countries to which Pan American would soon be establishing regular service.

Focused and determined to tend to the various business obligations with which he was charged, he nonetheless engaged in a number of singularly Whitney-esque adventures during this Pan American endeavor.

On a stopover at the island of Java, Whitney and another Pan Am founding director, Eddie McDonnell, were invited to spend the night in the interior village of Joc Jakarta, which was ruled by a young sultan.

As Whitney wrote about it in *High Peaks*, he and McDonnell grilled the Javanese guide who had been dispatched to escort them to the sultan's palace, and the two Americans became more intrigued with each detail disclosed. The young Oxford-educated sultan had recently, upon the death of his father, moved back to the island to assume the throne. As was customary, he had inherited not only his father's kingdom but also his father's numerous wives. He now lived a rather isolated existence behind the palace walls with only a huge white elephant and his coterie of wives, ladies-in-waiting, and an assortment of exotic dancing girls as divertissements.

"I had a fairly vivid imagination, so the prospect of a night spent in a sultan's palace proved more than a trifle exciting," Whitney wrote in *High Peaks.*[10]

As dinner talk with the sultan meandered from discussions of the South Pacific to the joys of flight, Whitney and McDonnell were practically vibrating with anticipation. Finally, after numerous courses and several bottles of wine, Whitney wrote, "our host sighed heavily and confessed, 'I am bored to death here. All I can do is ride my elephant around and visit the wives I did not select.... And the evenings. My God! I have to watch every night nothing except native dancing girls. Ah, but tonight it will be different, Mr. Whitney.' Different? How different? What exotic entertainment, I wondered, did the sultan have in mind? Perhaps for a pair of worldly Americans, he had concocted something really extraordinary."[11]

As Whitney pondered the possibilities, the sultan snapped his fingers.... And then he announced they would engage in a game of Ping-Pong.

Stunned and deflated, the two Americans followed the young sultan to a game room where a new English Ping-Pong table had been installed. The games began.

Still, the two Americans thought, all hope might not be lost. "From outside the window some of the most sensuous music imaginable wafted into the room. More than a little distracting to the game. But promising," Whitney wrote. "I thought to myself: it won't be too long now before we go outside and join the fun. Ping-Pong, I told myself, was simply a preliminary to more sophisticated entertainment."[12]

The sultan, however, was a strong and tireless player, and when the games finally concluded in the early morning hours, he bade his guests good night and had them shown to their rooms.

Other aspects of his tenure with Pan American were even more confounding — and trying.

In slightly more than a decade, Pan Am — under Juan Trippe's management and with Whitney

as chairman of the board — had exceeded even the most optimistic expectations. By January 1, 1939, according to author Daley, Pan American "served 54,072 route miles in forty-seven countries with 126 airliners and 145 ground radio stations. It had over five thousand employees. Pan Am and its subsidiaries constituted by far the largest airline in the world."[13]

The numbers were undeniable. But they did not tell the full story of the various undercurrents, dramas, and tensions that existed behind the scenes.

Over the years the board of directors had gone through periodic cycles of disgruntlement with Trippe, almost always because of his autocratic compulsion to forge ahead under almost any circumstances and his excessive, habitual secrecy. Often the board had no idea what he was planning or what he had done, and expansions were often undertaken long before the board voted to approve them.

Juan Trippe, president of Pan American, used to calculate the distance Pan Am's planes could fly by stretching string between two points on his globe and translating the string measurement into inches. *(Photo courtesy Pan Am Historical Foundation.)*

In 1936, C.V. Whitney — along with Henry Morgan, Marshall Field and seven other elite businessmen — developed the Grumman Model G-21 Goose. The versatility of this eight-person, twin-engine amphibian aircraft made it quite popular with the Army, Navy, and Coast Guard.

This had been going on for the better part of a decade, since 1929, when John Hambleton, the pilot who had been one of the triumvirate of founders, was killed in a private plane crash while traveling on business for Pan Am. It was one of the rare times, according to Merylin Bender and Selig Altschul, who wrote a book on Pan Am, that Hambleton had "violated his precept of not surrendering the controls to any pilot other than his equal, like Charles Lindbergh."[14]

Hambleton had been the stabilizing force, the quiet but firm voice that Juan Trippe always listened to when he refused to hear others. Hambleton's death hit Trippe and Whitney hard, and Whitney wrote a poignant tribute that was published in an aeronautical magazine: "He was what most of us wish we could be, modest, sincere, loyal to his friends, decent in his ways, balanced in his actions and, in short, what has been described as a very perfect gen-

tleman. It is a pity that this young man could not have lived longer so that many more people might have benefited from personal contact with him."[15]

The equal pity, biographers later concluded, was that without his steadying hand, Trippe's natural tendency toward sovereign rule went unchecked.

For quite some time, Trippe managed to get by with it. His genius was undisputed, and besides, he had handpicked the board over the years, biographer Daley pointed out, so he always managed to have sufficient support when discord erupted. But in early 1939, the company was in poor financial shape. It was losing heavily in the Pacific and investing heavily in the Atlantic with no return yet to pay off the enormous loans required for the massive expansions it had undertaken and would soon undertake. Moreover, dividends had been due stockholders two months earlier, but Pan Am had been unable to declare any.

On March 14, 1939, a special meeting was convened in the boardroom of corporate headquarters on the 58th floor of the Chrysler Building. The directors were bristling over the current state of financial affairs, and when the meeting was over, Sonny Whitney had been installed as chief executive officer and Trippe had been demoted to president, reporting to Whitney.

Even though Whitney, with 154,432 shares (worth about $3 million) of Pan Am stock, was the single largest stockholder and had served as chairman of the board for years, he was an improbable figure in any coup to topple Trippe. Whitney, according to Daley, had, over the years, "backed every one of Trippe's dreams" and "sometimes he was the only support Trippe had."[16]

Precisely what was said and what transpired behind those closed doors that day will never be known, for it was not recorded. Trippe had a long-standing policy of keeping meeting minutes extremely vague, a practice strictly adhered to that day. And Whitney, Trippe, and the other board members disclosed very little about the sudden turn of events.

Trippe said many years later that Whitney had indicated he was contending with a second wife who had high ambitions for him and that his life would be immeasurably improved if only he could serve as chief executive for awhile. "I handed it to him [Whitney]," Trippe said. "He wanted it and I handed it to him."[17] And in another account, Trippe said Whitney "needed it for his self-esteem."[18]

Whitney told a different story.

"[The press] played up that Juan and I had disagreements," Daley quoted Whitney as saying. "We did. We just put it to our board of directors and they made the decision."[19]

On another occasion, Whitney presented a few more details. "The board didn't feel it was being fully informed and so they put me in charge. But it was a temporary thing."[20]

In any event, whatever the details, it was the fervent hope of the board that with the change, the company, which may have been expanding too rapidly and dismissively, would begin to take on a higher level of fiscal responsibility.

Whitney immediately moved into the corner office that had been occupied by Trippe, and Trippe, sullen and silent, moved to an office down the hall.

Determined to supplant the secrecy that had been the hallmark of Trippe's reign, Whitney immediately instituted twice weekly meetings of the operations committee, requiring full disclosure of all that was being executed or contemplated. Trippe, as president, was part of this meeting, but, unaccustomed to subordinating

himself to anyone, he "sat stony-faced at the other end of the table, and for week after week he spoke not a single word," Daley wrote.[21]

It was a tense period at Pan Am, as employees constantly sniffed out the shifting winds of power, trying to establish where to place their allegiance and how to carve out a safe haven. Although Trippe later said he didn't take what could only have been interpreted as a demotion personally, he resolutely refused to engage in planning or strategy sessions with Whitney, tending instead to the various projects he had started before the Whitney reign. Whitney, stunned that a company man could seem so utterly unconcerned with the company's well-being, "didn't know how to cope with Trippe's attitude," wrote Daley. "Soon the two men were no longer on speaking terms at all, which upset Whitney terribly."[22]

As Pan Am officials sought to move forward, they kept discovering deals that Trippe had cut that no one else was aware of. And they sorely needed information that was not part of any records, only in Trippe's head.

By year's end, Whitney was weary of the strain and could see no way to propel the company forward when the man who knew more about it than anyone was acting as a roadblock at every turn. Moreover, he had in recent years become increasingly involved in the film industry and the horse business, and that, coupled with his other ventures, both old and new, along with the various Whitney family enterprises he headed, created a heaping platter too massive to manage. As biographers Bender and Altschul pointed out, Whitney was constitutionally a whirligig, "physically and emotionally unable to stay put for a sustained period of time."[23] Contending with the daily grind at Pan Am was not the ideal situation for a man of roving nature and entrepreneurial bent.

On January 9, 1940, the board voted to change the bylaws to designate the president rather than the chairman as chief executive officer. Trippe moved back into the big office, Sonny took a respite — a yachting vacation in the South — and he and his cousin Jock began selling their stocks for a return on their investments. By Pearl Harbor Day, most of Sonny's stocks had been sold, and he had resigned as chairman of the board and joined the Army Air Corps.

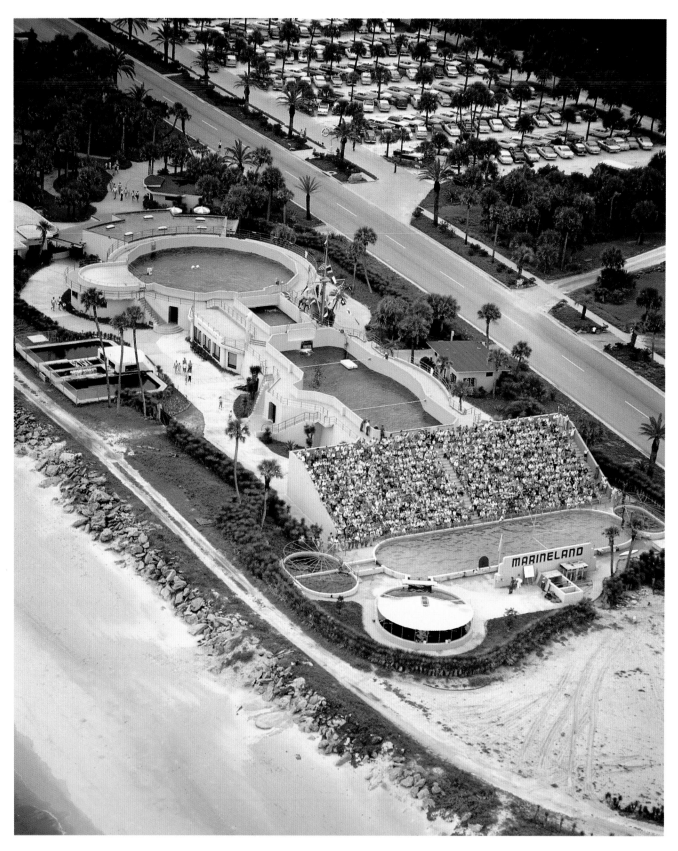

Whitney founded the world's first public oceanarium, Marineland, which quickly became Florida's premiere tourist attraction. *(Photo courtesy Marineland.)*

CHAPTER SIX

MOVIES AND MARINELAND

P AN AMERICAN WAS BUT one of more than forty significant ventures, avocations, and life changes that occupied C.V. Whitney's time, energies, and psyche during the post-Depression era. The 1930s were defining years, a decade of extraordinary successes and accomplishments fringed with disappointment, heartache, and grief.

When the decade began, he was involved with Pan American Airways, already a multicountry enterprise. He also had Flin Flon, his venture in the Canadian wilderness, soon to be known as the Hudson Bay Mining & Smelting Company, the "third-largest producer of copper in Canada and second-largest zinc producer and the source of millions of dollars in byproducts."[1] At the same time, he was tending to the metals exploration company and bank his father had handed over and was growing increasingly involved in arts patronage.

He was thirty-one years old, a millionaire in his own right, recently divorced, and taking on more of the Whitney family responsibilities. The Great Depression had a solid lockhold on the nation, but this affected the very wealthy very little. There continued to be world travel, summer vacations in the Adirondacks, hunting expeditions, and now that he was single again, many pretty young women eager to take his arm. "Oh my God, he was so wonderfully handsome," one woman who knew him in the 1930s and 1940s

told a writer for *Town & Country.* "Very winning. And extremely nice."[2]

He had survived scandals and penance and had come into his own, ever more determined to continue to make his own imprint on the world.

Late in that first year of the 1930s, in October, Whitney family patriarch Harry Payne Whitney came down with a cold after a weekend outing at Old Westbury. He was feeling poorly when he returned to his office in the city on Monday, and within a couple of days, he had taken to his bed. Doctors pronounced it pneumonia. Harry did not respond to any treatment, and by week's end, the family was called. Sonny and his two sisters and their husbands huddled about their father's bed for most of the weekend. On Sunday night Harry died. He was fifty-eight years old.

Harry's various holdings were worth about $65 million, a substantial increase over the $10 million his father had left him.[3] When the will was read, Sonny received about $2 million outright. He would receive an additional $18 million, but not for four more years, when he reached the age of thirty-five. The rest of Harry's money went

---

Over the years, Whitney posed for many pictures in front of the Marineland monument, which stands near the opening gates of the park.

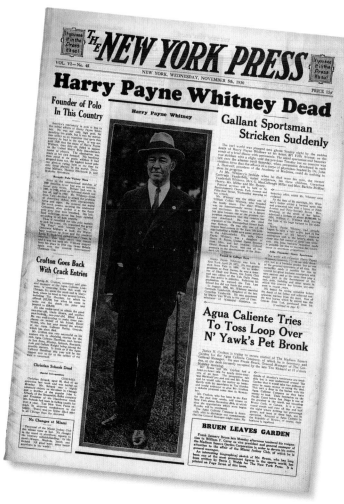

mostly to his daughters and to trusts set up for his grandchildren.

It was not customary for a father to withhold a son's inheritance for a period of years. But as Whitney family biographer Hoyt pointed out, "Harry Payne Whitney had never been close to his children, so it was nothing person-

Above: C.V.'s father, Harry Payne Whitney, died in 1930 at age fifty-eight.

Right: During the 1930s, Whitney presided over his various ventures and those of his family from a suite of offices on Park Avenue that his father had occupied before his death.

al, but Harry Payne had a look at the wastrels of society and he did what he could to prevent Sonny … from squandering his birthright."[4]

It seemed of little consequence to Harry Payne that Sonny had spent nearly a decade rising above his earlier transgressions and proving himself an adept businessman. Harry seemed obsessed with protecting his son from himself.

As biographer Hoyt saw it, Harry did what he did because his son, "unlike his father and his grandfather, had been born when the family was really rich" and "this third generation represented something new, a danger point to inherited wealth."[5]

Others saw it quite differently. In their minds, the punitive hand of Harry Payne was emerging from the grave, to give a final signal to the son he regarded as never quite good enough.

"His father didn't like him at all," Sonny's fourth wife, Marylou, said years after Sonny had died.[6] If that was true, and Sonny seemed to believe it was, it probably contributed mightily to much of what transpired in Sonny's life, including his many successes.

"He wanted to do everything better than his father," Marylou said. Whitney's apparent conviction that his father had little regard for him "was the best thing to ever happen to him. He did a lot of interesting things, but that's the reason he wanted to excel in everything he did, because of his father."[7]

Whatever the realities of the motivations and emotions that compelled Harry Payne when he made his bequests, Sonny Whitney became, at age thirty-one, a multimillionaire, assured of receiving many millions more in a few years.

This seemed to affect his life very little. Although he did move into the ancestral suite of offices at 230 Park Avenue, the seat of the Whitney business empire for many years, he continued the course he had set for himself years earlier, sniffing out opportunities and investing in those things he found personally exciting. If he now had the resources to enter into games where the stakes were higher, so be it. Money was to him simply a way to be involved in greater challenges, not a cushion upon which to recline and live the lagabout, ne'er-do-well existence Harry seemed to fear.

Indeed, the chief impact of Harry's death was not that Sonny had access to far more money, but rather that he would never again be thought of or referred to as "Sonny Whitney, presumed heir to the Whitney fortune." Harry's death, said biographer Hoyt, was Sonny's "coming of age." He was now the head of his branch of the Whitney family, charged with protecting the Whitney holdings along with tending to and expanding his own.

In 1931 Sonny married again. Gwaladys Crosby Hopkins, known as Gee, became the second Mrs. Cornelius Vanderbilt Whitney. A blonde Main Line beauty with unerring style and a rich, sensuous voice, she had been introduced to Sonny by his cousin Jock Whitney. A socialite by upbringing, she

Right: Whitney and his second wife, Gee, the gorgeous Philadelphia socialite and horsewoman, were married only ten years.

Below: Sonny would sometimes take Gee dogsledding while he was overseeing his mining operations in Flin Flon.

THE POLITICS OF PROMINENCE

WHITNEY'S RUN FOR CONGRESS in 1932 spawned a flood of press coverage that was quite copious, even by New York standards. During the six-week period that marked the opening of the campaign — from his August 17 announcement that he would seek the seat held by Republican Robert L. Bacon until September — more than nine hundred newspaper articles on Whitney appeared. In the subsequent weeks before election day, there were thousands more.

The emphasis in the stories tended to be less on his political positions than on his heritage, his reputation, and his motivation. The *Daily Mirror* pointed out that Long Island voters were stunned by his entry into the race, eventually attributing it to a rich boy engaging in diversion. But his close friends fervently denied that he sought public office "as one more hobby that he can easily afford."[1]

Moreover, the press pointed out with fierce regularity that this race presented an awkward challenge to Long Island blue-bloods because Whitney had chosen to run against one of his/their very own, the monied and socially prominent Mr. Bacon. "The social registers are all astir," cried the *Auburn Citizen Advertiser.* "The select social countryside is in confusion. The country clubs are divided against themselves and the vast country estates are in variance over which candidate to support."[2]

Whitney, who had endured a lifetime of unfortunate press coverage in his twenties and had assiduously avoided newspapermen in the decade since, found himself in the unhappy position of having to speak with them at length,

FOR CONGRESS

CORNELIUS WHITNEY

often about topics he had hoped he would never have to discuss again. Now it was necessary to defend his family, his wealth, and his background. He was not a playboy, he insisted, nor was he a silver-spoon-fed laggard who knew nothing but a life of privilege.

He had made his fortune through grit and gumption, he asserted, and he felt he should do what he could to help others. "In times like these I felt that it was the duty of young men to take an interest in public life and politics," he told the *New York Herald-Tribune.*[3]

As it turned out, many other men of breeding were just then becoming involved in politics. The nephew of J.P. Morgan was running for office, and Vincent Astor, head of the American Astors, was an executive on the campaign finance committee of the Democratic Party in New York. But this did not prevent the press from giving Whitney the lion's share of attention.

"He has to crack through the glamour of his position as grandson of Cornelius Vanderbilt and batter down the false glory and random animosity occasioned by his being a multi-millionaire," noted one newspaperman. "He is desperately anxious to be just an ordinary fellow, like you and me."[4]

Whitney dropped the Vanderbilt from his name, calling it "incongruous," lobbied heavily for family, friends, and reporters to stop referring to him as "Sonny" (without a bit of success) and insisted at every campaign stop that he was in politics, not as a lark, but to stay.

He campaigned without stop for fourteen to sixteen hours a day, and, in fact, Whitney and his wife Gee spent the first anniversary of their mar-

riage on an eleven-stop campaign tour of Long Island's North Shore villages — a personal tidbit duly noted by the press.

The reserved Gee, invariably referred to by the press as an "indefatigable campaigner," traveled with him virtually every hour of the campaign. This husband-wife campaign effort came during an era when

spouses did not generally take to the stump, making only occasional podium appearances before very important crowds. So unusual was her intense, sleeves-rolled-up participation that the society women of the North Shore found themselves scrambling to write letters of apology when they discovered that the young Whitney campaign worker loaded down with literature, whom they had so unceremoniously turned from their doors, was none other than Mrs. Cornelius Vanderbilt Whitney herself.

One of the highlights of the Whitney campaign befell when, just before election day, Franklin D. Roosevelt, then governor of New York, appeared in the district to encourage voters to cast their ballots for Whitney.

But while much of the press seemed taken with Whitney, and while several of the area newspapers endorsed him, politics was an arena in which Whitney did not have instant success and one that he chose not to pursue for the long term.

Opposite: Whitney ran for Congress when he was thirty-three years old, and the newspaper reporters frequently observed that he looked much younger than that.

Above: Whitney was known for making short, to-the-point speeches, which most rally attendees and all newspaper reporters appreciated.

Below: Even Franklin D. Roosevelt, then governor of New York, got behind Whitney's campaign. Here, Whitney (far left) waits for his turn at the podium during a political rally.

nonetheless trekked obligingly along the distinctly off-the-beaten paths Sonny often chose, just as Marie had done. She accompanied him, when invited, on many of his arduous Pan American exploratory trips and was a regular on many of the hunting expeditions he organized almost yearly into the most remote mountains of Mexico.

After returning with his new bride from a honeymoon in Central America, Sonny decided to try his hand at politics. He got the nod from the Democratic Party to run for Congress against a Long Island incumbent named Robert Bacon, who had been serving since 1923. Whitney hired a passel of public relations men who, according to biographer Hoyt, "taught him how to kiss babies and shake hands and ride around in an open car (as Roosevelt did so well), waving and smiling and greeting people."[8]

Whitney and Gee worked tirelessly, she, always beautifully clothed and coifed, driving the open Packard through the huge district as he gave speeches demanding reform, veterans' bonuses and repeal of Prohibition. When the speeches were over, they passed out sandwiches

as a band that traveled from stop to stop with them played "Happy Days Are Here Again."

The district had been solidly Republican for years, so it was an uphill struggle, and besides, Whitney was not the most effective Democratic candidate, most agreed, given his extreme wealth and his regular appearance on the society pages of the staunchly Republican *Herald-Tribune*.

On election day he lost by twenty-five thousand votes. He never ventured into elective politics again. It was his first real defeat in life, and it was an especially grueling and public one. He and Gee retired to Whitney Park, the sprawling acreage in the Adirondacks his grandfather William C. had purchased decades earlier and where several Whitneys — Sonny's sisters and cousins — had cabins. It was the remote safe haven of his childhood, just as primitive as and

Whitney campaigned in an open Packard, and Gee (in dark suit and hat in the back) was always with him on the campaign trail.

barely changed from many years earlier, when he had learned to fish, hunt, and swim there. He had returned there often in his twenties, to decompress and regain balance and, often, to reconnect with an extended family that had the usual share of misunderstandings and squabbles. In the fresh air and sunshine of the mountains, bruised feelings and egos were quickly healed, and a great feeling of familial appreciation settled over everyone. "Uncle Sonny gave us a great deal of fun as children," his niece Pamela Tower LeBoutillier told a writer for *Town & Country* in 1981. "He was a marvelous storyteller; nobody ever told better ghost stories than he did around the campfires in the Adirondacks."[9]

As Whitney propelled through his twenties, his visits to the Adirondacks became more frequent and longer in duration. For with maturity he recognized something about himself that most people did not see in him. His easygoing sociability notwithstanding, he was an intensely private man, even a little shy, and the never ending business and social contacts drained him to the very bottom of his reserves. The Adirondacks became the place where he could engage in soli-

For Whitney, fishing was a means of relaxing and connecting with nature. He fished chiefly in the Adirondacks and the streams of eastern Kentucky and would often get dropped off in the mountains of Colorado, where he stayed for days on end, hiking from stream to stream and staying in remote farmhouses at night.

tary reflection and shore up his energy reserves for the next round of adventure and enterprise.

He and Gee remained at the camp in the Adirondacks for weeks, he fishing mostly and hiking silently through the forests. When the snow got too high, they would go to a spa in the West or to Sun Valley or on one of their various hunting expeditions.

About this time, he was also entering a new venture, one regarded to be nearly as high-risk and fanciful as the air transport business. He and his cousin Jock Whitney formed a production company called Pioneer Pictures, which helped advance the infant technology of Technicolor and film making and financed four pictures that Hollywood wunderkind David O. Selznick directed. In fact, the company's first film, *La Cucaracha,* became the first "three-color, live-action short."

THE OLD WESTBURY CHAMPS

LATE IN THE 1930S, WHILE HE WAS founding various ventures and tending to others that he had created or that had been in the family for a generation or more, Whitney decided to have a serious go at an avocation he had only toyed with for years — polo.

He was well into his thirties, an age at which most serious polo players begin looking to other sport, but he became engrossed with the idea of taking the big title. He had been part of the Meadow Brook team that took the United States Polo Association Championships in 1928, but he regarded that as a lucky fluke. Now he was serious; he would not accept failure.

It was a goal born partly, no doubt, of a man's need to prove himself still vital as he approaches that watershed age of forty. But mostly it was a matter of family pride. His father, Harry, had won the world cup when he was nearly forty, and that might have been motivation enough. But there was more. His cousin Jock, five years his junior, had headed up the polo team that for the preceding two years had won the national championships.

Sonny and Jock had summered together and had been close when they were children. As adults they were involved in a number of business ventures together and had even introduced each other to various promising young women. But as men in their thirties, their relationship had taken on some sharper edges. This may have been partly because society columnists and the world at large often confused one for the other, an understandable error since the similarities were many. In addition to the shared surname, both men attended Yale, rowed, invested in Pan Am and motion

Polo became a passion for Whitney when he was approaching the age of forty.

pictures, were involved in horses, were frequent column fodder and were generally popular with women.

For one cousin to one-up the other was, as they approached middle adulthood, increasingly difficult to bear. Suddenly, in Sonny's mind, the weekend sport became a vehicle for surpassing Jock.

"I was actually a mediocre and not a serious player until I got the urge to overthrow my cousin Jock Whitney's champion Greentree team," Whitney wrote in *High Peaks.*[1]

The Greentree team was "held almost in awe by the polo-playing world," Whitney wrote. "I felt an urge to compete every time I read about them in the press or met with them socially."[2]

Sonny set about recruiting a strong team of players and building an incomparable string of polo ponies. But he wisely recognized that he was the weak link and set about remedying that. He hired a former prize-fighter to condition him, fixed up an old polo field near his home in Long Island, hired Ivor Balding — the brother of one of the nation's top polo players — to condition the ponies, and practiced every evening.

In mid-July he went to Whitney Park in the Adirondacks for several weeks, and there he boxed six rounds every day, jumped rope for thirty minutes, and rowed a boat for three or four miles. By the time be returned home, he was ready.

His team, Old Westbury, reached the finals of the U.S. Open with no difficulty. He found himself competing, not unexpectedly, against Jock's team for the championship. The game see-sawed back and forth. At one point, Sonny was cracked over the right eye with a mallet swung by none other than his cousin. The cut was severe, but he got stitched up and went back in the game.

The score was tied, and the referee called for a sudden-death conclusion. Sonny ordered

Ivor Balding to ready Tournasol, one of his favorite ponies, for the final minutes, even though the horse was already exhausted from being involved in earlier rounds. Unbeknownst to Whitney until after the game, Balding poured a quart of whiskey down the horse's throat and sent him onto the field, where he blocked a goal, allowing for a quick point by Old Westbury and the capturing of the trophy.

The following year, his Old Westbury team again beat Jock's Greentree team in the U.S. Open Championship.

After that, Sonny lost all interest in the game. "I sold my ponies at public auction and never played polo again," he wrote in *High Peaks*. "Having won the Open Championship I had achieved my goal."[3]

Sonny Whitney, left, and his Old Westbury team accept the trophy for the U.S. Open Championship after their triumph over Jock's Greentree team in 1937. They successfully defended the trophy the next year.

There is some question about which cousin approached which first. Jock always maintained it was he who looked west and saw the possibilities, first of the Technicolor technology, then of movie-making with Selznick. Sonny maintained it came about when his friend Merian Cooper, one of the pioneers in the making of outdoor adventure films, including *King Kong*, approached him to provide the financial backing and guidance that would allow him to reframe his talents and make films of classic dimensions. Sonny told Cooper he did not have the time to become so intimately involved in such an enterprise, but he approached his cousin Jock. Jock had been a film buff since his teen years, when he and his sister would take in six movies a week every summer by appropriating the family automobile and driving themselves to one of the area's three moviehouses each afternoon (although each was below the age at which they could be licensed to drive). Jock had begun backing New York theatrical productions almost as soon as he was out of college, and he promptly agreed to be president of the new venture.

Whoever had the idea first, Jock and his sister, Joan, along with Whitney and his two sisters, agreed to a family arrangement whereby each of the two Whitney branches would provide half of the necessary financing.

In quick order, the Whitneys linked up with the talented young Selznick, and soon they all united into Selznick International, which rapidly turned out *Becky Sharp*, *Rebecca*, and *A Star Is Born*, which was billed as the first full-length Technicolor film.

Each of the three movies was met with strong critical acclaim and solid box office success, but,

as Whitney wrote in *High Peaks*, "we not only did not make a profit but found ourselves several million dollars in the red" because "Selznick was such a perfectionist that our production budgets were monumental."[10]

The two Whitneys realized they had to come up with a blockbuster and put everyone in the company on notice to seek out a script that would accomplish that.

In 1936 a woman in Sonny's New York office declared she had found the perfect manuscript and believed she could obtain it for under fifty thousand dollars. Upon hearing her synopsis of the as-yet-unpublished manuscript, Selznick International purchased it on the spot. It was titled *Gone With the Wind*.

Selznick laid down four conditions: The novel must be faithfully adhered to, the production cost would run about $4 million, the movie's length would be about four hours, and the leading man would be Clark Gable.

The Whitneys, who had been aiming to do a film that would finally get them into the black, had instead committed themselves to a "staggeringly expensive motion picture," Whitney wrote.[11]

While the movie script was being written, the novel was published and became

Above: The race for who would play Scarlett O'Hara in *Gone With the Wind* was at last won by British actress Vivien Leigh. (*Vivien Leigh provided courtesy of The Roger Richman Agency, Inc., Beverly Hills, CA 90212.*)

Right: Decades after the movie's release, Olivia de Havilland (far right), who starred as Melanie, attended a Gone With the Wind–themed party given by Whitney and his wife Marylou.

could disappoint and turn off the thousands of fans of each of the others, thus leading to box office calamity.

An unknown must be found, Selznick declared, and for months the press breathlessly reported each development, or lack thereof, in the search. Every woman who had ever acted or ever thought of acting stepped forward to express her interest in playing the role of Scarlett.

Columnist Walter Winchell later asserted, according to Jock Whitney biographer E.J. Kahn, Jr., that "1,400 young women had been interviewed and ninety of them actually tested. The known roster included Miss America candidates, debutantes, shop girls, high school drama majors, cheerleaders, Junior Leaguers and the more or less nubile daughters or younger sisters of just about everyone who thought he or she had influence."[12]

The casting became a national fixation. "Even the White House got into the act," Kahn wrote. "For the role of Mammy, the lovable Negro maid in the book, Mrs. Roosevelt proposed her maid."[13]

But it was the Scarlett issue that captivated everyone and kept company officials up late into the night, considering, rejecting, and reconsidering — all of which prompted columnist Louella Parsons to carp, "Selznick and his aids kept looking in tree-tops, under bridges, in the Social Register and on lists of parolees in reformatories."[14]

an instant bestseller. Now the public was viscerally connected to the book and had very strong feelings about who should play Rhett and Scarlett. Readers inundated Selznick International with letters and wires. Almost everyone demanded Gable in the role of Rhett (except for Southerners, who regarded him as entirely too Yankee-like). Thus, Selznick's initial leading-man instincts turned out to be correct, and casting Gable could be expected to fan the already blazing fires of interest in the movie.

Scarlett was another matter entirely. There was no public consensus. Many of the leading starlets of the time, including Joan Crawford, Bette Davis, Katherine Hepburn, Lana Turner, and Loretta Young, were considered for the role, but Selznick feared that choosing any one of them

One day, finally, the ideal Scarlett presented herself. "She was young, beautiful and she could act," Whitney wrote in *High Peaks.* "Furthermore, almost unbelievably, she had an authentic Southern accent."[15]

But it was not to be. The beautiful young woman would not be permitted to play Scarlett. The motion picture censorship bureau, which in the 1930s had full power over the casts and scripts of any picture produced in the United States, declared that the young woman simply would not do. They had researched her background and discovered that her grandmother had Negro blood.

"There was no arguing her case," Whitney wrote. "The decision was final."[16]

Eventually, Selznick found Vivien Leigh, a green-eyed beauty who looked the part but unfortunately, for the purposes of this film, was British and sounded it. She was sent to a speech coach for six weeks to develop something approaching a Southern accent.

Just when it appeared production could finally begin, the censorship people reared their heads again. They were not at all pleased with Rhett's final exit line: "Frankly my dear, I don't give a damn."

The word "damn" was profane, they asserted. Rhett would have to say he did not give a darn.

"We presented a carefully thought out case to them," wrote Whitney, who became the primary leader in convincing the censorship bureau. *"Gone With the Wind* was already an American classic, and the line in question was in common usage. Would they change the language in a Shakespeare play? And certainly the Bard used some rougher language than damn. Margaret Mitchell was a Southern lady herself and she used the word damn. Rhett himself certainly would have used the word; it was in keeping with his character. In fact, we argued, it would be out of character for him to say darn."[17]

At last the discussions ended. The movie was made with a British actress as the Southern belle, Rhett was allowed to be mildly profane, and the movie became a huge success.

Sonny Whitney's part in the making of *Gone With the Wind* went virtually unnoticed. As he wrote years later, "I must admit that today I boast more about my role in producing *Gone With the Wind* than I did then, for it is not generally known that I was involved, as Selznick took most of the publicity."[18]

After the enormous success of *Gone With the Wind,* all of the Whitneys left the motion picture business. But Sonny was the only one of the original backers not to sell off his interest in the movie, a decision that led to his pulling in millions of dollars in royalties in the years to come. Again, Sonny's business judgment and timing proved superb. Years after his death, in fact, his wife Marylou Whitney remained the largest private owner of the film.

Whitney's Hollywood activities during the 1930s also led, rather improbably, to a pioneering effort clear across the country, in Florida. This new effort became that state's single-largest tourist attraction for a time. The venture was born out of what Whitney saw as a need to educate the public about nature, and the idea took wing with his notion that movies might be the way to do it.

It all began in the mid-1930s when Whitney and his explorer/adventurer cousin Douglas Burden, both trustees of the American Museum of Natural History in New York, concluded that the museum's stated purpose, to "collect, catalogue and display," should be revised to "collect, display and educate." Although both men were avid sports hunters, they had a profound appreciation for nature and its creatures and believed the way to preserve the abundance that nature offered was to educate the public about its richness and its fragility. This was Whitney's first step into what would become decades of conservation efforts, and it was taken at a time when most men were not at all concerned about promoting or protecting the environment.

Whitney, by then deeply involved with moviemaking, and Burden, who had produced a movie in Canada, concluded movies would be the way to accomplish their goal. Their friend Ilia Tolstoy, the grandson of the famous Russian author, was also involved in moviemaking, and he too became involved in the discussions. The three decided that they would focus on the creatures of the sea, for this was a largely mysterious and untapped realm of nature.

One of the key attractions at Marineland was the leaping porpoises, and thousands of visitors had their photographs taken with them.

What would be required, they decided, would be for them to build a giant glass home for sea creatures. Burden had studied various outdoor adventure movies and knew that corralling wild animals in the proper-sized area allowed film-makers to capture very natural behaviors on film. This glass enclosure would be the "corral" that would allow filming of a variety of different sea-based movies, the first of which would be a feature film starring Johnny Weismuller and an assortment of sharks who wind up somehow aiding or saving Tarzan. The actor would pull in moviegoers, and the focus on sharks would provide the public with insights into this glorious if reviled sea creature.

Florida, with its abundant offshore fauna and year-round good climate, seemed the logical place to start. So in the summer of 1936, Whitney began the process of getting sharks captured for study off the coast of Montauk, New York; Tolstoy began exploring appropriate Florida sites; and Burden devised a business plan.

By summer's end, Tolstoy reported that he had found the ideal site fourteen miles south of St. Augustine. Here, the inland waterways came together just a few hundred yards from the ocean, ensuring that fish could be brought in with little delay.

If the aquatic confluence of the spot was perfect, nothing else about it was. It was, at the time, a soggy, primitive area with no fresh water supply, no telephone service, and a tendency to flood when ocean storms blew a little too hard. It was accessible only by a one-lane sand road.

It took two years and enormous engineering skill, but in 1938, Marine Studios, the first oceanarium in the world, was completed. By now, Sherman Pratt, a John D. Rockefeller descendent who was connected with RKO pictures, had joined the threesome and was contributing some of his considerable wealth, as well as naturalist sensibilities, to the venture.

Thousands of fish representing hundreds of species swam together in glass enclosures, providing an unparalleled view of rare fish and fish behavior. It was exactly as the men had dreamed, except that the notion of using sharks as the focus of their first film had been scrapped.

"We found out sharks are the dumbest animals in the world, and we were unable to train them," Whitney told a writer for Town & Country many years later. "We were groaning, 'What the hell are we going to do?'"[19]

Fortunately, Whitney had then, as was always his practice, a suggestion box installed at the site, and one of the employees asserted that it was his strong belief that porpoises could be trained to do just about anything asked of them. They were bright, they were sensitive, and they were man-friendly, unlike the sharks. Within weeks, a sufficient number of porpoises had been

June 24, 1938

Nearly 30,000 People Jam Ocean Front As Marine Studios Open

A Portion of the Tremendous Crowd

Traffic Blocked for Miles By Huge Throng Gathered for Ceremony

NOTABLES SPEAK

Spectacular Tourist Attraction Is Thrown Open to Public

The pioneer development inaugurated many years ago by Henry Morrison Flagler, creator of Florida's famed East Coast, might be said to have reached culmination yesterday—through the disclosure to a fascinated, thrilled public of the modern-day miracle that is Marine Studios.

Despite the torrential downpour just prior to the opening ceremonies crowds conservatively estimated at between 25,000 and 30,000 people blocked traffic for miles along the Ocean Shore Boulevard to the north and south of Marineland. Massed cars stood for hours unable to move an inch, yet their occupants apparently did not think of departing before getting at least a glimpse of the undersea wonders revealed by the world's largest and

Caught by the camera in the above picture is a portion of the record-breaking throngs which massed from many localities yesterday at Marineland to witness the formal dedication of the $500,000 Marine Studios. This scene, which gives an indication of the size of the crowd, estimated at nearly 30,000, was snapped from the western side of the Ocean Shore Boulevard, looking eastward across the automobile-packed highway to the gigantic tanks swarming with men, women and children.

Above: The grand opening of Marine Studios, which later became Marineland, drew a huge crowd that, according to this local newspaper, blocked traffic for miles. (Photo courtesy Marineland.)

Left: Marineland's opening was very big news in St. Augustine. The local newspaper devoted much of its front page to biographical sketches of the founders and other key personnel.

captured and trained, and the group knew they were onto something.

The idea still was to use the facility for moviemaking. But Burden's early research had indicated that the moviemaking potential would be limited and therefore insufficient to support the facility. Upon examining some of the recent developments in Florida, he concluded that there was a chance of drawing some tourists, and he proposed that bleachers, a restaurant, and a gift shop be constructed. There might be only an outside chance of drawing large numbers of visitors, he acknowledged, given the public's limited knowledge about and interest in fish, but it was worth trying to bring in whatever additional income they could.

When the gates to Marine Studios, the first public oceanarium in the world, were opened for the first time in 1938, nearly thirty thousand people thronged past, much to the amazement of the men who put the venture together. "One of our directors ... who had charge of public relations, seized this opportunity to give us national publicity and from that day forth we found ourselves in a growing and thriving business," Whitney wrote.[20]

But it was not the business they had conceived. "We decided to forego the motion picture," Whitney recollected in 1988 when Marineland, which is what it had been hastily renamed, invited him as a key speaker for its fiftieth anniversary.

Stories about Marineland were featured in the *Saturday Evening Post, Woman's Home Companion, Life,* and *Vogue.* First Lady Eleanor Roosevelt visited the park and wrote about it in her syndicated newspaper column, "My Day." Within months Marineland was Florida's premiere tourist attraction.

The porpoises, which had been trained to perform in movies, were now doing leaps and dives for amazed audiences. Marineland was the first facility in the world to use performing porpoises, and much of the subsequent fascination with these sensitive sea creatures grew from Marineland's focus on them in the 1930s and 1940s.

In the years to come, Marineland would suffer a decline before being infused with new vitality. When the United States entered World War II, Marineland was taken over by the U.S. Coast Guard and closed to the public so the military could develop a shark repellent that downed aviators could attach to their uniforms. In postwar years, the staff set about restocking fish, all of which had been released, and added some new programs to entice tourists, but the park, then nearly twenty years old, was no longer the glittering attraction it once was.

In the 1960s and early 1970s, as Florida was undergoing a population and tourist boom spurred by Disney World and other attractions

that followed, the Marineland directors launched a $6 million program to update and expand.

At the same time, Whitney piloted an initiative that elevated the facility to a new plane. Marineland had been attracting marine biologists since its beginnings, and to meet their needs, a small research lab had been constructed at the site soon after the war ended. It was growing ever more clear, however, that the research potential was far greater than anyone had anticipated. In 1972, newspapers around the country announced there would be a limited union between Marineland and the University of Florida. Whitney and his partners donated two and a half acres near Marineland, and Whitney put up $150,000 — to be matched by the University of Florida — to construct a leading-edge marine research lab.

The Cornelius Vanderbilt Whitney Laboratory for Experimental Biology and Medicine of the University of Florida was dedicated on January 30, 1974. Thirteen years later, the lab, which by then was specializing in cellular and molecular biology, became known as the Whitney Laboratory.

In 1983, when he was eighty-four years old, Whitney sold his shares of Marineland to a group of investors. He did not, however, lose interest in the facility or the lab that bore his name.

Whitney gives a speech at the dedication opening of the Cornelius Vanderbilt Whitney Laboratory on January 30, 1974. *(Photo courtesy Marineland.)*

Whitney's war activities included intelligence work in North Africa and several positions in the Pentagon.

CHAPTER SEVEN

WAR AND PROMOTION

HE CONSTANT TRAVEL, ADVEN-
ture-seeking, and interest in
beautiful women the world over
took a toll on Whitney's marriage. His
relationship with Gee was collapsing in
large chunks with each passing month,
and by 1941, not quite ten years after
they had married, they were divorced.
They had produced one child, a daugh-
ter named Gail, who had the blonde tresses of her
mother and the clear blue eyes of her father.

Within months of the dissolution of his second marriage, Whitney was at the altar again, this
time with Eleanor Searle, an aspiring singer who
began working in the reception area outside
Whitney's Pan Am office almost immediately after
Juan Trippe had been deposed and Whitney had
taken over the executive corner.

An attractive brunette from the Heartland,
Eleanor had stirred talk among the secretarial
pool soon after her arrival because of her habitual
dating of Pan Am's senior executives, according to
Pan Am biographers Merylin Bender and Selig
Altschul.[1] It came as little surprise to anyone when
Eleanor and Sonny began keeping company.

Eleanor had none of the society credentials of
her predecessors. She was a doctor's daughter
from Plymouth, Ohio, who had alighted in New
York to pursue a singing career and had taken the
Pan Am job to earn money for voice lessons. But
soon after her and Sonny's modest little wedding at

the Lutheran church she had attended
as a child, the bride, pretty in pink, had
no difficulty vaulting into the orthodoxy
of the very rich. Indeed, for the seventeen years they were married, they lived
a life far more lavish than had been
Whitney's habit. They built the magnificent mansion in Old Westbury, socialized with Hollywood glitterati, appeared
with all the right international luminaries, and
glided among Washington's top echelon.

But it must have been difficult for Eleanor to
follow Gee as Sonny's wife, for Gee was a favorite
of the Whitney family and was very popular on
Long Island. Unlike Eleanor, Gee meshed well
with Whitney's friends. She had fox hunted with
them at the Meadow Brook Club and had been
raised in ultrachic mainline Philadelphia.

Whitney said in later years, after a spectacularly acrimonious divorce, that Eleanor became
"a different girl" after their marriage. He also
maintained that he had married her because she
was pregnant and that he rejoined the military
because he needed time to get away from
his present life. Prior to his divorce from her
in 1957, he listed his grievances — those

Although Whitney was too old to be a pilot in World War II,
he sometimes went on bombing missions.

"continuous general practices and acts of Mrs. Whitney that caused great unhappiness to me, affected my health and peace of mind, and made me suffer beyond my ability to continue with the marriage."[2]

Still, these grievances, he said, did not begin until April 1943, after he returned from his World War II service. While serving his country overseas, he was much like the other fighting men half his age: a man of uncertain future proud to serve his country and hopeful of returning home.

His writings to Eleanor during this time were filled with fond references to her. He was buoyed

when one of her letters would finally make its way to him at one of his foreign posts, and he was distressed when mail was held up for long stretches and he heard nothing from her.

Whitney went to war when he was nearly forty-three, well beyond the age when the government would have called him up to serve. The government didn't have to. The day after the Japanese attack on Pearl Harbor, in December 1941, Whitney enlisted in the Army Air Force, for he felt it was his duty to serve his country.

He was too old, he was told, to serve as an active pilot. As with the first war, when his age also was a hindrance, he came up with a strategy he hoped would propel him close to the action. This time he applied for combat intelligence.

After the requisite three months of training, evidently concerned that his specialty might not take him as close to the lines as he had hoped, he volunteered to go as a gunner with a squadron whose mission was to bomb Tokyo.

His first flight as a major in the Army Air Force was fraught with bizarre mishaps, including a harrowing incident over the jungles of Brazil when the emergency raft blew out of its locker and lashed itself to the left stabilizer. The plane and its crew also spent an afternoon mired in quicksand near the Red Sea. By the time they finally got near their destination, eighteen days after embarking on the mission, they were grounded. The Japanese had already taken the airport in China where they would have landed

for refueling before heading out for Tokyo. He and the crew would have no part in a decisive action against the enemy.

It was a supreme disappointment for the man who had already spent one war far from enemy lines and had planned to make up for it this time out.

However unfulfilling the mission turned out to be, it did serve an important purpose. It quickly prepared a New York businessman for the realities he would be facing in the years ahead. "I had become far removed from the luxury and contented ways of civilian life," Whitney wrote in *Lone and Level Sands,* a book about his World War II experiences. "I could fly a Fortress, handle its guns, and sleep on a cold metal floor with the deafening roar of engine and wind in my ears. I could live out of a B-4 bag, shave with cold water, sleep in a barracks with the light on and men talking. I was further astounded to discover that I could sweat on the ground, shiver in the air, drink a lot of beer and still be up at 5 a.m. ready for another day."[3]

With his first mission aborted, Whitney was ordered to New Delhi, India, to serve as liaison

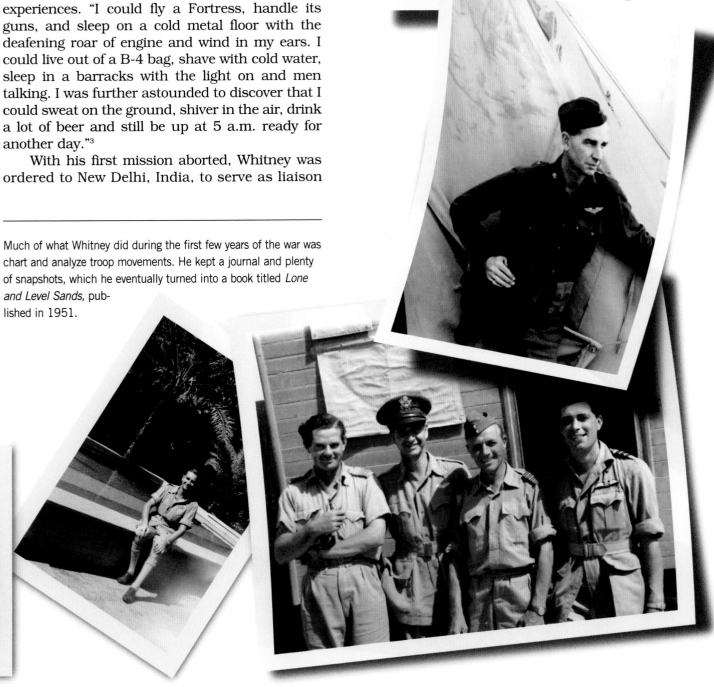

Much of what Whitney did during the first few years of the war was chart and analyze troop movements. He kept a journal and plenty of snapshots, which he eventually turned into a book titled *Lone and Level Sands,* published in 1951.

between the U.S. and British air forces. It was his job to study situation maps, sort through intelligence reports, and make sure that the Americans and the Brits each knew what the other was doing. It was not hazardous duty, but it was a tough time of year to be in India. The heat was unspeakable — 100 to 120 degrees Fahrenheit every day — and dust storms churned through

the city every few days. "We all broke out in some type of prickly heat for which there seemed to be no known remedy," Whitney wrote.[4]

Far from the action, stuck in an assignment secondary to the British, Whitney grew morose. "I suffered from the disappointment of having volunteered for foreign duty on a combat mission and finding myself assigned to a desk job in a rear area. At this point it seemed as if I would spend the next years here in New Delhi, a crushing outlook. I had never been a desk officer and never wanted to be one. I cursed the Army and the ill fortune which had brought me to this end. If I had to be away from my family, I wanted a combat mission."[5]

To add to the misery, he received the worst possible news from home. His mother, Gertrude, had died of an embolism at the age of sixty-four.

Eleanor had tried every way possible to reach him and break it gently, but her efforts were not successful. He learned of his mother's death from Claire Booth Luce, wife of publishing magnate Henry Luce. Luce had heard the news on the radio, and during the course of their catching up on mutual friends, she told Whitney (mistakenly believing it had been Whitney's aunt, not mother who had died).

Gertrude's death was noted in the *New York Times* in the sort of obituary almost always reserved for men of a certain station or accomplishment. Her legacy was twofold:

First, she had fostered and nurtured a widespread interest in American art and artists through ceaseless support and promotion of them. At the time of her death, the Whitney Museum on West 8th Street had become highly popular, as had many of the artists who had created the works showcased there. And it was a popularity destined to continue long after her death. By 1957, the collection was so large it was moved to a building adjacent to the Museum of Modern Art on West 54th Street, and eleven years later, the collection was moved to a new home on Madison Avenue.

Second was Gertrude's own sculpture. In Washington, her Titanic Memorial and Mayan

Whitney and his cousin Alfred G. Vanderbilt, who skippered a PT boat in the Navy and, like Whitney, was an aristocrat of horse racing.

fountain were considered stellar examples of twentieth-century American sculpture, as were her statues of Peter Stuyvesant, displayed at Second Avenue and 16th Street, and her War Memorial, at 167th Street and Broadway in New York. One of the most ambitious and striking was her massive memorial to Buffalo Bill in Cody, Wyoming. The Western town so impressed her while she was working on the project that she purchased two acres of land and presented it to the town for a park. Years later the Whitney Gallery of Western Art and the Buffalo Bill Museum were built on that property by her only son, C.V. Whitney.

Whitney, of course, was unable to get away to pay a final tribute to his mother. He was trapped in the heat of New Delhi, left to grieve in solitary seclusion.

His assignment there was to last only three months. At the end of June, he was to leave India — just as a famous Indian fortune teller had predicted only a few days earlier. He received orders to go to Cairo, Egypt, to serve as assistant chief of staff intelligence.[6]

Cairo was not the front. It was 135 miles from El Alamein, upon which the crafty general known as the Desert Fox, Field Marshal Rommel, who commanded the Nazi armies in North Africa, was advancing at an alarming pace. If El Alamein fell, it was feared, the fall of Cairo soon thereafter was almost certain. Whitney could satisfy himself with the knowledge that he was contributing more directly to what was shaping up as a major and potentially pivotal war effort.

Soon after his assignment to Cairo, he received a promotion to lieutenant colonel and moved into a quite decent room at the Shepherds Hotel. The war was being fought only a few score miles away, but in Cairo, the officers lived a reasonably comfortable life, according to Whitney's reports. Liquor was still plentiful, American cigarettes were available, and there were fine race tracks and polo fields. Whitney played tennis two or three times a week and took a swim in the pool every day before lunch.

When the fighting forces managed to stop the enemy at El Alamein, Whitney was assigned to Headquarters, U.S. Desert Air Task Force, which was to coordinate with the British to develop strategies for pushing the Germans back. Whitney spent a long, hot summer camped in the desert north of Cairo, where the sand and the bugs were equally vexing, the bombings by the Germans fairly regular, and the food quite awful.

By fall the pushback strategies were in place, and on October 19, Whitney received word he would be assigned assistant chief of staff, intelligence, to participate in the Allies' plans for driving Rommel out of the area before winter settled in. "At last my hopes had been rewarded," Whitney wrote. "I would see action first hand. I wrote my wife that she might not expect to hear from me for a long time."[7]

Three days later, after a final ice cream soda at Groppies in Cairo, Whitney and a band of officers hit the dirt road for their secret destination near El Alamein. "Gone were the golden nights of luxury," Whitney wrote. "Gone the scent of flowers and ladies' perfume. Gone the gossip and chatter of a great metropolis. Gone the typewriters and yards of carbon copies. Gone the routine I had gotten to know so well. And ahead the lone and level sands stretching far away. Somewhere camped in those sands were hundreds of thousands of men waiting to spring at each other's throats. What would life at the front be like? I was keen to find out."[8]

The task force set up a few miles from where the fighting men were converging to begin their assault the next day. And for the next several days the Allied bombers made significant hits, clearing the way for the grounds troops to inch ahead, claiming territory once held by Germans.

For Whitney, the sifting of information, the debriefings, and the report filing continued, though, he acknowledged, this was an operation in which the British had the primary role. "American intelligence officers did embarrassingly little," he wrote. "Our job was to learn as much as possible without getting in the way. We were being trained for the future. We were chiefly observers and liaison officers between the R.A.F. and the U.S. Air Force. We kept our records and joined in the strafe meetings and discussions, but we did not command."[9]

At night the men in Whitney's little encampment lay on their cots listening to the booming of artillery fire, the drubbing of bombs, and the droning of airplane engines.

By the end of the month, many of the enemy pockets had been cleared, and the Allies were in position now for the final breakthrough.

On November 4, Whitney asked for and received permission to join one of the daytime air bombing missions. As the plane surged into the air, the cabin filled with smoke and the stench of burning rubber. The copilot ordered Whitney to prepare to jump — to certain death since they were only fifty feet above the ground, not nearly high enough to allow the parachute to unfurl and be of any value. But then a fire extinguisher was pointed into the general vicinity of what seemed to be the source of the smoke, and the air in the plane cleared.

Crisis averted, the B-25 surged forth to take its place in the bombing formation. Once they reached their bombing site, the crew unloaded their bombs — manually, since very little of the electrical system of the plane was operable after the fire — and then headed back to their desert hideaway. Asked back at camp if he enjoyed participating in the mission, Whitney's grim response was "Parts of it."[10]

The next day they received word that the enemy retreat was in full swing and that Whitney, four other officers, and seven enlisted men were to break camp immediately and set out for a location close to what was believed to be the new Allied front line. Communication had broken down during the many days of battle, and it was difficult to know precisely where the enemy had retreated and what lands now belonged to the Allies, but there was a general sense of where the lines had been formed, and it was toward these that the group set out.

Heavy rains had turned the sands to mud, and Whitney and his company spent a day slogging through the rain-soaked ruts left by the retreating Germans and Italians, dodging the tanks, vehicles, and field kitchens hastily abandoned by them.

When it was possible to go no farther because of shelling ahead, Whitney settled in on a rock for a rest and was soon joined by a British colonel, who offered, of course, a spot of tea. The Brit set about preparing the tea, Whitney scrounged up some C rations, and soon, Whitney wrote in *High Peaks,* "the tea was boiling and the colonel and I, crouched down among the rocks, were sharing some good American meat and vegetable stew, along with sweet biscuits and chocolate bars. What utter contentment I felt."[11]

Suddenly, a sleek staff car pulled up. Inside was General Montgomery, commanding general of the Eighth Army.

Whitney and the Colonel leapt to their feet to salute, sending the biscuits and candy bars flying into the sand. The two officers expected to receive a dressing-down for loafing, but the general found no fault with them and, indeed, invited them to join him for tea. This time there was no crouching in the rocks. As the three shared tea in a hastily erected tent, the general's men were sent forth to get a bead on the situation. What they discovered was that Whitney and his group, then Montgomery and his men, had arrived at the site before the Allied troops who were to have cleared the area of the enemy. "It seems, General," Montgomery was told by his aide, "you are the spearhead of the Eighth Army. There is a strong German position ahead and we will have to clear it out before we can advance."[12]

And so, Whitney wrote, "ended the historic day after the defeat of General Rommel's army at Alamein, the turning point of World War II. And Lieutenant Colonel Whitney, U.S. Desert Air Task Force, together with General Monty Montgomery, Commander in Chief of the Allied Forces, had actually been the spearhead of the victorious Eighth Army and were alive to tell the tale."[13]

For several days the officers were forced to stay in their position, since the disruption of communications had rendered it impossible to ascertain where the various units were. The supply situation became acute. Whitney and his group were put on minimum British rations and two pints of water per day.

Eventually they began to make their way to the new front, Halfaya Pass, with the intent of completing the decimation of Rommel's army before it could retreat into Tunisia, where it could join up with other German forces. Pommeled by fierce windstorms, Whitney's group advanced slowly across the desert, a few miles behind the fighting men.

There was much to endure: the raging winds slamming sand into their eyes and ears, intense cold at night, the bleakness of the landscape, regular bombings and strafings by the enemy, and the meagerness of the rations. But perhaps the most difficult, Whitney wrote, was contending with "the ever-present differences in temperament of the American and British soldiers — differences which often made the sparks fly."[14]

For two months during the winter of 1942–43, a critical stage for the war, Whitney was at the front, collecting intelligence to help air fighters fly their sorties and continue the rout of Rommel. By the time his trek across northern Africa was over, Whitney weighed 148 pounds, twenty-two pounds less than his normal 170.

He looked and felt quite ragged, and his commanding officer, General Brereton, ordered him to Cairo, where he shared a flat with his cousin Whitney Straight, a commander in the British Air Corps, and another British officer and longtime friend, famed portrait painter Simon Elwis.

As might be expected, there was another singularly Whitney episode during his days in Cairo with his cousin and friend.

King Farouk, the young ruler of Egypt, favored the German cause over the Allied one. The British high command wanted very much to convert Farouk to its way of thinking and devised a plan. Elwis would paint a portrait of Farouk's young queen, a woman of incomparable beauty who was never seen outside the palace walls. The British rationale behind devising this particular plan has been lost to history. Possibly the Brits believed that during the sittings Elwis would be able to influence the queen sufficiently that she would go to work on her husband. Or possibly they believed that Farouk would be so impressed with Elwis' brilliant work that he would begin to rethink his position on all things British.

In any event, for reasons unknown, Farouk agreed not only to allowing Elwis to do the por-

When the United States entered World War II, Whitney was too old to enlist as a pilot, so he opted for intelligence work.

trait, but also to having the sittings take place in the queen's quarters of the palace harem.

Over the course of many sittings, the young queen and Elwis developed a cordial relationship, he regaling her with stories of his various adventures with his two Cairo roommates. The young queen decided she must meet those two men, and she and Elwis came up with a plan. At an upcoming party at the palace, Whitney and then Straight would be secretly taken to her private chamber by her most trusted servant.

On the night of the party, when he was escorted to her chamber, Whitney discovered that "Simon had not exaggerated her fatal beauty," he wrote in *High Peaks*.[15]

As the "music from the ballroom below filled the incense-laden air,"[16] the two sipped champagne and talked about jazz and current events.

"I could not resist asking her to dance with me, and she happily accepted," Whitney wrote. "So in this romantic setting we danced a waltz and a foxtrot."[17] Finally Whitney's thirty minutes was up, and it was his cousin's turn.

His cousin, however, was caught by the king's bodyguard, who announced the king would be informed. Back in their apartment, the two men discussed the calamity well into the night and decided they would await further developments before reporting the turn of events to their commanding officers.

Several nights later, there came a pounding at the door. It was the king.

After two hours of conversation, the king approached the portrait painter and said, "Captain Elwis, I do not think you are familiar with our Eastern customs. I shall enlighten you. When a man displeases us his body is found floating in our mother river, the Nile, with his throat slit open, and the serpent of the Nile is happily devouring him. And now gentlemen, I thank you for your hospitality and bid you goodbye and a good night's rest."[18]

Elwis had evidently overstayed his welcome during all those days of painting in the palace. The three men decided that night they would report all that had transpired to their commanding officers the next morning.

Whitney and Straight received sympathetic hearings and were allowed to remain at their posts. Simon Elwis was dispatched that very day to Madagascar.

A few months later, in March 1943, Whitney received orders to return to Washington. He was assigned to the Pentagon to draw up endless strategic plans to coordinate the Army's, Navy's, and Air Force's roles in various offensives.

The war was still raging, and there was much to be done. The following year he became chief of projects for the Army Air Force, representing the Air Corps on various military committees and helping to plan the redeployment of air power from the European theater to the Pacific.

It was a tense time and an intense environment. Virtually everyone assigned to the Pentagon worked fourteen-hour days, according to Whitney, who received a promotion to the rank of colonel a few months after arriving in Washington. "I had no time for the much publicized social activities in Washington; we burned many hours of midnight oil," he wrote.[19]

Whitney and Eleanor and their son, Cornelius Searle Whitney, who was born in November 1944 after Eleanor had several miscarriages, had taken a frame house in Chevy Chase, a quiet community with broad tree-lined streets and sweeping lawns, about a thirty-minute drive from the Pentagon. They socialized rarely, and when they entertained, it was usually people from Whitney's office.

These were the best years of their marriage, Eleanor wrote in her book, *Invitation to Joy*. "That happiness stemmed, in large measure, from the fact that my husband was occupied in Washington with responsibilities worthy of his time and energy."

Whitney was utterly and completely focused. He was considered a solid part of the military team, and he was about to get his reward. Early in 1945, on February 9, Whitney received a call from his friend Jim Forrestal, secretary of the Navy, asking if Whitney wanted to join him on a top-secret journey. Whitney agreed, and that day Forrestal had him appointed the Navy's Army Air Force advisor.

The next evening, Whitney joined Forrestal on his DC-4 for a flight to Saipan, then boarded a ship headed for Iwo Jima. Whitney was about to observe the Navy's invasion of Japan.

On a stopover in Pearl Harbor, a ship's captain treated Whitney with obvious coolness. The

reason was quite clear. This was to be a Navy invasion, and an Air Corps man had no business being around. Forrestal realized it would be necessary to have a word with the captain. One sentence cleared up the matter. Whitney's grandfather, Forrestal explained, had been secretary of the Navy. "This altered the situation considerably," Whitney wrote.[20]

Whitney and Forrestal continued their journey west, and nine days after they had left Washington, they stood aboard the command ship SS *El Dorado*, anchored about one mile off the landing beaches, and watched the invasion.

"We could see the whole beach area in a mass of flames and smoke," Whitney wrote.[21]

It was not a fast or simple victory.

The following day, his 46th birthday, Whitney passed the cold, windy hours in the joint operations room of the *El Dorado* as the troops fought through violent rainstorms, continuing to try to take their positions.

The battle on shore raged for three days. "On the fourth day," Whitney wrote, "when it appeared that our forces would finally rout the Japanese, Mr. Forrestal invited me to accompany him on a trip along the shoreline of Iwo, and if conditions were satisfactory, to land on Red Beach."[22]

The Forrestal group arrived just as the Marines were scrambling up the sheer walls of Mount Suribachi, where, against the bright blue of the Pacific sky, they planted the American flag. "A cheer went up from the men around us," Whitney wrote. "I turned to look at General [Holland] Smith and saw tears streaming down the face of this seasoned veteran. 'I told you they'd do it,' he said."[23] Again, Whitney had been on hand to witness history in the making.

He returned to headquarters in Washington and served three more months, leaving in May 1945 shortly after Germany surrendered. He had served three and a half years in the Army and had been decorated with the Distinguished Service Medal for the strategies and operations he developed for the Ploiestri raid, the Legion of Merit, a bronze battle star for the European theater, and a bronze star for the Pacific invasion.

Upon his leave-taking from the Army, the C.V. Whitneys and their young son returned to New York. Finally they would move into the Greek Revival mansion in Old Westbury whose construction Eleanor had overseen while Whitney was off in the war. Although Whitney also owned a duplex in River House in Manhattan, houses in Saratoga and Kentucky, and camps in the Adirondacks, to him Old Westbury was home, so as soon as the old William C. Whitney mansion

Commanding General Carl Spatz awards Whitney the Legion of Merit for his outstanding service during the war.

had been torn down in 1940, Whitney had begun making arrangements to build another.

The new C.V. Whitney house in Old Westbury had "24 rooms, plus great halls, breakfast porches, open patios, closed patios, two walk-in safes, storage, laundry and pressing rooms," Eleanor wrote in *Invitation to Joy.*[24]

Building such a house in wartime would have been impossible but for the fact that the lumber came from Whitney Park in the Adirondacks and most of the plumbing fixtures came from the torn-down remains of William C.'s old house. It was a glorious intermingling of the past and the present, testament to a new patriarch and a new style.

Indeed, the whole estate took on a new post-war vigor with Whitney's return. After Gertrude's death, Whitney had bought his sisters' shares of the property at Old Westbury. Although Barbara and Flora kept their houses, Sonny took over the grounds. "The estate was like a feudal manor, almost self-contained, a lovely, somewhat unreal world," Eleanor wrote.[25]

The stables, which had been virtually empty during the war years, were replenished with riding horses and polo ponies and race horses and

hunters. The feed for them, as well as for the herds of dairy and show cattle, was grown on the estate by agronomists. The dairy was made operational again; the greenhouses overflowed; vegetables, chicken, ducks, and hens were raised on the grounds. Overall, it took more than a hundred full-time employees to keep the house and estate running.

Whitney was pleasantly surprised that Eleanor enjoyed living at Old Westbury, for she always told him she'd like to live with just Whitney and their son, Searle, in a traditional house surrounded by a picket fence. Whitney reveled in the new home, and it seemed to have spawned in him an interest in home and property acquisition that surpassed that of his grandfather William C. and that did not wane until the final years of his life. Over the next four decades, he would buy and sell scores of properties from New York to Florida to Majorca.

As Whitney settled in at Old Westbury, he resumed tending to his various business enterprises, including the mining and timber operations, as well as the bank and Marineland. He became especially attentive to the thoroughbred breeding and racing operation that he had taken over on the death of his father.

And there were social obligations as well. The couple was drawn into the society swirl — charity balls in the city, luncheons for their moneyed

After the war, Whitney, his wife Eleanor, and his son Searle moved into the Old Westbury mansion in New York.

friends, or trips abroad, "for Sonny always liked to be on the move," Eleanor wrote.[26]

In July and August they would go to Whitney Park in the Adirondacks, where Sonny's children from his two previous marriages — Harry, Nancy, and Gail — sometimes joined them for a few weeks. On August weekends, Sonny and Eleanor would leave the mountains for their Saratoga house, Cady Hill, so they could attend the racing meets.

And Sonny continued the philanthropies that had been started by his father and grandfather, including the Metropolitan Opera and the Museum of Natural History. He also took an interest in a variety of special projects, such as a maternity wing at the community hospital in Glen Cove, which was built in memory of his mother.

Eleanor, meanwhile, made regular shopping trips to Paris, and she was photographed for the cover of *Life* as she drove two horses pulling her in a cart. She was in great demand as a singer and model at various charity events and was a regular client of the design houses of Dior, Elizabeth Arden, and Givenchy.

Whitney did not join her in these ventures, for two years after the couple had established themselves in Old Westbury he was beckoned back to Washington. The Air Force had been made a separate service of the military, and when Stuart Symington, the senator from Missouri, was appointed the first secretary of the Air Force, he asked Whitney to become an assistant secretary. Whitney agreed without hesitation, and on September 26, 1947, he was appointed to the post by President Harry Truman.

In the years just after the war, the Air Force, so critical in many of the key victories, held new prominence. Whitney was eager to see that the United States did not ultimately undervalue and underfund this important resource. His official charge was to oversee civil and military/diplomatic affairs, but his reach and influence were broad. He was a member of the president's Air Coordinating Committee and the Committee on Civilian Components of the Defense Department, and he also functioned as an administrator of Air Force business relating to the National Security Council and the War Council of the State Department. After he had been in the job for several months, the *New York Times* reported that Whitney had "helped form

Above and below: After serving in the U.S. Army Air Corps, Whitney spent some time in Washington, D.C., first as assistant secretary of the Air Force and then as undersecretary of commerce.

Right: President Truman, under whom Whitney served as assistant secretary and undersecretary, considered Sonny to be a personal friend.

policy and supervise the role of air power as an instrument of national policy."[27]

The couple took a suite in the Shoreham Hotel during their first year in the capital, then moved to a house on 30th Street in fashionable Georgetown, where they entertained the likes of Vice President Alben Barkley, General and Mrs. Dwight Eisenhower, and General and Mrs. Omar Bradley.

The Whitneys became regulars at the White House, invited to a variety of the president's private and social events. And in 1949, eighteen months after becoming an assistant secretary for the Air Force, Whitney was appointed undersecretary of commerce, an appointment that required a substantial amount of travel abroad. Amid his many trips to boost tourism and trade with the United States, Whitney helped the minister of tourism in Spain establish the parador system, which opened up tourism to that country by turning castles into hotels. After a year as undersecretary of commerce,

Cornelius Vanderbilt Whitney was the second Whitney in his family to serve in Washington. His grandfather had served as secretary of the Navy.

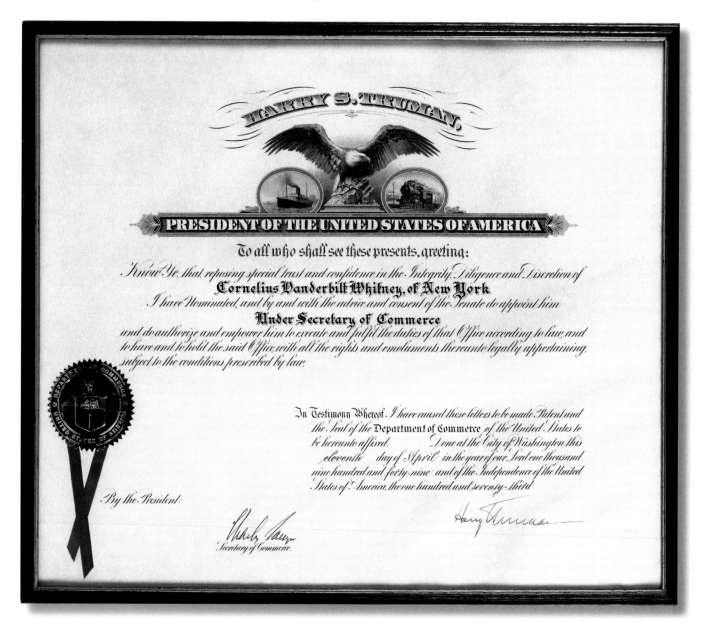

Whitney resigned, stating the reason later in his 1957 divorce documents: "Due to the continuation of my poor health, brought on by the unhappiness of my home life, I was unable to continue my job, and therefore resigned."[28]

The couple returned to their home at Old Westbury, where, Whitney wrote, "the situation at home grew increasingly worse.... It was a continuous hope of mine that our marriage could be saved."[29]

In the fall of 1950, "upon further deterioration of my health and peace of mind," Whitney left Old Westbury with the intention of never returning, and

As undersecretary of commerce during the Truman administration, Whitney spent the better part of the year traveling abroad, encouraging tourism to and trade with the United States. He retired after only a year in the position, however, citing poor health brought on by his troubled marriage with Eleanor.

in March 1951 he asked Eleanor for a divorce. The negotiations were well underway when he decided to give the marriage another try.[30]

Whitney was a regular in the winner's circle, but horsemen said he was as gracious about losing as he was about winning.

CHAPTER EIGHT

THE REINS OF VICTORY

EVERY SPRING WHITNEY could be found prowling quietly about the foaling barns — the tall, straight lord of the manor, eager to examine the latest spindly-legged additions to the fold. All year long, he would study bloodlines and race performances and feed mixes and talk to the jockeys and exercise boys for hours on end, ever seeking the novel approach or unturned page that might prove to be the Rosetta stone of racing. He would arise before first light and bundle up in herringbone tweeds against the bone-biting chill to observe the dawn workouts at the track.

These were activities that did not attract the newspaper columnists. There were no microphones and no photographs, just a man, almost inevitably in a jaunty hat, going about the business of developing thoroughbreds.

And ultimately, this was the enterprise in which Sonny Whitney made perhaps his greatest, and certainly his most enduring, mark. For all his involvement in high-profile and highly successful ventures over the years, it was horse breeding and racing where he penetrated the public consciousness and distinguished himself in ways that spoke to his skill, diligence, and character, not just his wealth.

"A success in spite of his money," proclaimed *Sports Illustrated* in 1961, calling Whitney a "thoroughbred purist" and a "far cry from the popular tintype of the rich American sportsman and socialite."[1]

Whitney was indeed quite unusual in the thoroughbred world. While it was not uncommon for wealthy men to get into the horse business, it was usually the accoutrements of racing — the parties, the glamour, and the celebrity — that drew them in and kept them there. Most were equine dilettantes with little knowledge about or involvement in any aspect of the business away from the glitter of the track. Most had very little interest in learning.

Whitney, conversely, was "very involved and he was very good," said Joe Hirsch, a highly regarded turf writer for the *Daily Racing Form.* "He had an awful lot of good horses over the years.... The only race that ever defeated him was the [Kentucky] Derby. He never had a Derby winner although he tried. He must have tried twenty times. But he won the Belmont, the Preakness, and almost every other big race.... He was a very good breeder, and he was very active in the procedure, too. He knew pedigrees, and he was very conversant with the horses."[2]

It was an expertise born not of passion for the sport, but of a determination to do well by it.

Tompion was regarded as one of the best stallions from the Whitney Farm in the early 1960s.

From the Horse Breeder's Mouth

SONNY WHITNEY DEVELOPED A KEEN knowledge of horses and racing over the years and was known for his frequent utterances on the topic — some humorous, others offering valuable tips. Among them:

• "Kentucky is the greatest place in the world to raise horses and just for three very serious and profound reasons: (1) the good bourbon; (2) the beautiful women; and (3) there's not much else to do."[1]

• "All foals should be weaned together whenever the youngest is ready so they can get the benefit of competition amongst themselves. But the bully should be separated from the others."[2]

• "Breed the best to the best and hope for the best."[3]

• "She looks like a girl and acts like a girl. Like all of them, she's temperamental and hard to handle when she gets her feelings hurt." — on his famed filly Silver Spoon, considered, in 1959, the first female since Regret with a strong chance of winning the Kentucky Derby[4]

• "There is no formula for breeding champions. One year we bred Top Flight to the best horse

Unlike many rich horse owners, Whitney was a regular in the training paddock, and he was relentless in keeping informed about his horses and the industry in general.

in the world at that time, Man-o'-War. The foal arrived on the day the Kentucky Derby was run. It seemed everything was just right. But the foal, named Sky Raider, could only win two small races. What one might have expected from that mating is anyone's guess."[5]

Whitney was to the stables born. His grandfather, William C. Whitney, had entered the racing business just before the turn of the century, determined to develop the finest stable in the nation. He accomplished this with astonishing speed. By 1901 his racing stable topped all other owners' earnings, a record he repeated in 1903. He also purchased the Saratoga Race Course, the oldest race course in America, and converted it from "a ramshackle country-fair operation into what has become the dowager queen of American racing," in the words of turf writer Bob Stokhaug.[3]

Firmly convinced, unlike other breeders of the time, that the route to championship racers was found in the dams, William C. scoured the country to find prospective brood mares that had proven racing performance. He quartered them in the more temperate hills of Kentucky, where he leased a farm in the Bluegrass region outside of Lexington.

By the time he died in 1904, William C. had constructed a solid foundation of breeding stock through which his sons became highly successful.

Harry Payne was the chief purchaser at the dispersal sale of his father's stable and established his operation, Brookdale Stud, in New Jersey. For years he conducted his breeding from that farm, but just as his father before him, Harry Payne eventually concluded that the Bluegrass was the most favorable environment, so in 1914 he bought 1,000 acres in Kentucky and moved his breeding stock there.

For many years, Harry Payne was the inarguable ruler of the turf. No other breeder came close to his record of wins. But to him, sportsmanship was even more important than victory.

"He often allowed friends to buy whatever yearlings they chose from his entire crop in the hope that they might emulate his successes on the turf," according to writer Stokhaug. "At times those yearlings defeated his own horses in important stakes, but this didn't bother Whitney. On more than one occasion when his horses were sweeping the boards in leading stakes, he withdrew them in order to give his friends a chance at a purse which was probably entirely at his mercy. Certainly there has been no such sporting gesture as this in the annals of the turf."[4]

Between the years 1913 and 1930, Harry Payne Whitney was America's leading owner six times and leading breeder eight times. He set an American record for breeding stakes winners.

Oddly, although horse racing was perhaps the greatest of Harry's many passions, it was something he did not think to try to convey to his only son until Sonny was nearly thirty years old.

Sonny Whitney had grown up around horses — he was a fine horseman and a weekend polo player — but the racing side of his father's life was one Harry held in protective secrecy until 1927, when Sonny was invited to make his maiden visit to a race track. The place was Churchill Downs, and the race was the Kentucky Derby.

The events of that day became one of Sonny Whitney's favorite stories, one he told again and again, and one that he wrote about in *High Peaks.* Sonny had accompanied his father on the journey

south in Harry's private Pullman assuming, reasonably enough, that the two of them would attend the races together. Once they arrived in Kentucky, Harry disabused him of that notion. "You'll be going to the Derby alone. I get too nervous," Harry said.[5]

Harry had a promising stallion called Whiskery entered into the Run for the Roses. He also had a habit, which Sonny would have had no way of knowing, of absenting himself from important races in which he had a favored horse entered.

"If Whiskery wins, you'll have to go to the winner's circle and make a speech," Harry told his son.[6]

With that, the old man pressed a hundred-dollar bill toward Sonny, clearly not realizing his son was already a millionaire in his own right, and suggested he might want to make a bet.

Once he arrived at the track, Sonny drifted about in search of food and drink and made the acquaintance of a group of men, including the famed writer Ring Lardner. They all settled cheerily into an afternoon of scotch and sodas.

Moments before the start of the race in which Whiskery was to run, Whitney gathered what he could of his wits and set off for a good vantage point. But the noise was intense, the crowds were bedlam, and he got hopelessly lost. He didn't even know the race had been won until a man, deliriously happy that he had placed a winning bet, grabbed Sonny's arm and began chanting the name of the winning horse.

Whiskery had won the race.

Sonny had not seen any part of the run. He had made no bet and had made no winner's speech. He didn't even collect the trophy.

This inauspicious introduction to the world of fast horses did not entice Sonny into believing he had to get a piece of the excitement.

When Harry Payne died in the waning months of 1930, Sonny was not at all inclined to take over where his grandfather and father had left off, but he was prevailed upon by other horsemen.

"I didn't go into horses because I really wanted to but because when my father died the leading thoroughbred breeders and owners came to me and said I must carry on the tradition of fine, honest, thoroughbred sportsmanship," Whitney told a writer for *Town & Country* magazine.[7]

He purchased his father's horse operation for $1.26 million — since his father had not willed it to him — and began immersing himself in books about racing and bloodlines. He made application to the Jockey Club to race under the Eton blue and brown, which had been the Whitney colors for more than three decades, and stated his intent to race his father's prized stallion Equipoise, the champion two year old of 1930, in the Pimlico Futurity on November 5.

The race took place only a few days after Harry's death, and Whitney had anguished a bit over the propriety of his engaging in such an activity so soon after he had buried his father. But the chairman of the Jockey Club, a longtime and very close friend of Harry, phoned Whitney and encouraged him to run the steadfast little horse, as he was certain that is what Harry would have wanted.

"So I traveled to Baltimore dressed in a mourning suit with a bowler hat and with mixed emotions," Whitney wrote in *High Peaks.* "Ordinarily it would have been a happy occasion. This was the first horse to run in my name."[8]

Whitney had absolutely no familiarity that day with Equipoise, the horse known to the racing world as the Chocolate Soldier because of his deep brown coat and his unflagging need to win every race even though he had a deformity that sometimes gave him great pain. There was nothing Equipoise would not do to take a trophy, and he had been disqualified from several races for biting another horse on the neck while trying to pass it.

Whitney was about to get a fast lesson in the character of his father's most spunky racer. Equipoise had a bad start out of the gate that day and was left behind by about twenty lengths. This did not seem to trouble him. He methodically gained

on and passed every horse in front of him. He simply wore them down. And he won by half a length.

Whitney, unfailingly proper and reserved in public settings, found himself, he wrote, "jumping to my feet and shouting."[9]

With little knowledge of racing, breeding, or bloodlines, Whitney became the owner of a race horse that knew no equal in the early 1930s. Thus it came as little surprise to him when he received a call one day from the brother of Al Capone. The man owned an important race track in the Chicago area, and he wished to challenge Whitney's Chocolate Soldier to a match with Gallant Sir, the pride of the Midwest. Whitney agreed immediately, with the proviso that the race would be open to other horses as well.

As the race day approached, Equipoise was having progressively more trouble with his deformed foot, and on the day before the race, his trainer told Whitney he would prefer not to run him. But fearing that an eleventh-hour scratch would send the message that Whitney was afraid of being beaten, they agreed to run him anyway.

Equipoise won the race after having to fight off a horse in the backstretch that repeatedly bumped him. As Whitney made his way to the winner's circle to collect his trophy, he noticed the Capone brother who had set up the race and nodded briefly at him. "I rather imagined that was

Equipoise, also known as the Chocolate Soldier, had a deformed foot, but he was one of Harry Payne's most prized stallions.

going to be my last encounter with the Brothers Capone," Whitney wrote.[10]

It was not, of course. The following winter, while playing poker with some friends at the Bahamian Club in Nassau, he was approached by a young mobsterish-looking man who announced "the Boss" wanted to speak with him. The young man guided Whitney through a maze of hallways to a back room, and "there at the table sat Al Capone, a bodyguard close behind him," Whitney wrote. "His black hair neatly combed, his rather considerable bulk encased in a striped silk shirt, he certainly didn't look fierce.... He seemed extremely low key, almost gentle. Close up I thought he seemed like a sorely tired overweight barber on a much needed holiday."[11]

Whitney was mystified by the invitation to join the notorious gangster at his table, but he was driven by curiosity. So he chatted amiably with the man and drank his champagne, biding his time until Capone might tell him what was on his mind.

Finally Capone said, "When I heard you were in the Club I wanted to meet you."[12]

This was not at all illuminating.

Above and right: The Bull was one of Whitney's early stakes winners, taking the Breeders Futurity in Latonia, Kentucky, in 1931.

Capone seemed to be having difficulty with how to proceed. Finally, he said, "You've produced some great horses, but none greater than Equipoise. And I asked you here, Mr. Whitney, to apologize for something I did. My conscience will never be free until I do."[13]

Capone then admitted that during the race in Chicago, it was his jockey on his horse acting on his instructions in the backstretch, who almost led to Equipoise's demise. "I had a big bet on Gallant Sir. I did an injustice to your truly great horse, Mr. Whitney. I don't expect you to forgive me."[14]

With that, Capone invited Whitney to be his guest at the Sharkey championship fight in Miami the next month, an invitation that Whitney declined. This wee-hours-of-the-morning confession and invitation ended up being Whitney's final encounter with the Brothers Capone.

Equipoise was Whitney's star during those early years of the 1930s, but Whitney's racing success was not dependent exclusively on the scrappy colt. For four successive years — from 1930 to 1933 — C.V. Whitney led the owners list in earnings. It was an extraordinary run, but when it was interrupted, it took him twenty-seven years to head that list again. In 1960, he amassed $1.03 million in earnings, only the second time in history at that point that a stable had earned over $1 million.

After those first four stellar years, Whitney's stable not only failed to top the lists, it suffered several highly undistinguished seasons. Whitney

was otherwise occupied — in movies, in Flin Flon, at Marineland, and with Pan Am — and in 1937 he announced he would retire from racing. He sold virtually all the horses he had in training, and the following year there were, for the first time in thirty-five years, no Whitney horses in action. He did, however, keep a handful of the breeding stock and yearlings that were on the farm in Kentucky.

The horses in training he sold did very well the next couple of years at the track, and this restored his confidence in his ability to breed winners. By 1940, he was extracting himself from Pan American and was ready to commit himself to the horse business.

The reentry after retirement seemed odd to many. Whitney had always openly acknowledged he had never felt deep passion for the sport or great enthusiasm for the business. His chief motivation for reentering the horse business, Whitney told a reporter for *Sports Illustrated*, was "a sense of duty."[15]

Although many observers found this insufficient reason to become involved in such an expensive and risky endeavor, Whitney's intimates regarded it as perfectly plausible. For they understood the depth of the importance Whitney attached to tradition.

"Both my grandfather and my father had loved the sport and they have devoted a great deal of care to building up our bloodlines and breeding stock," Whitney told a writer years later.[16] This was something not easily dismissed by Whitney.

Then, too, there was the matter of the ever-present competition with his cousin Jock, who was experiencing some significant success with Greentree Stud, the Bluegrass farm adjoining Whitney's, owned by Jock and his sister.

Having made the commitment, Sonny did not settle for simply playing at horse breeding and racing. He was determined to make the family heritage proud. He hired Ivor Balding, the young Englishman he had enticed a few years earlier to manage his polo ponies and serve as a substitute on his polo team. He sent Balding to Cornell for an agronomy course, then put him in charge of the farm. One of the first moves Balding recom-

For a time in the 1950s and 1960s, Whitney Farm had one of the top Black Angus herds in the country. His cattle on the show circuit captured virtually every top award.

ANGUS PRIDE

WHITNEY WAS WELL KNOWN AS A horseman. What was not so well known is that for many years he had one of the leading cattle herds in the nation.

Early in the 1940s, at farm manager Ivor Balding's insistence, Whitney got into raising Black Angus cattle, primarily as a means of fertilizing the grazing pastures for the horses. Soon Whitney Farm had assembled a top-notch herd. The gleaming black cattle, hauled to competitions throughout the Midwest and Middle Atlantic regions, were inevitably top prize winners, the envy of larger-scale cattle breeders throughout the 1950s and into the 1960s.

Whitney was quite proud of his herd and never failed to show it off to guests. But one day in 1963, without preamble, Whitney ordered the herd's dispersal. Kenneth Haines, the farm manager at the time, was instructed to immediately put them up for auction, every last one of them. Whitney intended to get out of the cattle business, and he intended to do it completely.

"Mr. J.C. Penney himself bought our top bull," Jouett Redmon said proudly in an interview years later.[1]

Redmon and everyone else on the farm were baffled by Whitney's decision. But not for long. "Mr. Whitney had an uncanny way of knowing, long before anyone else, when to move on things," Redmon said. "He knew exactly when to get rid of them."[2]

The month the cattle were auctioned, prices were at a peak. A few months later, the cattle would not have commanded nearly the dollars — three million of them — they did when Whitney sold them.

"And Mr. Whitney, when they were all gone, sat right on that porch and cried," said Redmon.[3]

But once Whitney regained his composure, he looked at Redmon and confided, "You know, Jouett, I had no idea they were worth that much."[4]

Several years later, Whitney made a similar decision with his horses, and he made that one at precisely the right time as well, according to Ted Bassett, chairman of Keeneland race track in Lexington, where Whitney raced many horses. Whitney had "a unique sense of timing. He was always ahead of the curve in terms of the choices he made," Bassett said.[5]

Soon after his horses were auctioned, there was a fast and dramatic downward spiral in the prices people were willing to pay for thoroughbreds, a depression that lasted for the next several years.

If Whitney had not made the decision to sell at that time, Bassett said, "he would have lost money on them."[6]

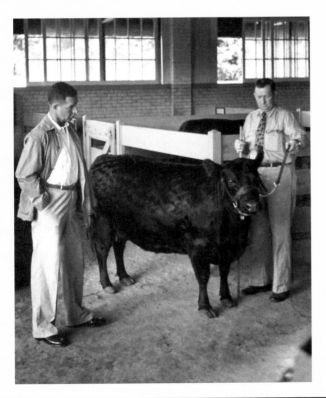

At farm manager Ivor Balding's recommendation, Whitney kept a herd of Black Angus on the farm to naturally fertilize the pasture for the horses.

THE GIFT HORSE
THAT KEPT ON GIVING

WHITNEY'S SPORTSMANLIKE BEHAV-
ior was matched only by his generosity
with friends. His longtime friend and
personal physician, Dr. Benjamin Roach, was
lucky enough to be one of the beneficiaries.

Roach saw Whitney's filly Song Sparrow
run in a stakes race at Keeneland in Kentucky
and told Whitney that if he ever wanted to sell
the horse, he'd like to buy her. "The next day,
I had a call from him, and he said, 'I'm going
to sell this filly to you for $7,500, but I'm going
to deduct $5,000 for your taking care of me,
for being my doctor. You don't have to pay me
the remaining $2,500 until you sell a yearling
out of that filly.'"[1]

Roach took the filly and bred her, and two
years later, he sold the first yearling from her
for $18,000 — not a bad return, as Roach
pointed out.

Another of Song Sparrow's foals was
Comorant, whom Roach sold as a yearling
and who became a multiple stakes winner and
the leading sire in New York state. Moreover,
Song Sparrow foaled a filly named Queen of
Songs, which Roach kept. That one won
$600,000 for Roach.

mended was starting a herd of Black Angus as
a means of naturally fertilizing the rolling
Kentucky pastureland.

Whitney began looking for a sound stallion
with speed and staying power, and when he and
Balding learned that the Aga Khan was willing to
sell his English Derby winner Mahmoud for
$80,000, they made the decision to purchase him.

It was a bold move on Whitney's part — some
said a foolhardy one — to settle on this stallion.
Mahmoud was a gray, and in American racing circles, this was a bane every bit as repulsive to
horsemen as bad knees or no courage.

There were those who declared the arrival of
Mahmoud would be the certain end of Whitney
studs. And for a time it appeared their prophecies
would be realized. Once Mahmoud was imported
and installed on the farm, Whitney could find no
one interested in breeding to the stallion. Finally,
one bold breeder broke the trend and brought all
the mares he was breeding to outside lines to
Mahmoud. The results were very good. The gray
produced some sound yearlings, and eventually
other breeders turned to him as well. Six years
after Whitney acquired Mahmoud, the gray stallion led the American sire list and dispelled the
gray-horse myth.

When Balding and Whitney had first
embarked on rebuilding the horse operation in

Whitney dispelled the superstition that a gray horse couldn't
make a good sire after Mahmoud, shown here in 1960,
produced a string of top-quality yearlings.

1940, they had agreed it would take at least ten years to get the farm into top-notch shape and reputation. It actually took less time than that. By the time World War II had ended, the farm had produced several outstanding horses, and Whitney Farm was again beginning to be seen as a force to be reckoned with.

By 1947, Whitney's big come-from-behind horse Phalanx won the Belmont and the Jockey Club Gold Cup, came in second in the Derby, and was voted top three year old of the year.

In 1951 his glorious chestnut Counterpoint won a handful of stakes races, took the trophy at Belmont and was named Horse of the Year.

As his commitment to horses and racing grew, Whitney purchased Maple Hill house (which later became known as Whitney House) and the surrounding sixty acres in 1951 to add to the nine hundred acres of Kentucky horse land he already owned.

Throughout the 1950s, Whitney bred and raced a string of impressive horses, including Silver Spoon, a gray filly who beat the best colts in California during the winter meet in Santa Anita and was the sentimental favorite to win the Kentucky Derby, just as Harry Whitney's stalwart filly, Regret, had done decades earlier. (Silver Spoon was not successful in that bid.) Other Whitney winners included Fisherman, a small bay who won the Washington, D.C., International; Tompion, the temperamental colt who easily won the Bluegrass Stakes at

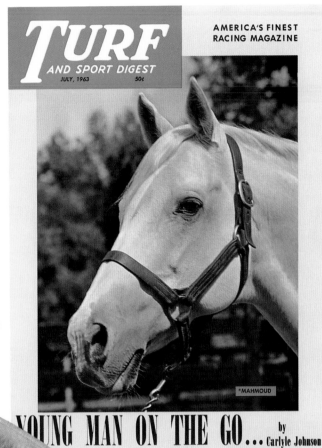

Above right: Mahmoud became Whitney's first breeding stallion and was hugely successful, siring twenty-four stakes winners for Whitney and becoming a cover boy for *Turf* magazine.

Right: Tompion was an irascible but winning horse for Whitney. Bred and trained in the 1950s, he took the purse at Belmont in 1961.

Keeneland; and Career Boy, victorious in the United Nations Handicap against a field of far more seasoned horses.

Whitney was clearly on a winning streak. But he was beginning to be known as much for his sportsmanship as for his ability to win, much as his father, Harry, had been.

Indeed, Whitney's defining characteristic was that he was "an exemplary sportsman," said thoroughbred writer Hirsch.[17]

"He sent two horses to Europe [to the Prix de l'Arc de Triomphe at Longchamp in 1956] to run against Ribot ... at a time when Ribot was the dominant horse in the world and nobody stood a chance against him, really.... It was considered a very sporting gesture," said Hirsch. "Then he had Fisherman standing by as an alternate to the International Race [near Washington, D.C.] one year when the American-designated horse, High Gun, was injured and had to be retired. Fisherman stepped in as an alternate and won the race.... He was the first American winner of the International Race."[18]

Top: Whitney was not content to supply the money and sit in the stands. He regularly discussed strategy with the jockeys.

Above: Whitney and his wife Marylou were regulars at the Keeneland track in the 1960s and 1970s and often socialized with friends and other horse enthusiasts there. Pictured from left: Whitney's friend and farm manager, Ivor Balding; Mary Jane Gallagher; Whitney; Marylou; and Whitney's brother-in-law George Headley.

If the horse business was an endeavor that did not reach Whitney's soul, it was one in which he was able to expose much of what resided there. The millionaire businessman, always so correct, was suddenly seen as less monolithic, more interestingly complex. His ability to connect with all strata who populate the track suggested an unpretentiousness rarely seen among those born to extreme wealth.

"He moved in all company, from grooms to millionaire bankers," said writer Hirsch. "He was a very democratic fellow, and everyone liked him. He was a very popular man."[19]

And his behavior was regarded as exemplary at a time and in an arena where pride and egos often displayed themselves in most unfortunate ways.

"He took defeat very gracefully," said Hirsch. "He was very experienced at both winning and losing. He was a gracious winner and a gracious loser."[20]

Once Whitney became involved in the horse business, wherever he went in the world he could count on being approached by people who knew him and appreciated him because of that association. One time, near the end of World War II, when Whitney was on the SS *El Dorado* observing the Marine takeover of Iwo Jima, he was approached by a ship's cook.

"Aren't you the Colonel Whitney who has a farm in Lexington, Kentucky?" the smiling black man asked.[21]

Whitney replied that he was, whereupon the cook grinned broadly and asked about Yankee Maid, the successful racing mare who had been retired to brood status a few years earlier. Whitney was amazed that out in the Pacific, during the final days of the war, there was someone who knew of his horse. The cook, as it turned out, had been a stable hand at Whitney Farm, and he had a particular affection for the mare.

Over the next several decades, the horse business would bring Whitney into contact with thousands of people, from grooms and trainers to presidents and British royalty.

In 1966, after more than thirty-five years in the business, he sold about half of the acreage of Whitney Farm, as well as about half of his mares. But he produced 141 stakes winners, and until midsummer of 1977, he ranked as the leading breeder of stakes winners in the world. In 1983, when he

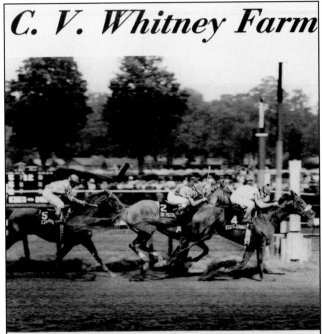

State Dinner-Winning The Whitney Stakes

C. V. Whitney Farm is continuing its great tradition of breeding for 1981 with the stakes winning mares SILVER BRIGHT (Barbizon - Silver Fog) dam of STATE DINNER and BANQUET TABLE now at stud. In Foal to EXCLUSIVE NATIVE.

INCA QUEEN (Hail to Reason - Silver Spoon). In Foal to BOLD BIDDER.

PLAINS AND SIMPLE (Twist the Axe - You All). In Foal to FOOLISH PLEASURE. Along with these three mares, he has just retired from racing seven fillies for the 1981 breeding season.

P. O. Box 890   **Lexington, Kentucky.**

An advertisement for C.V. Whitney Farm, long considered one of the top breeding stables in America.

was well into his eighties, he announced he was getting out of the horse business completely.

To break the news to the public, he turned to his friends Ed and Maureen Lewi, who owned a public relations firm. "He called us and said, 'I must get out of the racing business. I'm not as sharp as I used to be, and I don't have the stamina or energy to put into it. But I don't want to saddle Marylou with these stables and all of that because it's a major business,'" Maureen remembered. "He asked our opinion as to how to go about letting the public know, so Ed suggested he do a press conference. He took our advice, and we wrote a basic press release, and he made an announcement in the press box at Saratoga that he was retiring from the horse business."[22]

Although Whitney ultimately passed most of his remaining enterprises to his wife Marylou, the horse business was one he did not, believing, by all accounts, that this was an arena where women had no business. As it turned out, his timing was impeccable, as it had been throughout his life, and his decision not to turn the business over to his wife was a wise one. The thoroughbred industry took a major nosedive only three years after he dispersed his bloodstock.

He never did have a horse win the Kentucky Derby, although he tried repeatedly — nominating four of his horses in 1969 — and came heart breakingly close several times. Moreover, he never produced a horse of the exceptional quality and racing record of Equipoise, Regret, and Top Flight, bred in the Harry Payne regime. What must be remembered, according to Abram S. Hewitt, author of *The Great Breeders and Their Methods*, is that "Consideration must be given to the vast dif-

Even after he retired from the horse business, Whitney still took an interest in watching the races and would occasionally venture out to the tracks with Marylou.

ference in conditions which prevailed between the era of the father and that of the son."[23]

During Harry Payne's reign, the thoroughbred foal crops ranged in number from about two thousand to something less than five thousand. During Sonny's years, the foal crops were almost always above twenty thousand, and in the 1980s, the numbers soared to more than thirty-five thousand. "Hence," Hewitt pointed out, "the sheer numerical probability of getting a champion out of any given crop has been unfavorable" by significantly higher odds.[24]

"Still, he was extraordinarily successful," said Whitney's nephew Leverett Miller, the Florida thoroughbred breeder to whom Whitney turned over his Eton blue and brown colors. Whitney's horses, Miller noted, were never really conformationally correct. "Many of them were crooked legged and yet they ran like the wind. He was extremely successful, and it was a success a lot of people couldn't figure out."[25]

Whitney broke all the breeding rules, sought out blood- lines almost no one else found appeal-

ing, and had magnificent foal crops year after year. "I know how hard it is to breed good horses, and he did it consistently," said Miller. "One of the things that used to drive us all crazy was the fact that he would never talk about his methods or how he did it, and I specifically would question him, and Marylou did too, and say, 'How did you come up with this?' or 'How did you come up with that?' And he would always sort of smile distantly and say, 'Aha, that's my secret.' So we really never did find out."[26]

Whitney missed a few of the golden rings of racing for which he reached, but he found himself in possession of many more he didn't intend. For more than half a century, he was regarded as something of a standard setter in the business he very nearly did not enter.

His reputation for fair play was recognized by the National Museum of Racing (which he cofounded) when he was named an Exemplar of Racing, one of only five men ever so honored up until that point, for setting an example for good sportsmanship.

C.V. accepted the Exemplar of Racing award in 1991 for his contributions to the thoroughbred and racing world over the decades. Holding the award are (from left) Sonny's nephew Whitney Tower, Sr., and John Von Staade, president of the National Museum of Racing and Hall of Fame.

The New York Turf Writers named C.V. Whitney Outstanding Owner in 1952 and 1957 and Outstanding Breeder in 1960. In 1984 the group gave him its Distinguished Service to Racing award, and since 1991, it has presented the annual C.V. Whitney Achievement Award to a variety of outstanding jockeys, trainers, horses, and others involved in racing.

The Thoroughbred Club of America also honored him with an honorary life membership for his contributions to the industry.

And when he retired from the horse business in 1984 at age eighty-five, he left it as he had entered it — with the certain knowledge that his timing was right.

On January 24, 1958, C.V. Whitney married Marylou Hosford, a talented and beautiful woman who brought to their marriage an excitement and stability that Whitney had not before experienced.

CHAPTER NINE

STARSTRUCK

ELEANOR SEEMED OBLIVIOUS TO their marriage's falling apart. After Whitney resigned from his post as undersecretary of commerce, she wrote that "We returned to a life centered in our home and estate at Old Westbury and our River House apartment in New York. We went to the opera, entertained our friends, participated in benefits for charity, went to the races in New York, Kentucky, Florida and California, cruised on our yacht, summered in the Adirondacks and traveled abroad."[1]

Whitney had his stables, his mining interests, the timber business, and his Marineland responsibilities to attend to, and he worked on his book about his war experiences, *Lone and Level Sands,* which was published in 1951, the year he first asked Eleanor for a divorce. Eleanor kept busy with her charities, and their son, Searle, attended the Greenvale School just across the way from Old Westbury. Whitney's children from his first marriage, Nancy and Harry, spent a few weeks each summer with them, and his daughter Gail, from his second marriage, spent most summers and an occasional winter vacation with him.

Life settled into a routine, but "then slowly the situation that had existed previously took over again," Whitney wrote. "I again consulted doctors and specialists in the fields of medicine and psychiatry. I was advised that the only way I could preserve my health was to be away from my home as frequently as possible. In pursuance of this recommendation, I started businesses elsewhere."[2]

One of his first outlets was in painting — in creating huge, brooding oils, mostly of nature scenes.

Then he created another outlet in Hollywood. He linked up with his old filmmaker friend Merian C. Cooper to make historically authentic pictures of an upbeat nature that celebrated the strength of the nation and of the human spirit, and in late 1954, he announced the formation of C.V. Whitney Pictures, Inc. His films, he said, would serve as a counterbalance to the dour hopelessness that had penetrated Hollywood in the doom-and-gloom post-McCarthy years. He was weary of negativism, he declared, and he vowed to present a series of films of substance to offer a "truer understanding of life in the United States."[3]

"No C.V. Whitney picture will ever misrepresent or paint a false picture of the United States or its people," he told the *New York Times.*[4]

The film industry and the public at large took him seriously, for not only had he enlisted respected

---

C.V. Whitney Pictures produced such films as the critically acclaimed *The Searchers,* starring John Wayne, and *The Missouri Traveler.*

filmmaker Merian Cooper, but he and Cooper had signed four-time Academy Award winner John Ford to a multipicture contract, and megastar John Wayne would star in their first effort, a film adaptation of the best-selling Alan LeMay novel, *The Searchers*.

"Get the best," Whitney had commanded Cooper as the filmmaker prepared to put *The Searchers* into production. That resulted in the signing not only of Ford and Wayne but also of Natalie Wood and Vera Miles. It resulted in taking the entire company to Monument Valley, where real Navajos were hired to portray the Indians in the film. And it meant hiring the top stuntmen in the country.

Whitney spent most of the fall and winter of 1955 in Monument Valley on location, often joined by Eleanor, who was given a short walk-on part as a hymn-singing graveside mourner.

The film company's publicity machine worked tirelessly throughout the production, cranking out endless tidbits seized by the trade press like bait thrown into a tank of starving sharks.

By the time the film was released, the critics and public were in a lather of anticipation. They were not disappointed. The movie received rave reviews, and box office numbers were impressive. "Strongly authentic," the critics cried. "One of the finest westerns to come along in years," "straight and strong," "a little rugged for queasy stomachs," "compelling and suspenseful," "an auspicious beginning for the recently formed production organization of C.V. Whitney and Merian C. Cooper," "a contender for big-money stakes." Indeed, more than four decades after the film

was released, it was considered among the best three westerns ever made and was ranked the thirteenth best film ever made by the editors of *Entertainment Weekly.*

As *The Searchers'* ferment played itself out, Whitney was enjoying some additional acclaim. In July 1956, a few weeks after celebrating his fifteenth wedding anniversary, he went to London. There he was honored by the Jockey Club in England, which is the exclusive British turf organization, and afterwards, the U.S. ambassador feted him with a gathering that included the Queen of England.

Three months later, he was once again back in Europe. He and Eleanor encamped in a suite at the Ritz in Paris, where they celebrated her birthday and his latest racing venture. The thoroughbred world was abuzz over Whitney's decision to fly two of his best horses (Fisherman and Career Boy), two of the best jockeys in America, and a week's worth of food and water to France for the Prix de l'Arc de Triomphe. He was the first American stable owner to fly horses into the country specifically for that race. Neither of Whitney's horses won the race, but that was really not the point. He had shown a supremely sportsmanlike gesture of American participation in international races. Whitney, in fact, pioneered the practice of shipping horses abroad to race, and for this, scores of newspapermen, including Art Buchwald, who was then with the *New York Herald-Tribune,* paid homage.

His filmmaking plans, meanwhile, continued to

command great attention. He had acquired the rights to a Civil War story called *The Valiant Virginian,* which caused a good deal of excitement among the citizens of Lexington, Virginia, where the filming was to take place. He had also acquired the rights to do the story of Chuck Yaeger, the first man to break the sound barrier. And he had signed a contract on *William Liberty,* an upcoming novel by Frank Clemensen, which Whitney declared would be the West's version of *Gone With the Wind.* There was even talk that he was negotiating with Marilyn Monroe for the female lead in *William Liberty.*

But the next film to go into production, he announced, would be *The Missouri Traveler,* based on the novel by John Burress. This film, he said, would prove that it is possible to make a "picture about American youth without resorting to switchblade knives and marijuana."[5] *The Missouri Traveler,* according to the trade press, was to begin shooting in January 1957.

His marriage to Eleanor, meanwhile, was again fraying at the seams. He was spending more and more time on the West Coast without her, and she was feeling a growing unease over their life. "Life was busy and interesting, with endless variety and opportunity," she wrote in her autobiography, *Invitation to Joy.* "My marriage had brought me all the worldly possessions one could think of.... I cannot deny that during my sixteen years of marriage my life was full of pleasures. But those pleasures were on the surface. They had no cohesion, no depth, no sure foundation."[6]

In the summer of 1957, Eleanor, a lifelong, regular churchgoer, met the Reverend Billy Graham after a friend asked her to invite him to a garden party. Soon thereafter, Eleanor attended a crusade Graham was holding at Madison Square Garden, and she found herself drawn to

Opposite: Even today, many critics consider *The Searchers* to be one of the best films ever made.

Right: *The Missouri Traveler* brochure included vignettes about all the actors and actresses and pointed out that "newcomer" Mary Hosford was appearing for her first time on the big screen.

leave her chair in the audience and walk to the front, ready to commit herself to God and to a course of evangelism.

Eleanor had found something of importance in her life — which was just as well, because Whitney had too. Early in the summer of 1957, "My husband made it clear he wanted a divorce," she wrote.[7]

Whitney, at fifty-eight years old, had become utterly smitten. The object of his affection was Marie Louise Schroeder Hosford, a vibrant, attractive woman of thirty-one, who was separated from her husband and was supporting four children.

Hosford was a product of the Midwest, the third of four girls, born on Christmas Eve 1925 in Kansas City. Her father was a corporate lawyer of German extraction, a disciplinarian with high standards, and her mother was a doting housewife of Scottish descent.

Marie, as she was known by her family, grew up in storybook style. As a child, she was a slight, blue-eyed tomboy who passed happy family holidays with adoring grandparents, learned to cook at the elbow of a cherished black housekeeper called Jane, and competed vigorously with her sisters.

Marie knew from her earliest years that her father, surrounded by a gaggle of females, desperately wanted at least one son, if for no other reason, she cheerfully acknowledged years later, than "to feed his masculine ego."[8] And when he tapped his third-born to be his surrogate son, Marie felt honored. She was, even in childhood, she acknowledged, an "ego feeder,"[9] and it was a characteristic she fine-tuned as the years went on. But even as a tiny girl with knobby elbows, she understood there was an advantage to being the one person in the family who "would lend an eager ear to his narration of the daily chores and his business troubles."[10]

Although the family was reasonably well-off, her mother felt there was no excuse for girls not learning at an early age the finer points of tending to a household, so she put her daughters through a rigorous course in home economics — sewing, knitting, embroidering, and cooking. Marie distinguished herself as the most careful of budgeters, planning the menus and buying the items that could be had at the most reasonable prices. It was a trait "that stuck to me to this very day," she wrote in the 1950s, after she was already divorced from one millionaire and on the brink of marrying another. "I'll drive miles to three or four markets for a sale on a head of romaine lettuce or five cents off on a can of coffee with a newspaper coupon."[11]

By the time she was approaching her teens, she knew what she wanted to be when she grew up — an actress. She came by it honestly enough. Her mother sang in choirs and at weddings, and young Marie and her sisters would put on performances in the garage, using their mother's red velvet drapes as curtains for their makeshift stage.

As soon as she finished high school, Marie set off for the University of Iowa and enrolled in theater arts courses under the tutelage of Edward

Opposite: After the war, Marylou moved to New York, where she was the belle of society and the object of many men's affections.

Above: Even at a very young age, Marylou had visions of becoming an actress.

Charles Mabie. Her first role as a college thespian was that of Sally Jackson in *Letters to Lucerne.* She joined Kappa Alpha Theta (largely, she said, because of the exquisite chocolate dessert served at the sorority rush party)[12] and made the social rounds of fraternity row, becoming pinned twice in two weeks.

She stayed in Iowa for a year, and when she returned to Kansas City, she was speaking a jargon of three accents, "one acquired from my speech course in college, a broad-A derived from Theta's Housemother Anderson, who came from Boston, and a lazy Southern drawl from my Sally Jackson role."[13]

When the war came, she didn't join the WACs or WAVs because, as a child, she had battled high fevers and aching joints during a bout with rheumatic and scarlet fever. Her parents objected that her constitution was "too frail and delicate to withstand the rigors of boot camp."[14] So she took the aspiring actress route and toured Army and Navy camps, playing various ingénues. She was, for several years, a disc jockey at KCKN radio station in Kansas City, where she had a very successful show for servicemen called *Private Smiles.* During her lunch hour, she would stand on a bandstand dressed in her private's hat and sell war bonds. She was so popular with the servicemen that she appeared twice on the front page of *Stars and Stripes* newspaper, once posing in an oversized pajama top as the "pajama girl" and again in a two-piece bathing suit. Later, she was honored as New York's USO Woman of the Year, and her picture is still displayed in a Kansas City radio station museum for her efforts during the war.

Soon, however, brighter, bigger lights beckoned, and off she went to New York City, where she lived in Sutton Place, became friendly with a host of high-profile characters (including Patrice O'Neal and John Forsythe), renamed herself Marylou, and almost immediately began showing up in the society gossip columns, inevitably identified, for some reason, as a Kansas City cattle heiress.

She became friendly with composer Gian Carlo Menotti, world-famous harmonica player Borrah Minnevitch, and Peruvian Prince Augui, who sent her a never-ending stream of flamboyant, flashy, and very expensive gifts, including, one time, a horse.

She was linked romantically in the columns to Count Vincent Orssich (who she admitted was calling her from Mexico nearly every day), famed tenor Frank Parker (who columnist Cholly Knickerbocker reported was so head-over-heels that he would soon ask her to marry him), and Sir Cedric Hardwicke. Now she was identified not only as a cattle heiress but as a playgirl and girl-about-town.

She was living the sort of carefree, urbane life that was the envy of most young women who read the gossip columns — and many who appeared in them.

But just before Valentine's Day in 1948, she married Midwestern millionaire Frank Hosford, a descendent of tractor and farm equipment magnate John Deere. She was introduced to Hosford by silent movie star Richard Bartholmus, and the couple hit it off immediately. The way the columnists told it, the two had been lunching and decided to elope to Brooklyn. News of her marriage, it was claimed by columnist Dorothy Kilgallen, plunged much of New York's bachelor contingent into deep mourning.

The couple lived in a large mansion in fashionable Greenwich, Connecticut, where he had a foreign car dealership. By April the society columns were announcing that the young Mrs. Hosford was busily knitting baby clothes, and at the end of November, Marion Louise, called Malou, later changed to M'lou, was born. Additional children arrived with great regularity. Two years after the birth of their daughter, Frank Hobbs Hosford, called Hobbs, arrived, and the October after that, Henry Deere, called Hank, was born.

The Hosfords appeared to be the epitome of the prosperous young couple, living within striking distance of New York City and partaking of all that thriving 1950s America had to offer. They made frequent jaunts to New Orleans, had a two-month holiday in Europe, and regularly spent their winters in Phoenix.

In 1954 they moved to the Phoenix area — lock, stock, children, and four dogs. Hosford gave up the car dealership and announced plans to develop a manganese mine. Later, the couple did a man-and-wife television show. Their daughter M'lou became the only girl enrolled in the Judson

School for Boys. And the large but time-worn adobe house they bought and renovated was regarded as such a triumph of rehabilitation that the local newspaper did a story on it.

Their fourth child, Heather, was born in August 1955. But the marriage was coming to a close. Marylou, who by then was starring on television with a popular cooking show, also began selling real estate.

Her husband, she said, "didn't want to work. I was supporting him working two jobs, and he was having a good time at the bars." The much-touted millions, she said, were gone. "He inherited a lot of money, but he never knew what he was doing with it. He'd stand in a bar, and somebody would sell him all sorts of stock in some mine that didn't exist. He was taken to the cleaners by many people."[15]

Marylou was struggling to come to terms with her separation from Hosford when her friend Deering Davis, who played polo against Sonny's team and was Gee Hopkins' cousin, strong-armed her into going to a dinner theater one night to meet a gentleman who, he told her, was "blue and lonely and needs someone to pep him up."[16]

Cornelius Vanderbilt Whitney had also been a reluctant participant in the set-up, but when he arrived at the place, he looked through the window at Marylou, liked what he saw, and decided to join them. He found himself utterly enchanted with her very essence. She was "blonde, petite and very feminine yet outgoing, outspoken and efficient," he wrote years later.[17]

He asked her to lunch, but she refused, saying, "I can't have lunch with you. I cook on television at noontime. You watch me, you'll know where I am at lunch."[18]

To which he replied, "Oh, I've never seen a woman cook before."[19] As far as he knew, none of his wives had ever entered a kitchen.

They spent hours that night talking about how each of them was at a very low ebb in their lives. He told her that he was planning his own suicide. He had recently spent some time in a cabin in the desert painting, and it was his intent to return there sometime soon to end his life.

In 1948, Marylou married Frank Hosford, and they moved into an astounding mansion called Deerecrest Hall in Greenwich, Connecticut.

"He was miserable," said Marylou. "He'd wanted to get a divorce from Eleanor,... and he told me, 'She won't give me a divorce.... This is the worst thing that has ever happened to me.'"[20]

By now it was three o'clock in the morning, the time when even strangers, if sad enough and tired enough, will confess almost anything. She, too, was miserable, she told him, and she admitted having considered suicide herself. But her children had kept her going through the darkest moments, and in the light of morning, she had realized that suicide was against everything she believed in. She would not date him again, she said, if he continued to entertain any suicidal thoughts.

They covered a lot of ground in that first, long night. Whitney told her he was planning to make a picture in California called *The Missouri Traveler*, and, he told Marylou, "I think you'd be the ideal person for it."

He asked her to go to California to try out for it. At first she demurred, saying she was happy selling real estate and that she had given up her young girl's dreams of acting years ago.

"Please do it," he pleaded. "It will give me an excuse to see you again or for you to see me again, and you can get away from this life."[21]

She eventually conceded that it might be possible and left the children with a girlfriend in Colorado for a few weeks to make the trip to California. "So I went out there," Marylou recalled, "and the producers and directors all hired me for a part in the movie.

[Whitney] wasn't there. He went back to New York to go to work in the office for awhile. He didn't want to be there to influence the days I did my testing. He came back when they said, 'We're hiring her.'"[22]

So she packed up and headed west, bought a house and moved the children out. *The Missouri Traveler*, with Lee Marvin, was shot mostly in the Warner Brothers lot in Burbank, and her relationship with the film company's president blossomed.

"And that's how it started out," she said years later. "Two people who were very low."[23]

When the film was released, it was promoted as the screen debut of Miss Mary Hosford, "one of the most interesting newcomers Hollywood has welcomed into its midst for many years."[24] Now she was Mary, at least to the film world and Whitney, if to no one else. For reasons that even he said he never really understood, Whitney called her Mary from the time they met and continued calling her Mary for the rest of his life.

The picture company's press information made much of her discovery. "There she was,

beautiful and charming, thirty-one years old and the mother of four children.... Then lo and behold, the magic world of moviedom reached far out and touched her. Presto! She was a movie star."[25]

Marylou's divorce was finalized soon after she made her move to California. Whitney, however, was struggling with his own.

Though Whitney had started divorce proceedings in 1951, Eleanor always maintained that she had no hint of Whitney's desire for a divorce until the summer of 1957, when he unceremoniously stated his intent, left the house, and did not see her again. So she spent most of the summer in the Adirondacks and "took no action toward the divorce" as she tried to get a grip on her emotions and come to terms with what had befallen her.[26]

Mary Hosford (her stage name) on a publicity junket with Minnesota Governor Orville Freeman, C.V. Whitney, and Mrs. Freeman.

Left: One of the first things Marylou, now Mrs. Whitney, did once filming of *The Missouri Traveler* was complete was write a cookbook with that title.

Top: In 1959 and 1960, she did several promotional shoots to garner publicity for her cookbook.

Opposite: Marylou and Sonny soon after their marriage. Many who knew them said they were made for each other.

During a press conference about the filming of *The Missouri Traveler* later that summer, Whitney announced that he had found the star of a movie in Arizona and fallen in love with her. "This is the first woman I've really ever loved in my life," he said. "As soon as I get my divorce we're going to be married."[27]

This, Whitney and Marylou later acknowledged, may have been an unwise proclamation at the moment. It did not serve to make Eleanor particularly cooperative.

In November, Eleanor went to court. She was out of funds, she said. She needed money to keep up with the routine maintenance bills, and she was demanding a vast sum. A couple of weeks later, Whitney, who had moved to Nevada to establish residency, filed for divorce in that state.

Eleanor found this unacceptable. She filed suit in New York, seeking to enjoin him from obtaining a divorce anywhere but in that state, and, in a second part of her action, sequestered his New York funds and property until the matter could be resolved.

Whitney was suddenly flat broke, in reality if not on paper. "So I paid for everything," Marylou said. "Here's one of the richest men in the world, and I'm paying for everything. It was tough. It was really tough.... He didn't even have a car. He had to use my car to go to work. Every weekend, I would go back to Arizona to sell real estate, and Sonny would stay with my children."[28]

On January 24, 1958, Marylou and Sonny married in Carson City, Nevada, shortly after Whitney had been granted a divorce in that state.

Eleanor, however, did not view that event as the conclusion of her matrimonial connection to Whitney. Her injunction had essentially accomplished the feat of making the marriage invalid in New York. Sonny and Marylou were married in all states except the one in which Whitney had grown up and spent most of his life. It was not until seven months later that the New York Supreme Court announced a settlement in the divorce of C.V. and Eleanor Whitney.

By that time, Sonny had grown somewhat accustomed to living a middle-class life. "We lived well but on a tight budget," said Marylou. "So Eleanor, with her many lawsuits against us, did Sonny a favor, for he learned to live like a middle-class family — something he found novel, new, and relaxing."[29]

After the settlement, Sonny and Marylou remarried in California. "Eleanor said we weren't really married, so we had to remarry," said Marylou. "We had a house full of guests, and after breakfast we told them we had to go and do some business.... So we went to the Methodist Church and got remarried."[30]

With Marylou by his side, Whitney became a changed man, and the couple were virtually inseparable, whether at parties or camping in the wilderness.

CHAPTER TEN

TRUE HAPPINESS

THE COURTSHIP AND MARRIAGE of the fourth Mrs. Whitney may have been pure Hollywood — young working mother discovered in the desert by rich producer becomes his star and then his bride. But the postwedding bliss followed no predictable script.

"Most people married in January honeymoon in Palm Beach, Palm Springs or under a palm in Honolulu. We honeymooned in the land of ice and snow," Marylou Whitney wrote in the narrative-style cookbook she assembled in conjunction with *The Missouri Traveler*.[1]

The newlyweds flew to Flin Flon, Manitoba, where Sonny was still president of the mining operation, then even farther north, to Island Falls, where they landed their ski plane on a frozen lake. It was thirty-six degrees below zero when they donned their caribou parkas and slammed themselves onto a dogsled for a breakneck race to an Indian encampment where a campfire luncheon of moose-kabobs awaited. Everyone thought it fortunate that the temperature was much warmer than usual for that time of year.

The Whitneys, accompanied by C.V.'s oldest son, Harry, and his wife, Axie, spent their nights in a Spartan Flin Flon cabin during their interlude in the frozen northlands. Once Marylou managed to assemble a reasonable assortment of furnishings, Whitney declared it was time to move on. This time they were headed to Kentucky for Marylou's introduction to his horse farm and the Bluegrass State, for he had acquired an additional sixty acres with a pioneer house on a small hilltop overlooking Elkhorn Creek and was eager for his new bride to see it.

The couple arrived in the middle of an ice storm, which at first made passage impossible. But when the weather calmed, they proceeded to have a look at the homestead in question.

"I think she expected a Southern mansion," Whitney wrote in *High Peaks*.[2]

What lay before her was an old red brick farmhouse in a sorry state of disrepair, "flanked by a tangle of chicken coops and pigsties," she wrote.[3] But she loved the farm from the moment they drove through the gates. "I was enchanted with how the ice storm had left icy fringes on the gates," she said.[4]

Whitney wished to see the estate made livable for the seven to ten days a year he generally spent in Kentucky and looked at her beseechingly.

The Whitneys were painted by long-time friend and famous Spanish artist Alejo Vidal-Quadras. The artist's intriguing style emphasized the blue eyes of each of them.

"With my imagination and your money, we'll do it," declared Marylou, who became caught up with the setting and the historic value of the house. She envisioned a federal-style facade, a round portico, and white-painted bricks. This place would be turned into the Tara-like house she had imagined it would be.[5]

The preliminary plans began to take shape, and three months later, when the Whitneys returned for the Kentucky Derby, they decided the hilltop house would be more than a one-week-a-year residence. They would live there. But it was quite some time before that would be possible.

In the meantime, they returned to Marylou's house in California, there being no other place to go because his New York residences were tied up in the continuing divorce litigation for the next few months.

"That year, after Eleanor said we weren't married, we had to be very tight knit because she said she was going to put Sonny in jail," said Marylou. "So we stayed at home, and I cooked, and we had a lovely time together. I showed him a different time than he'd ever had before in his life. I took him to the supermarket for the first time in his life. It was like teaching a foreigner a new world.... And we found out," she concluded, "you could live on very little money and be very happy."[6]

Top: Sonny and Marylou embarked on a ski plane (left) to their honeymoon love nest in Flin Flon, where they took a dogsled (right) to a Cree Indian settlement, along with Whitney's son Harry and Harry's wife, Axie.

Left: Three of Marylou's children — Hobbs, M'lou, and Hank — enjoy an Easter Day with their mother and new stepfather of five months, in front of the Coronado Beach Hotel in California.

Mary," he would frequently say over the next three decades.

She gave him the kind of homelife and unflinching support he had not experienced in his previous sixty years. She understood the enormous role ego played in his life — that he was the kind of man who needed constant excitement and stimulation. And she understood that their long-term happiness together would depend on her ability to make him the center of her cosmos.

"Sonny was a spoiled child, and Marylou continued to spoil him — and she loved it," said Budd Calisch, the couple's public relations consultant and longtime friend. "Whenever she was away, she always wrote little love letters to be on his breakfast tray every morning."[7]

She never won a foot race they had, not because she couldn't, but because "I know you have to let a man do everything first.... Men have to have their egos built up," she said years later."[8]

She never caught the biggest fish for the same reason or upstaged him in any way that would matter to him.

She, much more naturally sociable than he, broadened his circle. She, much more congenitally optimistic than

Whatever the skeptics might have said (and they said plenty) about Whitney's marital history, his lifelong fascination with beautiful women the world over, his oft-expressed belief that a wife generally lasts about seven years, and his repetitive pattern of courting his next wife before he was completely relieved of his current one, the fact remained that his fourth bride was the ideal woman for him, and he knew it.

"The best money I ever spent in my life was the two dollars I paid for the license to marry

Whether dressing up for social parties, attending the races, or simply enjoying the sun and breeze, the Whitneys made a splendid couple.

he, helped him to see the rosier sides of things.

He blossomed under her care and tutelage. His tormented stomach, brutalized by a lifetime of intensity and nerves, calmed down enough that he could abandon the ulcer diet he had abided by for years. Moreover, he was seen smiling, widely and often, after nearly six decades of photographs in which he always wore a slightly wistful, slightly melancholy expression.

"Everybody in Long Lake loves the fourth Mrs. Whitney," said Marjorie Short, wife of one of Whitney's closet friends, Dave Short. "She's the nicest lady in the world."[9]

"He chose very well when he chose Marylou," said Whitney's niece Gerta Conner, daughter of Whitney's sister Barbara. "There was a big change in him when he married Marylou."[10]

Conner had observed Whitney from a distance for years, first as a child, then as a young girl who, like all females, found him "charismatic" and "sort of alluring."[11] What Conner noticed once he had settled into his fourth marriage was something that all his friends and relatives saw and spoke of. "He would gaze at her [Marylou] in a very intense way and a very tender way, and that never ended from the very beginning to the end of his life. It touched me a lot, especially from him, because he was rather spoiled and blasé about women," she said. "It was amazing.... I've never seen anyone change so much, and he always acted as if he was still on his honeymoon."[12]

Even Marylou's children observed the couple's happiness. "Uncle Sonny and my mother were good for each other," said Hank Hosford, Marylou's youngest son. "They helped one another by giving what was necessary for their relationship."[13]

Whitney's daughter Gail visited the couple soon after they were married and told Marylou she was astonished by what she saw. "She was looking at the swimming pool out at my house in California," recalled Marylou. "[Sonny] was out there teaching the kids how to swim and doing all sorts of things. Being a walrus in the water and doing all those games with them and then getting out and playing ball with them, and they're racing all over the place. She said, 'What have you done to my father? He hates children. I really wanted to warn you that you were going to have a tough time.... He never had anything to do with children.' I said, 'Gail, he never had a homelife before.'"[14]

To Marylou it was no doubt just that simple. That he was approaching sixty now, the age by which even the most self-absorbed men can usually wrestle themselves into some semblance of maturity in relationships, especially after a venomous divorce, did not seem to occur to her. She was prepared to take full responsibility for whatever would happen in their future, and she approached the next three decades with all the resolve of a skilled courtesan determined to outdo all others. This determination did not lessen with time.

"I cater to him," she said after she had been married to him for a quarter century and Whitney was well into his eighties. "If I didn't look after him, some other woman would, and I'm not going to let that happen."[15]

She found him utterly fascinating and was grateful that he had accepted a woman with four small children, a fact she made frequent references to for decades to come.

After a few months on the West Coast, the newlyweds left the house in California — with Whitney concluding that Hollywood and filmmaking held no further fascination — and retreated with the children to the Adirondacks.

The year they spent in the Adirondacks was something of a hardship for the Whitneys, given

Sonny and Marylou at home not long after they married.

that they were nine miles from a main road and winters could be quite severe. The school bus did not venture onto their property, so the daily transport of children became Marylou's job. "I had to take the children to school in a second-hand World War II Jeep every morning," she told a magazine writer. "It was a lumber road, and the children and I always said it was like Russian roulette, not knowing whether we were going to be run off into a snowdrift when the lumber trucks came."[16]

But finally, the house in Kentucky was sufficiently renovated for them to move there. They returned to California long enough to collect their belongings, then loaded the children up to head east — via the Panama Canal. Their means of transport was the *Orcades,* the largest steamship to pass through the canal, and not without some close calls. But it was a smooth enough sailing, which was fortunate because Marylou was pregnant. She gave birth a few months later to a daughter, whom they named Cornelia Vanderbilt Whitney.

Whitney, who had little to do with his children from previous marriages, was much more involved with this daughter and his four stepchildren.

"There was an incredible bond between Cornelia and her father," remembered Budd Calisch. "Cornelia had a way of communicating with him that was kind of unique. It was as if they were talking a foreign language. They loved to go off in the Adirondacks together with backpacks for days on end."[17]

Although Sonny and Marylou only had one child together, some of the stepchildren called him Dad and regarded him as the only

Marylou and the children smile for a Christmas portrait in the early 1960s. From left, Cornelia, Heather, Hank, Hobbs, and M'lou.

IN TOUCH WITH TRANQUILITY

FISHING, ESPECIALLY FLY FISHING, WAS a Whitney passion, a sport he took very seriously. He had learned the skill young, he had learned it well, and throughout his life, it was an anchor activity that brought him peace.

"He really loved fishing better than anything in the world," said his wife Marylou.[1] "He would awaken on a morning full of spring sunshine and say to Jouett Redmon and me, 'Let's go to Pine Mountain to catch a trout, stay at the State Park Lodge, and smell the great mountain air!' So off we would go in the old van, full of fishing gear, to Pineville [Kentucky]."[2]

"He [Whitney] often said that the drive through Cumberland Gap to Middlesboro and Pineville was one of the most majestic and splendid sights of scenery in all seasons on earth," said Mason Combs, who often accompanied Whitney on his Pineville fishing outings.[3] Once when Combs' son John commented that he found it strange that Marylou was being entertained by the king and queen of Thailand while Sonny was fishing, "Sonny turned around and said, 'Yes, but I would rather be here right now.'"[4]

But like most serious fishermen, Whitney was not necessarily easy or fun to fish with. Dr. Ben Roach of Midway, Kentucky, recalled the first time he ever went fishing with Whitney in the Adirondacks. He was filled with excitement and eager to cast his line. He, Whitney, and guide and friend Dave Short had been out in the boat for only a couple of minutes when a trout latched onto Whitney's line. "Most of us,"

said Roach, "we get them in as quick as we can. Sonny says, 'Now here's what you do.' He must have played that fish for twenty minutes. Let it run one way, then run the other." Finally Roach had had enough. He couldn't cast again while Whitney was still playing his fish. "I said, 'Hurry up and bring that thing in so I can cast.' But no, indeed, he had to see the whole routine. He was very proud of his abilities."[5]

Whitney was also very specific about when and where and how long to fish. Roach was often invited to drive to eastern Kentucky on trout-fishing trips. "They would be very organized. He'd leave at a certain hour, and we'd drive down there and find the place to fish. He would say, 'Well, now, we'll fish for an hour and fifteen minutes,' or 'We'll fish for two hours.' At the end of the time, even if the fish were bit-

---

The Adirondacks was where Sonny could relax and have a go at his beloved fishing. Whitney casts his line from the lake bank (opposite page), and (above) he and Dave Short display their catch of the day.

---

father they had, and indeed, after Marylou's divorce from Frank Hosford, the children never saw their father again. "There is a man out there who biologically created me," said Heather Mabee, the youngest of Marylou's children prior to marrying Whitney. "But there was only one father in my life, and that was C.V. Whitney, and there couldn't have been a better one.... He always knew the right things to say. He always knew how to smooth down the rough moments."[18]

"He was my Uncle Sonny, a stepfather in name but a good and devoted father to me and my brothers and sisters," said stepdaughter M'lou Llewellyn, years after Whitney's death. "He brought magic and enchantment into my life as a pre-teenager."[19]

Whitney was, however, a father in his sixties and a man who had been brought up in a certain way, realities that young boys seem far more likely

ing, no matter what was going on, when he had decided it was time to quit, he quit. We all quit."[6]

And in Whitney's mind, fishing was for fishing, not for chatting. Stepson Hobbs recalled a time he joined Whitney and Short for one of the fishing outings. "They were serious fishermen. As a kid, in the boat, you didn't talk. You didn't say anything. They concentrated on their fishing. I think they could communicate amongst themselves without a whole lot of words being said. Neither one of them was a great teacher in fishing. They'd say, 'Okay, here, put this lure on and cast out there, and you might catch a fish.' But they didn't get into a whole lot of details on the whys and wherefores."[7]

Still, most people understood that to Whitney, while the sporting aspect of fishing was important, there was a bigger issue.

Cornelia recognized this fact even as a young girl. "I didn't really fish much, and he did fish a lot, but a lot of times when he'd get all of his gear and go fishing, it wasn't about fishing. It was more about getting out in nature and listening to nature. He always felt like that's where the real wisdom of the world was. We'd go out together, and sometimes he'd just sit by a stream and smoke a cigarette and watch the birds, watch the wildlife, talk to other fishermen, and then go get ice cream. Those were really good times."[8]

Fishing was, as much as anything, a means of possibly gaining some deeper understandings. Whitney was always convinced that raw, basic nature was where the real answers to life lay.

"He taught me to appreciate the very simplest of things," said stepdaughter M'lou. "He taught me to listen to the variety of sounds in the woods, to reflect, and to access situations and surroundings. He taught me to respect the woods."[9]

Often on fishing or hunting trips, it would be clear to his companions that Whitney was deep into some quest for insight. "We would be out in the wilderness," said Jouett Redmon, "and he would look up at the evening sky and say to me, 'I wonder what the early people thought of that moon.'"[10]

"Sonny used to tell me that he liked to come up to Deerlands and spend the afternoon or the night," said Marylou. "It was a long trip, but he always said, 'You know, these are the healing woods. I look up into the trees and the mountains, and it gives me strength.'"[11]

to perceive. "He was more like a grandfather/uncle-type figure than a father type, at least in the same vein as you might see in the 1950s television sitcoms," said Hobbs Hosford, Marylou's oldest son. "I think some of it had to do with social position and obligations."[20]

But when he was there, there was a ritual that delighted all the children, and one that became an enduring memory, etched in each of their minds.

"In the evenings in Kentucky, we would come into the den and sit around Uncle Sonny eagerly, while mother worked contentedly on her beautiful needlework projects, to hear him read from *The Jungle Book* or one of the *Just So Stories*," said M'lou. "He brought Kipling's India alive, all of the characters leaping out of the pages. When we were older, his dramatic readings of Robert Service's poems had us totally spellbound, and we were transported to the wild, untamed world of the Yukon. Even the fire would crackle and spark on cue! He read this with such compassion that I can still hear him reciting it."[21]

He also played cutthroat cribbage games with the kids. And they had picnics, which became something of an obsession for the man who was introduced to his first one by Marylou when he was nearly sixty. "Picnics were one of his favorite things to do, so we would all get together and go on picnics, no matter what the weather, what the season," said his daughter Cornelia Vanderbilt Whitney Tobey.[22]

"Uncle Sonny loved toasted marshmallows," remembered M'lou. "Every picnic basket included a bag of them."[23]

The children lived a privileged existence but not a spoiled one.

"In the kitchen, when we were kids, there was our chore chart," said Heather. "It was on the staircase going up to our wing of the house. And we had chores that all of us kids had to do every week, whether it was going down to the laundry and working with the laundress or being in the kitchen and working with the cook. Or whether it was working outdoors with the gardener or washing dishes after the meals. Whatever it was, we had our chores. We would get stars according to how we did them. At the end of the week, the servants and my parents, they would all sit and decide how well we did our chores, and then they would decide what our little star would be, and the stars represented what allowance we got."[24]

"As we grew up, we were expected to work hard, to try to succeed at whatever we put our hand to and expect no handouts," said M'lou. "If you fell off that horse, you were expected to get back on again."[25]

Even when they got older, there was no open-wallet safety net. "He never set up trust funds for any of us kids. There was never a bank account out there that we could always rely on," said Heather. "Every single one of us, when we got out of college, whatever money we made had to pay for our apartments, had to pay for our own meals, had to pay for everything."[26]

For a time, while most of the children were still young, Kentucky was the homebase. This would not, however, be the middle-class definition of homebase.

"Mr. Whitney used to say, 'I can't stay too long in one place,'" said Jouett Redmon, the Kentuckian who was elevated from farm manager to one of Whitney's three closest friends. "I wore out three Volkswagen vans on that man."[27] Whitney preferred the van over the Mercedes or the Jaguar for his frequent hunting and fishing forays with Redmon because he could sit up high and see everything, and, more importantly, he could appear like everyone else when they stopped to buy bait or have lunch at some roadside joint.

"He was a man's man, but he wanted to be looked upon, when he was among most people, as just somebody regular," said Louie Nunn, who served as governor of Kentucky from 1967 to 1971. "In the South, they'd call it a good old boy.... He could appear just as comfortable in the finest appointed living room reading poetry as he did at a fishing hole or out in the woods. Of course, when he spoke with that sophisticated or well-educated Yankee voice, he stood out when he was among some people in Kentucky."[28]

As Nunn told it, Whitney's "Yankee voice" could sometimes be troublesome, at least while he was in Kentucky. "One time up there in the hills of Kentucky, they thought he was a revenue agent, a

The family enjoyed many family outings, even after the children were older. Above, Hank, Cornelia, Heather, M'lou, Whitney, and Hobbs prepare for a horse-and-wagon ride in Kentucky.

revenuer — hunting moonshine stills back in the mountains. He came back laughing about it. He explained to them, 'No, I'm not looking for any moonshine stills. I'm just trying to catch a fish.'"[29]

Sonny and Marylou would often make visits to Pineville, Kentucky, a small town about eighteen miles from Cumberland Gap, to fish in the mountains and attend the town's annual Pine Mountain Laurel Festival. Whitney was charmed by the area from the first time he visited it in May 1960 and made repeated visits in all seasons. The people of the town welcomed him as one of their own, eventually making him an honorary citizen of Pineville and naming a convention center after him.

"It was a charming town full of interesting people, who all became friends of Sonny," said Marylou. "We first went there when Bert T. Combs was governor. He asked us to go to the Pine Mountain Laurel Festival, where in a lonely, natural amphitheater surrounded by laurel bushes, they have the crowning of the Laurel Queen."[30]

It was at this festival where they met the town's honorary mayor, Robert Mason Combs, who owned the corner drugstore and was also cousin to the governor. Combs became a dear friend of both of the Whitneys and would take Whitney on fishing forays into the mountains. "Sonny and Jouett Redmon and I would play it by ear and go fishing where he wanted to fish in places he called the

ponds," remembered Combs. "He was the best fly fisherman I have ever known."[31]

Nature outings were by no means the limit of Whitney's travels. Whitney, by the mid-1960s, owned places in New York, Kentucky, Manitoba, and Florida, and his yen for travel had not diminished much over the years. He had taken possession of his father's private rail car, the opulent *Wanderer*, which boasted its own chef, observation deck, and monogrammed linens, and when train travel eventually struck him as too slow and

Above: Whitney was generous with his employees, not only in terms of salaries but also in gestures. Jouett Redmon (pictured) remembered how Whitney gave him a pair of snake-proof Gokey boots, the kind of boots that no farm laborer in Kentucky would ever be able to afford. "I wore those boots for forty years," Redmon said.

Left: Charlene Ecker (Marylou's sister), Sonny, Heather, and Hobbs enjoy an indoor picnic in the Adirondacks.

tiresome, he sold that and began leasing private jets. The geographical possibilities, like his checkbook, were practically limitless.

Marylou almost always accompanied him. One Whitney was rarely seen without the other, something that intrigued most of the people in their circle, where marital closeness was neither common nor chic.

"Normally, when he did things, she did them too," said Hobbs. "When I was a kid, if he was off doing whatever it might be, they'd both be gone, and when he'd be at home, they'd both be home. He typically came home for lunch every day whether he was working or not, so they normally had nice little lunches either on a terrace or porch. Generally, even when they went out in the Adirondacks, when they'd go fishing, they'd both go to the same place to fish."[32]

During the school year, the boys were at Kent in Connecticut, the girls were in private day school in Lexington (and later two of them went off to school in Switzerland), and there were plenty of hands to ensure that the children were cared for.

The Whitneys were social celebrities in every city they lived. Below, they dine with Marylou's good friend, socialite Anne Slater (left), at Armando's restaurant in New York.

The Whitneys' schedule fell into something of a routine. They spent most of summer in the Adirondacks with those children who were not in summer camp. August was racing season, so they were off to Saratoga. They spent September and October in Kentucky for the horse sales and the races and November in the Adirondacks for fishing and hunting. In December, they traveled to Manhattan for the social season but spent Christmas in Kentucky, followed by a post-Christmas week in the Adirondacks. They spent much of January and February in Florida, where they had places near Marineland and in Palm Beach. In early May, it was back to Kentucky, followed by a week or so in the Adirondacks when the ice left the lakes and spring fishing was at its best. Early June was spent at the apartment near Marineland with the children. They also took regular trips to Europe, Hawaii, or Acapulco and spent frequent weekends in New York City when situations called for it. They sojourned in Spain, where they renovated an old palace that Marylou purchased in Trujillo, and on the Spanish island of Majorca, where they owned a quiet little place up in the hills. In later years, they took regular vacations to Switzerland, where the girls attended school.

The Whitneys were jet-setters of the highest order, referred to in the press as international nomads. They spent no more than a few weeks at

a time at any one locale, gathering friends and acquaintances like wildflowers in a meadow.

Soon they were the toast of several towns. In New York City, they attended all the important arts and charity functions and did their share of fundraising as well. In Lexington, their Kentucky Derby parties were considered among the very best in the Bluegrass, and Whitney's donations and conservation efforts contributed greatly to the state's park system. The racing season in Saratoga came alive under their shining presence, and the town eventually underwent a social and cultural resurgence, in no small part through their efforts. In Palm Beach, they joined with the other extremely well-off during the winter months. "When the Whitneys get here, it's like the Duke and Duchess of Windsor arriving," one Palm Beach socialite declared to *Town & Country* columnist Earl Blackwell.[33]

Society people and society watchers were fascinated by them. Where once it had been Whitney's money and bloodlines that landed him in the columns, now it was the fact that he was

Above: Marylou (center) made sure that she and Sonny (third from left) were active members in whatever community they happened to be living. In South Florida, for example, they were members of the Palm Beach Bicycle Club.

Right: From time to time, the Whitneys took a winter respite on Paradise Island in the Bahamas.

everywhere and doing such interesting things. Moreover, he had a highly effective booster, who was herself quite intriguing.

"There's no question that he became much better known, everywhere, because of Marylou," said Dr. Ben Roach, a longtime friend and personal physician. "He had nice parties, and she was attractive, and she got into a lot of charitable things. It seemed she was chairman of everything that came along, and he basked in her glory. He was aware that she was making him more visible, and he liked it."[34]

Marylou was the consummate party giver, putting together everything from lavish dinner dances for 150 to Sunday evening movie-watching gatherings for their close friends, during which she handed out popcorn at intermission.

Indeed, so enthusiastic and indiscriminate a party giver was she that a *New York Times* society reporter once wrote that Marylou would "throw a party for the opening of an envelope."[35]

And when the Whitneys were not hosting their own big galas and little dinner gatherings, they were attending ones hosted by others.

Whitney had loosened up a bit, and this made him even more irresistible. "He was always game for something that was new and fun, like when the twist suddenly appeared on the scene," said Gerta Conner. "Marylou and Uncle Sonny came over for dinner to our apartment at Gramercy Park, and this person arrived and taught us all how to twist. [Whitney] threw himself into this like a boy. He had boundless enthusiasm for things. He was boyish in many ways when he was enthusiastic."[36]

Something else made him quite remarkable as a host and guest. Unlike most men who are rich or famous, Whitney "didn't want to be the center of attention," said Linda Toohey, who became friendly with the Whitneys in the 1970s. He did not work the room, and he did not glad-hand. He positioned himself in an out-of-the-way spot and spoke with whomever was nearby. He listened more than he talked, a rarity in his circle,

and when he was engaged in conversation, he gave his full attention as if there were no one else in the world of any more importance than the person with whom he conversed. "He was more interested in finding out about what other people were doing," said Toohey, than in using parties as a means to take center stage.[37]

The Whitneys — with Sonny's polite, gracious reserve, combined with Marylou's gregarious potency — quickly became the golden couple of high society.

In 1968 they were the cover couple for *Palm Beach Illustrated,* in a story touting the thirty-one canvases they had painted and donated to the Wally Findlay Galleries in Palm Beach to raise funds for the Good Samaritan Hospital. They were profiled in 1970 in a huge lifestyles-of-the-rich-and-famous spread in the *Washington Post,* which raved, with uncharacteristic abandon,

The Whitneys with his sister Barbara Whitney Headley and her husband, George Headley, at the Whitneys' home.

about his successes and her organizational efficiency. And they were often profiled in Robin Leach's popular television show, *Lifestyles of the Rich and Famous.*

Whitney even got published in a leading magazine. He wrote a long piece for *Field & Stream* about the week he and Dave Short spent hunting an elusive buck in the Adirondacks.

It was, however, his wife who commanded the bulk of the press, showing up in all the best publications. *Town & Country*, in its 1969 Christmas edition, declared she threw some of the "most imaginative and attractive parties in the world."[38] In 1970 she was described by *Ladies' Home Journal* as a "size 6 palomino blonde of 42 years with chiseled patrician features, little girl hands, a curious finishing school accent with Scarlett O'Hara and Boston overtones, five children and six houses."[39] This profile, prepared by one of the decade's top writers, Gael Greene, discussed the many faces of Marylou, pointing out that she is a Southern belle in Kentucky; "horsey, social, culture conscious and Eastern" in Saratoga; "a country squire's wife" at Deerlands in the Adirondacks; and a Girl Scout at Salmon Lake.[40]

Later that year, in April 1970, *Town & Country* crowned her the "summa cum laude hostess of Lexington."[41] She was a regular in *Bazaar* and *W* magazines and appeared on *Good Morning America* and in Delta Airlines' *Sky* magazine promoting her *Glorious Goober Cookbook*, which was inspired by a visit with Jimmy Carter in Plains, Georgia.

Still, Marylou insisted, she was just a woman doing what she loved most: taking care of her husband. "I'm fundamentally a housewife," she declared in the April 1976 issue of *Louisville* magazine. "I have ceilings leaking and plumbing breaking down all over the world — I'm the busiest housekeeper in the world."[42]

Whitney was happy, happier than he had ever been, he told everyone. His various businesses were doing well, his social life was exciting, his family life was satisfying, and he was contributing to causes of importance.

Suddenly, in 1970, he was forced to confront a reality that theretofore he had managed to avoid when, without warning, "the frightening specter of old age came to haunt me," he wrote in *High Peaks*.

Marylou, the Whitneys' friend and personal physician Dr. Ben Roach, Sonny, and Sonny's sister Barbara venture out to the Keeneland race track in Lexington.

The specter's appearance may have been unpleasant to confront, but its timing could not have been more fortuitous. Whitney and Marylou were having lunch at 21 Club in New York with their old friend-cum-personal-physician Roach and his wife. The Roaches rarely visited the Whitneys in Manhattan, but on this day they did. "We were sitting there eating and [Whitney] sort of lost consciousness for a second," said Roach. "He had a little seizure activity, and it didn't last more than twenty seconds maybe, and then he came to."[43]

Roach knew this meant there had been an interruption of the blood supply to Whitney's brain and immediately arranged for Whitney to be transported to the hospital.

A blood clot had formed in an artery leading from the heart through the right side of the collarbone toward his right arm, and, Whitney wrote, quick surgery saved him from having his arm amputated.

"The recovery was slow and painful, as it was accompanied by spells of real mental depression," he wrote. "When you have been very active both physically and mentally all your life, the relentless symptoms of age which do occur tend to depress

A Boost for Saratoga

THE WHITNEYS HAD AN IMPACT WHEREver they traveled and lived, connecting with communities and opening their checkbooks to various local causes. Nowhere was this more true than in Saratoga Springs, the place that began for them as a racing season stopover and evolved over the years to a several-weeks-a-year home. Ultimately, Saratoga became the town where the Whitneys voted and where C.V. Whitney passed his final weeks of life.

The Whitneys' impact on Saratoga started with the parties for which Sonny and Marylou were famous. They were lavish and outrageous beyond all that anyone in the monied set had ever experienced, spectacles of dancing gypsies, fortune tellers, dogs jumping through hoops, and all manner of frenetic mirth making.

The Whitneys held annual parties at the historic Canfield Casino on the eve of the renowned Whitney Stakes to usher in the beginning of the racing season. The festivities quickly drew regional attention, and, almost as fast, national attention. "They were by invitation only, and they were the most spectacular events in Saratoga and probably even in the country," said society columnist Jeannette Jordan.[1]

The parties always had themes, and Marylou invariably made grand entrances, for she planned and staged her arrivals to be wildly attention getting. Costumed, coifed, and bejeweled, she arrived in a hot-air balloon one year, in a horse-drawn landau another, in a two-decker bus, and in a pumpkin vehicle. Guests included the likes of super-rich oilman and horseman Nelson Bunker Hunt, Walter Cronkite, Joan Rivers, Ginger Rogers, and Liza Minnelli.

Although only the invited horsemen, socialites, celebrities, and political figures were granted entry, the route to the Canfield Casino was inevitably lined with hundreds of spectators eager to catch a glimpse of Marylou's latest incarnation and in some small way feel as though they had participated in the extravaganza.

The pubic relations benefit of those parties to Saratoga was incalculable, said public relations woman Maureen Lewi, who was also a friend of the Whitneys. Suddenly, the *NBC Nightly News, Lifestyles of the Rich and Famous,* and scores of others were on the scene vying for a little piece of the party. And just as suddenly, Saratoga Springs, which had suffered through a couple of decades of social malaise, began a resurgence.

"Without having a hook like Marylou and Sonny and without them being the type of people who would actually speak with the press, we never would have been able to bring in the national and international media," said Lewi.[2]

---

you. All the more in my case, as I am married to a younger lady."[44]

He feared his flaccid arm would remain unresponsive. "My right arm had served me so well in sports, in wartime and in writing and painting," he wrote. "I felt the only thing worse than this would have been the loss of my eyesight."[45]

He regained his strength in that arm, but the whole episode seemed to him a warning, one to be used as a catalyst for personal evolution.

He became a relentless researcher on the topic of aging and means of delaying it. And when he had settled on the anti-aging practices he felt were most promising, Whitney — who had always been quite disciplined about many of the routines and practices he followed — now became positively fervent.

Continue to innovate, with new businesses, new interests, new social activities, he demanded of himself. Make lists of long- and short-term objectives and meet them. Stick to proper nutrition, relying on simple, basic foods. Keep weight reasonable, and exercise every day, but rely on walking, horseback riding, swimming, stretching, mild calisthenics, and yoga rather than highly straining activities. And take vitamins, especially C, D, and B, along with megadoses of vitamin E.

Princess Margaret takes a peek inside the miniature version of the house where she is guesting. Cornelia's famous dollhouse was an exact replica of the Whitney House in Lexington.

founding members of the National Museum of Dance, housed in the spectacularly restored Washington Bath House, which was renamed in the Whitneys' honor.

Marylou raised enough money by displaying daughter Cornelia's famed dollhouse — an exact miniature replica of the Whitney place in Kentucky — to be able to buy a new Steinway piano for the Performing Arts Center.

It was a very top-drawer evening when the Whitneys presented the Steinway to the Performing Arts Center. Five thousand people watched as Eugene Ormandy led the Philadelphia Orchestra, accompanied by Andre Watts on the new piano. But three minutes before the end of the performance, the pedal of the piano fell off. Watts took this with good humor; Ormandy did not. Marylou, ever the social diplomat, was able to defuse what could have been an extremely tense situation, especially considering that Ormandy was already in a bad mood after getting locked in his dressing room just before the performance. The evening still turned out a success.

The Whitneys' largesse was directed not only toward the glossy side of Saratoga life, but to the bread-and-butter needs of the community as well. Over the years they contributed regularly to the YMCA, the Animal Welfare League, the Saratoga Hospital, Meals on Wheels, Skidmore College, and the Saratoga Emergency Corps.

With the increased attention came increased potential. The Whitneys drew even more people to the area by making contributions to various institutions. The Saratoga Springs Performing Arts Center and the National Museum of Racing were beneficiaries of their bulging checkbook, and Sonny installed $100,000 worth of air conditioning at the Canfield Casino as a birthday gift to Marylou. In addition, the Whitneys were

After a few months on this regimen, he was convinced he had discovered the proper route to vibrant longevity. "People tell me that I look 10 years younger today than I did a year ago," he wrote with pride. It did take self-discipline, he admitted, but it offered "spectacular results."[46]

With all this health fervor, he did not give up his ubiquitous cigarettes until he was in his eighties, though he did cut down a bit and spent as much time with a pipe as with cigarettes. His unique, often-commented-upon smoking style probably reduced his health risk from tobacco. "He was never a puffer like some

people," said Roach. "He loved to take a puff, and then he held it in his hand and waved it around some."[47]

Whitney, in his seventies, was sticking a little closer to the homefront now. The children were in their teens, and he rather enjoyed his influence in helping to shape them.

"Dad was strict," said Heather. "If I went out on a date, I had to be home by midnight. My brothers, when they would come home from college, if their hair wasn't above their ears, he wouldn't let them in the house. No mustaches or beards were allowed in the house."[48]

"He set high moral standards for all of us to follow," said M'lou. "There were house rules, and we were expected to obey them. If we were naughty, we were punished."[49]

In that, he was very much like many fathers of the 1970s. But any hope the children might have had of presenting him and themselves as just ordinary people was demolished the moment their friends or dates approached the Whitney home. "When a boy came to the door at my house, it was a whole lot different than with most of my girlfriends," said Heather. "I mean, my parents got dressed for dinner every night, my father in a smoking jacket, my mother in a long dress, so when a gentleman would come to pick me up on a Friday night for a date, first of all, he would come to the front door. There would be a butler who would answer the door, take him into the

back porch where my parents were having cocktails, and he would have to sit down for a couple of minutes with my parents, which was very hard on a lot of guys."[50]

Whitney was firm in his insistence that "he wanted his girls to be women who were taught about how to take care of a house and run a house," Heather said. "He was excited that we worked, but he did not really relish the idea of us becoming career women, and a lot of that just comes from the era and the time that he came from."[51]

"He would set the rules, and he was strict," said Cornelia. "When he said no, we didn't dare — even dare — to do whatever we were told not to do."[52]

"He had a smile on his face unless you did something to tick him off," said Heather, "and then you were in real dire straits. I would never want to get on the wrong side of him."[53]

All of Marylou's children agree that Whitney was a loving father, yet he did not spoil the children. He encouraged them to work hard and do the best they could in life. From left, Sonny, Heather, Cornelia, Marylou, Hank, and M'lou.

"He could raise Cain," said Whitney's long-time friend and employee Jouett Redmon. "Even with Mrs. Whitney."[54]

And as his wife knew, Whitney's temper was equaled only by his fabled jealousy. Many was the time that Whitney would approach a man he felt had been a bit too conversationally engaged with his wife or had danced with her one too many times. "I know you're a friend of mine," he would state in a controlled and steady tone, "but I just want you to know one thing. This is my girl and I own her." One of the recipients of this little speech was Henry Kissinger.

Even Marylou was sometimes grounded for what Whitney saw as inappropriate behavior. One time, it had to do with her making a brief appearance at the Turf Riders Ball in Saratoga, New York, after she had told her husband, who was to be out of town, that she would be staying in for the night. And that is exactly what she intended to do. But that afternoon her sister-in-law Barbara broke her collarbone and prevailed upon Marylou to hurry into the party and inform the guests at her table of the turn of events.

Marylou dashed into the dance, and while she was making the necessary excuses for Barbara, a jockey raced up and pulled her onto the dance floor. They both slipped and fell. The tangle of arms and legs on the dance floor was, unbeknownst to Marylou, captured by a photographer.

Marylou left the dance and went about her business, but the next morning a girlfriend called very early to inform her that the socialite-on-the-floor photo was on the front page of the newspaper.

This, of course, was something Whitney must not see, so she enlisted the help of three friends, who rode around in a station wagon for hours trying to collect every newspaper in the area. "We went everyplace," said Marylou. "We bought every newspaper in town. We went to outlying villages. We took them to the dump. We had four carloads of them."[55]

When Whitney returned, Marylou made no mention of the dance, the photograph, or the great newspaper collection effort.

That night, as the Whitneys roamed about at a party, a guest — perhaps the only person in town who had managed to get a copy of the paper — spoke of the picture.

"You're grounded." Whitney announced to his wife. "You're not to go out of the house for a week, and I'm going to see that you don't."[56] It was by no means the only time Whitney made this sort of pronouncement.

"He was so jealous," said Marylou, "but believe it or not, I kind of liked it. To think someone loved me that much."[57]

And no one doubted that he did.

"I always felt they were very much in love," said Cornelia. "It seemed to show through in the way they would hold hands or sit together. She'd sit on his lap, and they'd smile and kiss."[58]

"Mom and Dad had a very special relationship," said Heather. "He was able to expose Mom to a lot of things that she hadn't done in her life, a lot of traveling, meeting tons of new people. But at the same time, my father, even though he was brought up in the Adirondacks and had spent a lot of time in the woods, had never done things like go on a picnic, and my mother showed him how to go on a picnic. So they brought to each other different things."[59]

For all of Whitney's rules and adherence to routines and schedules, the family shared a lot of laughs. "I can just remember as a family laughing a lot, to the point where your jaw would ache," said Cornelia.[60]

The children experienced his dry, wry sense of humor, but adults and party goers experienced his jokes as well. His passion for joke telling was unparalleled. He was an enthusiastic collector who received jokes by fax from friends and associates the world over, and he was always at the ready to share one or several.

"I don't know how he did it, but he remembered more jokes than any human I've ever known," said Saratoga friend Linda Toohey.[61]

"He loved to tell jokes," said Jeannette Jordan, the society reporter for the *Saratogian*. "They could be a little off color or they could be just funny jokes."[62]

Whitney was also quite fond of limericks. One time, when Roach was invited to Saratoga for a weekend, he encountered Whitney and renowned horseman Admiral Markey involved in a front-porch competition. "Admiral Markey, of course, was much worse than Sonny," said Roach. "He had books of dirty limericks." But Whitney was holding his own in what had become a neck-and-neck effort to see "who could come up with the most dirty limerick."[63]

Whitney was settling rather comfortably into his older years, showing more mellowness than in years past. "He wasn't judgmental," said Cornelia. "He was helpful. If I wanted an opinion, he would give it; otherwise he would just listen."[64]

The Adirondacks continued to be the perpetual gathering spot in the summer, and sailboat races had become a Whitney tradition. There would be one big race every summer, then a banquet at which the person who won earned a trophy. Whitney was almost always the winner. "He was a very skilled sailor," said Hobbs, "and it's something he did even when we didn't have the competition. If he wasn't going out fishing during the day when he was up there, he normally would be going out sailing around Little Forked Lake."[65]

Others of the various branches of the Whitney clan would also gather at the Adirondacks during the summers, and, just as in Whitney's younger years, there were the inevitable campfire sessions. "He would come and tell a really scary ghost story," said his cousin Flora Biddle, who often summered there with her children, as her parents had when she was a child. "All the children would huddle around the campfire and be terrified. They loved it."[66]

"He had a wonderful voice," Biddle added. "He was a very fascinating presence to all of our children."[67]

Among his many talents, Whitney was quite adept at sailing. For many summers, family and friends gathered at Whitney Park in the Adirondacks, where the Whitneys hosted sailboat races — most of which Whitney won.

The Adirondacks was also the scene, in later years, of cold-month gatherings when a few of the Whitney friends would convene for themed dress-up parties or square dances. "These were not camp parties," said Roach. "Marylou would have the fine silver and china, and, of course, she always took three or four servants up there, a butler, and a couple of cooks."[68]

By then, Whitney's older children from his previous marriages no longer attended the family gatherings, in the Adirondacks or anywhere else. Gail had died of leukemia, and Whitney was estranged from all the rest. They had disappointed him, by most accounts, and he wished not to deal with them any longer. He had also severed relationships with many of his Whitney and Vanderbilt relatives or simply allowed these associations to peter out from lack of attention, expressing no interest in pursuing or attempting to maintain affiliations that were problematic.

Whitney had lifelong difficulties developing close relationships, but his reliability and skill as a social acquaintance and host were widely appreciated. Thus, in 1974, when Princess Margaret decided she wanted to visit the United States for the hundredth running of the Kentucky Derby, the organizers of the trip deemed the Whitney Farm the most appropriate place for her to stay.

Whitney had had earlier social encounters with the young princess. "The first time was when I went to London in post–World War II days as a representative of the American Jockey Club," Whitney recalled in one of his books. "Our American ambassador, Winthrop Aldrich, gave a magnificent dinner dance in her honor and I had the distinct honor of leading off the ball by dancing a waltz with the princess.... The second time ... was in 1964. Mary and I were spending a happy day on a tiny beach on the island of Spetzapula in the Aegean Sea where we were swimming and picnicking with our hosts, the Stavros Niarchoses. Princess Margaret had only recently married Anthony Armstrong Jones and they, too, were guests of the Niarchoses."[69]

The year 1974 was a turbulent one in world history, and there was great concern for the safety of the princess. Security precautions included requiring everyone at the Whitney Farm, including Sonny and Marylou, to wear identification badges.

The couple arrived on a Thursday and left on Sunday, and every minute of their stay was planned, including not only the outing to the Derby, but social parties, press interviews, and visits to horse farms. The royal couple were housed in the Whitneys' guest cottage, which happened to be a former slave house, a fact that the press found most intriguing.

During a limo ride to Churchill Downs, Princess Margaret divulged to Whitney that she had told her husband the evening before, "If I were not who I am, I would like to buy a small farm in Kentucky and live with these hospitable people forever."[70]

This was a year in which Whitney did not have a horse in the Derby race but did have one in the Debutante Stakes for two-year-old fillies. Sun and Snow was his most promising filly that year, and he was hopeful, but not really particularly confident, that she could take the race. But the Whitney filly won in a blazing finish to wild applause, a fitting turn of events on a weekend when he was hosting royalty.

The following year, when Whitney was in his mid-seventies, he published yet another book, *High Peaks,* a series of autobiographical short stories. Although Whitney was a skilled and rapid writer, this particular book had been years in the making. It had been conceived and started at Marylou's urging and began its life as a traditional autobiography. But because Whitney was constitutionally unable to relive anything of an unpleasant nature, he had great difficulty delving into much of his past. He finally decided that in this endeavor he would simply focus on and present the good things. It was most certainly a case of art imitating life. The proceeds from the book, which sold quite well in the places where Whitney had homes and was well known, went to the Filson Club, a group that collects books and other information on Kentucky.

Whitney was by now considered something of an eminence grise in many arenas and had become much in demand as a speaker. He had dozens of requests every year.

Although he was an excellent public speaker, he was a reluctant one. He loved giving wing to the thoughts and words of others in his after-dinner readings for guests, but he was much less

confident of his ability to captivate an audience with his own words.

Marylou suffered from no such reservations and often agreed to take the stage when the speech was in response to an award presented to both of them for philanthropic or other contributions. Saratoga public relations woman Maureen Lewi, who was a friend of the Whitneys for years, described how Whitney would watch Marylou gleefully make her acceptance speech, then turn to his friends or table companions and say, "I don't like to make speeches, you know. That's not my thing. I'm so happy Mary is able to do that."[71]

But there were times that Whitney was the requested speaker and the only appropriate

Though Whitney was not fond of making speeches, he was an undeniably gifted speaker. Above, he accepts the Distinguished Horseman tribute from the Thoroughbred Club of America in 1966.

speaker. And once he had made his commitment to take the stage, he prepared so carefully and fastidiously that no one in the audience had the slightest hint this was an activity he really quite dreaded.

"He always knew exactly what he wanted to say" once he approached the podium, said Roach. "There were no errs or uuhhs, none of that stuff."

Like most really good speakers, he understood the importance of preparation and rehearsal. "He put a lot of thought into what he was going to say," said Roach, who often served as Whitney's audience of one during the rehearsal phase. Whitney took similar pains with formal utterances that most people do by rote, for example, the blessings before dinners at his home. "He was aware," said Roach, "that it was important to say exactly what you meant."[72]

Whitney was similarly methodical and painstaking with his decision making. "He liked to analyze any situation and discuss all the possible consequences and why he should do this and why he should do that," said Roach. "He was very concerned about how people would react to what he said or did. That was always a big thing with Sonny." This was not because he feared making an unwise choice or a decision that would not play well with the public. "I never saw him afraid of anything, actually," said Roach. It was, quite simply, because he "had that old feeling that maybe our grandparents had that you had to live up to what was expected of you by the people you were around. Also there was an element, a tiny element of that thing all of us have — that we like for other people to appreciate us and look up to us."[73]

Well-known thoroughbred artist Peter Williams painted two of the Whitneys' main residences: the Whitney House (top) and Cady Hill.

CHAPTER ELEVEN

A HOME FOR ALL SEASONS

WHITNEY COLLECTED HOUSES with the same passion and abandon that many people collect stamps. Some, such as the places in the Adirondacks and in Saratoga Springs, he inherited from his father and his grandfather, but once they were recast in his own style, they served as geographical anchors throughout his life.

Others were added according to a momentary need or interest, then discarded when the need or interest faded. He bought a place in Lake Placid, for example, when he and Marylou were very involved in the 1980 Lake Placid Winter Olympics, for which they were the largest private donors. They also owned tropical havens in Palm Beach and a palace in Spain, into which they poured much energy and money during a period of fascination with all things Spanish (and when there was talk that Whitney might be appointed the U.S. ambassador to Spain).

Whitney's habitual homesteading was not motivated by the intrinsic investment value. To be sure, he always more than recouped his investment when he sold one of his multimillion-dollar properties, but residences of the size and grandeur of those in his collection were extremely expensive to furnish and maintain and could not be regarded as a sound money-making proposition.

For Whitney, these houses were not primarily a fiscal consideration. Quite simply, he, as a relentless wanderer, preferred the comfort of homes to the comfort of hotel suites. "It was the way he was raised," said stepdaughter Heather Mabee. "If there was a town or a city where he knew he would visit regularly, he wanted a place there. He liked having his own space and having his own things around."[1]

Also, according to many of his friends, Whitney believed in the virtues of entertaining one's friends and acquaintances in one's home rather than in an impersonal restaurant or country club. He wished to entertain in the manner he preferred. This translated to dressing for dinner and having solid, simple fare followed by after-dinner drinks, conversation in a sitting room or library, and, usually, a reading of some sort that he would conduct in grand and solemn style.

Marylou was the majordomo of the many manses, which always numbered at least a half dozen. An inveterate rehabber and an organizer of the highest order, she kept bulging files on each and every property, bought linens and other essentials in bulk, kept track of the inventories and state of repair of all the various homes through

---

Whitney Park's extended wildlife preserve offers a network of canoe routes, such as "Big Brook," shown here in early autumn.

the property manager or housekeeper installed at each, and commanded that every house be kept guest-ready at all times.

"Every house has practically the same kitchen, only the ones at Saratoga and in the Adirondacks are the best," Marylou often said as partial explanation to society reporters who were stunned by her ability to keep track of this array of homes and feel any degree of familiarity with whatever house she was staying in at the moment. "I like peach and orange and have them in most of the houses."[2]

The couple maintained necessary wardrobes at each residence, including the requisite tuxedos and gowns, and each place had some of the priceless accoutrements of Whitney's ancestors — such as the Vanderbilt gold-rimmed stemware or turn-of-the-century silver cups and bowls won by Whitney's father at the tracks — to lend an air of homeyness and stability.

The Whitney House

The twenty-room Kentucky farmhouse on its thousand acres was where the Whitneys raised the children in the 1960s, where they held their lavish Kentucky Derby parties in the pool atrium, and where they put up such guests as Princess Margaret, Anthony Armstrong Jones, the Ronald

Marylou (shown in inset with daughter Cornelia) oversaw the renovation of the stately Whitney House. The portico was designed by Whitney's late former brother-in-law, George Headley.

Reagans, and the Henry Kissingers. But it was in a sorry state when Whitney developed the urge to see it brought up to Whitney standards.

Situated on the rolling hills of horse country just outside Lexington, the red brick pioneer house had been built in 1794 by some of the area's early settlers and had undergone various renovations and degradations over the centuries. By the time Whitney acquired it, the farm sprawled across more than a thousand acres, but he later sold about half of that land.

Whitney was drawn in an odd way to the house, despite its derelict state, probably because of its pastoral setting overlooking the winding course of North Elkhorn Creek.

He had tried to convince his third wife, Eleanor, to have a go at renovating the place, but she had no interest in the project. Marylou did, however, and she immediately enlisted the design skills of Whitney's brother-in-law George Headley. Headley, the son of a prominent Kentucky family, had studied art and eventually established the Headley-Whitney Museum in Lexington. It was he who drew the plans for the imposing round portico with white columns and the Federal facade Marylou had envisioned.

The home would also need some expansion, she declared, including a children's wing attached to one side of the house. Marylou eschewed convention in the restoration. She wished to preserve the eighteenth-century nucleus, and the expansions resulted in some architectural quirks, she cheerfully acknowledged, including two land-locked rooms without windows. Also, the rooms, unlike those of many mansions in the region, were quite modest in size. The final result was a collection of comfortable, homey rooms, and the mood was not of a mansion but rather of a landed-gentry farmhouse.

A sitting room with walls of shelves displayed hundreds of silver trays, trophies, cups, and bowls won by Whitney horses over the family's nearly century-long run at the tracks. A casual breakfast porch overlooked the creek and pastures, and a library was built specifically to hold the paneling from an entire French room. The house also had a children's breakfast room with an Egyptian motif, purchased from a museum in Florida, disassembled there, and reconstructed in Kentucky. An art studio, built to look like an old

This portrait of Marylou, which hangs in the main living room of the Whitney House, originally hung in Marylou's Scottsdale, Arizona, mansion. Elvis Presley once commented that he would buy the mansion only if the woman in the portrait came with the house.

smokehouse, was constructed not far from the main house, and Whitney's offices were located in a two-story wood-and-stone building in the middle of the farm.

Furnishings included a table from Sonny's cousin, Consuelo Balsan, the former Duchess of Marlboro. And the huge Aubusson rug once owned by Whitney's mother, Gertrude, was placed in the peach and turquoise living room, along with several small-sized casts of her sculptures.

The couple also installed a pool in an enclosed atrium with Ionic columns and palm trees, and this is where they staged the dozens of huge parties they had over the years, usually installing a bridge over the water to seat guests of honor. Guests were put up in the former slave quarters, which had been redecorated in pastels.

The chapel on the grounds was resurrected from an old log cabin, circa 1802, that farm manager Jouett Redmon stumbled across on Two Mile Creek in Clark County. When Redmon stopped to inquire after it, the elderly lady who owned it told him that her son had promised to turn it into a garage for her. Redmon asked how much she figured it would cost to build a brand-new garage, and she said $800, acknowledging that she would

much prefer a new garage to a reconstituted one. Redmon handed her $800, dismantled the cabin, hauled the logs to the Whitneys' house, and used the best of them to build the log cabin–style chapel with plank floors. It was this chapel where the Whitneys, staff, and guests had services at 11:00 a.m. on Sundays.

This farm, like many Kentucky farms, but very much unlike country homes and stables of the very wealthy, always had eight to twelve big yard dogs of indeterminate lineage roaming the grounds and noisily announcing the arrivals of guests. They were all strays who arrived tired and hungry and found an agreeable environment. Although the Whitneys always had poodles as house dogs and traveling companions, they were not at all distressed when they returned to Kentucky after several weeks away to find yet another motley-looking farm dog in the brood. They figured a big farm needed a few dogs, and they couldn't bear to turn them away.

The place was known for many years as Maple Hill, but as new information came to light, Whitney renamed it the Whitney House. "I loved the old name, but it was already in use — you couldn't have two horse farms called Maple Hill," said Marylou.[3]

Cady Hill

Cady Hill, the rambling, four-story estate in Saratoga Springs, once served as a stagecoach stop, and it was ideal for the Whitneys for just that reason. It had been built in 1774 to accommodate many people at once. The main house alone had twenty-one rooms, and the 124 acres of land on which it was situated boasted a ten-car garage and five ranch-style staff homes. All told, it was exactly what the Whitneys needed during their August hosting activities in Saratoga.

The house had been in the Whitney family since the turn of the century, purchased for the summer seasons, but by the time Marylou and Sonny married, it was a down-in-the-heels dowager in need of a large measure of reconstructive surgery.

The Whitneys' swimming pool atrium in Kentucky was the site of many festive gatherings.

Above: Cady Hill was a former stagecoach house in Saratoga Springs, and portions of the main house date back to pre–Revolutionary War days.

Below: The formal gardens at the Whitneys' Cady Hill house were a spectacular display of flowers, fountains, walkways, and sculptures.

Whitney wished to sell it, but this was a house Marylou couldn't bear to part with, and she believed so fully in its potential that she told her husband she herself would buy it if he intended to follow through with his plans to sell. It remained with them, and Marylou went on a renovation binge, decorating in cheerful yellows, greens, and whites. Among other renovations, she enlarged the kitchen, turned the basement into a playroom, and built flower-laden walkways that led from the house to the glassed-in swimming pool.

White wicker pieces were installed on all the porches. And on the porch just off the living room, the focal point was a multicolored bird aviary, presented to Marylou by Elizabeth Arden Graham. Elsewhere in the house, some of the earlier-generation Whitneys' furnishings were put to use, including a massive dining set and generations-old gold rimmed stemware from the Vanderbilts.

Cady Hill, the scene of scores of elegant parties and gatherings, was also the site of the area's biggest and most publicized jewelry heist. In 1968, someone managed to abscond with $780,000 of Marylou's jewels, including the $500,000 diamond-and-pearl bracelet and earrings Whitney gave her when Cornelia was born and the turquoise owl he bought her in Arizona

when they first fell in love. Fortunately, the priceless, much-photographed diamond tiara from Empress Elizabeth of Austria and the giant pearls that once belonged to Empress Eugenie of France were overlooked. But the investigation was intense, the loss was huge, and it was the sort of tragedy that society types could sympathize with. Marylou received dozens of condolence notes, letters, and gifts. After the robbery, the Whitneys had an elaborate security system installed and hired twenty-four-hour patrolmen for all of their main residences.

In 1982, a chapel was built on the grounds, a Christmas gift from Marylou to Sonny. The chapel, seating forty, was built to resemble an 1810 Dutch house that the couple had spotted not far from the Whitney estate. The new chapel was dedicated with a blessing service attended by several Whitney friends and family members. "He was so pleased," Marylou recalled. "I wanted to move the original to our property. It would have been a perfect chapel, but the preservationists wouldn't let me move it, so we copied it exactly. It's very interesting how this sort of thing happens, but the original burned down about two months later."[4]

The chapel became the site of a new Whitney tradition. Just before Christmas they would convene a large group of their friends and children of their friends for a Christmas caroling party. "Entire families would sit together in the pews," said Linda Toohey, a regular at these events. "And [famed opera star Patrice Monsel] would

lead us in Christmas carols. Sonny and Marylou would sit facing the rest of us. It was sort of like a Quaker Friends meeting."[5]

Whitney Park

The most enduring and, until the end of his life, perhaps the most beloved of his homes was Whitney Park, the sprawling forestland, shimmering lakes, and countless homes, cabins, outbuildings, and lean-tos on the Adirondacks property.

Whitney was first introduced to the Adirondacks when he was nine years old and

Above: Whitney relaxes on the sunporch at Cady Hill. This one, like the rest of the porches, had white-painted wicker furniture.

Left: Hand-painted Chinese designs cover the walls of this dining room at Cady Hill.

spent the summer there learning about nature, sleeping on balsam boughs, and gaining skills in canoeing, fishing, and camping out. He never forgot the freedom and exhilaration he felt in the silent nights while staring up at the inky black skies and blazing stars.

Throughout his life, this was his safe haven, the place he sought out in times of stress, the place he returned to summer after summer and hunting season after hunting season to connect with nature.

It was wild and beautiful and unchanging — and remote. All of those characteristics were important to Whitney, especially, perhaps, the last.

"You see," he confided once to a reporter, "these mountains provide privacy, which is everything to a rich man."[6]

The eighty-five thousand acres of private boreal forests along with thirty-eight lakes and ponds had been part of the network of canoe routes the Indians used for hundreds of years, and the tempo and tex-

ture of the place has changed very little since then. The earliest settlers in the region did not move in until the 1870s, and these were extremely wealthy magnates whose mission was to develop pristine hideaways. So they were respectful of the land, wishing to keep it as natural and quiet as possible.

In 1897, Sonny's grandfather purchased about 100,000 acres for $1.50 an acre, making the

Below: Whitney Park encompasses so many miles that even this aerial shot of the property does not capture its full scope. (© EarthImagery — the photographs of John McKeith www.earthimagery.com.)

Inset: Whitney loved to go hunting and fishing in the untamed wilds, but as his longtime friend Jouett Redmon pointed out, "He never took any more than we could eat."

Whitney family one of the largest private landowners in New York state. Indeed, Little Tupper Lake, which sprawls along the northern border of the property, was the largest privately owned lake east of the Mississippi River. The extended wildlife preserve became known as Whitney Park, with Camp Deerlands, which can sleep thirty-five people and encompasses over a hundred miles of logging roads, as just one retreat among several the family owned.

The largest building on Camp Deerlands was a pale gray chalet that served as the main house. It was here, after a substantial pick-me-up infusion of fine French furniture, that Sonny, Marylou, and the children spent the first full year of their marriage. A massive lakefront lodge built for rustic entertaining, it was the focal point of the Whitneys' various outings there, including the summer vacations with children and other Whitney family members, fishing in the spring, hunting in the fall, and snowshoeing and cross-country skiing in the winter.

Whitney Park also encompassed camps Killoquah, Bliss, Togus, Francis, and Camp on a Point, all of which served as retreats for other members of the Whitney family; a rustic gazebo where Whitney's mother, Gertrude, was known to serve formal tea and which Sonny and Marylou turned into a chapel for Sunday services; Sunset Cottage, a tiny cabin covered on all sides by dec-

The Whitneys spent at least part of each year at Camp Deerlands (top), where a large lakefront house served as their main residence (middle). Also in Whitney Park, Sonny liked retreating to the rustic trappers' cabin on Salmon Lake (bottom), which was built in the 1800s.

orative twigs in mosaic patterns known as twig work (which Marylou donated to the Adirondack Museum in 1995); and what is widely thought to be the first A-frame house built in America, used by the Whitneys' children as a playhouse.

One of Whitney's favorite spots on the property was the Gun Room, a two-story structure complete with bedrooms and other necessities, where he stored his fishing equipment, rifles, oil paintings, hats, and camping gear. This was his place, and he liked going there to be alone sometimes.

"Women weren't allowed in it, number one," said Whitney's friend and public relations man, Ed Lewi. "It was his room, and no one could tell him that he had to pick it up. He could leave his boots where he wanted to, his green boots, or he could leave his flannel shirt lying wherever he wanted."[7]

The Adirondacks was a place for fun and relaxation, but it was also a place for which Whitney felt an enormous sense of responsibility. He was fervent about leaving the land exactly as he had found it and, if at all possible, better than he had found it.

Whitney Park also served as home base for the family's timber operation, Whitney Industries, which is considered the apex of forest management. The forest was thinned but not decimated, and great care was taken to obscure the cutting operations from the rest of the land.

The Whitneys allowed relatively few outsiders on the property and "encouraged a policy of fishing ethics that allowed for the taking of a few 'keepers' but discouraged greed," wrote one environmentalist. "They successfully prevented the introduction of predatory and competing non-native fish species."[8]

Maureen Lewi was told by more than a few conservationists that the Whitney land "was tremendously more well cared for than any property that was owned by the federal or state government or any other private owner."[9]

In June 1998, several years after Sonny's death, the Whitney family sold nearly fifteen thousand acres to the state of New York. At Marylou's insistence, the property was named the William C. Whitney Area, in honor of C.V.'s grandfather, and was studied by the Department of

This A-frame house in Camp Deerlands, which the children used as a playhouse, was designed to stay cool in summer and warm in winter. It is said to be the first such house ever built in the United States.

CORNELIA'S DOLLHOUSE

THE WHITNEYS' KENTUCKY HOME became perhaps the most recognizable of their various mansions and estates because an exact replica of it was displayed in various cities over the years in a fund-raising tour that raised hundreds of thousands of dollars for such charities as the Girl Scouts, the Good Samaritan Hospital, and the Saratoga Performing Arts Center.

It all started when the Whitneys' daughter, Cornelia, asked her mother for a dollhouse, one that would remind her of the home in Kentucky when she was staying or living elsewhere.

Marylou embarked on what turned into a years-long project, researching the history of the place and overseeing the work of the Kentucky farm staff who labored through the quiet winter months for several years to create an exact replica, right down to electricity, furnishings, and wall hangings.

The finished product, weighing four thousand pounds, was seven years and untold thousands and thousands of dollars in the making. By then, Cornelia was well into high school and had lost her need for a dollhouse. But it was a masterpiece of miniaturist precision. The parquet floor was 2,790 tiny pieces of wood, sanded with a dentist's drill, and the thumbnail-size furnishings were created from materials collected all over the globe. It was exhibited in several cities, including Chicago

Cornelia's dollhouse, which made fundraising tours and was housed for a time at the Headley-Whitney Museum, is an exact replica of the Whitneys' Kentucky home.

and Saratoga Springs, drawing enormous interest and huge crowds.

"When looking at it, you had the feeling that you could shrink everyone and put them

---

Environmental Conservation "to ensure that sound decisions affecting long-range management plans will be made."[10]

Other Homes

Cady Hill, Whitney House, and Camp Deerlands and its environs were the most enduring of the Whitney properties, the places where, over the years, the Whitneys spent the most time, but there were many others in their constantly shifting inventory.

In Manhattan, they had the elegant, two-story, thirteen-room terraced duplex once owned by Elizabeth Arden, which was on Fifth Avenue overlooking Central Park. This was an apartment they maintained for many years for those occasions when Whitney was in New York on business and for entertaining during the New York social season, when they hosted regular soirées for society swells, diplomats, and the New York establishment. In 1987 they sold the cavernous duplex for about $8 million, opting for a downscaled, though still magnificent, five-room pied-à-terre formerly

inside," said the Whitneys' public relations consultant, Budd Calisch.[1]

The dollhouse was installed in the Headley-Whitney Museum in Lexington for a period after Whitney donated $100,000 to the museum to build a wing primarily for the purpose of displaying the house. The Whitneys withdrew the dollhouse in 1981. "The people who ran the museum just didn't know that dollhouses have to be cleaned like regular houses," said Marylou. "They let children come in and play with all the handmade silver, the tables, the handblown glass, and all the furniture made to order. So I had to take them back, and then I had to refurbish them. Dollhouses are a responsibility, just like a regular home."[2]

Responsibility indeed. "It had a staff of workers who traveled with it," said Calisch. "Not only the men on the farm who created the dollhouse, but their wives had to come to dust it every day."[3]

The dollhouse ultimately was moved to the Kentucky Derby Museum at Churchill Downs in Louisville.

"Seeing Cornelia's dollhouse for the first time after having just come from the main house can be, I'm told, a rather unsettling experience," wrote Marylou. "For inside this tiny house ... is an exact replica of the very room you were sitting in a moment ago — right down to a gold filigree ashtray or Chinese bowl no bigger than an infant's fingernail!"

owned by shipping magnate Peter Grace. They did not give up the nature-in-the-middle-of-the-city view, but they did sacrifice a significant amount of storage, a situation which prompted Marylou to confide to the columnists that she sometimes had to resort to storing her beloved Moët-Chandon champagne in the dishwasher.

Also in New York they possessed, early in their marriage, a giant estate near Oyster Bay on Long Island. Called Oakley Court, this faintly brooding three-story Tudor home was perched atop fifty-three acres and sported manicured lawns, a heated pool, stables, two greenhouses, and croquet lawns. While it was a portrait of magnificence, it was never really a favorite of any of the Whitneys. The children missed their schoolmates and didn't find the perfectly kept grounds nearly as interesting as the rolling farmlands of Kentucky. Marylou herself told reporters that she found the place a little too imposing and that she always felt like a pampered guest who really did not belong there. So they sold it in 1970.

For many years they also maintained the house in Flin Flon, Manitoba, which Marylou had hastily furnished during her honeymoon so that Whitney could feel at home when he checked on the mining operations. The sun and surf of Florida also had some appeal for them. They owned a hotel near Marineland for their frequent stopovers there and, sporadically, a place in Palm Beach. The first of their Palm Beach homes went on the market in the late 1960s and was snapped up by a Texas millionaire, sight unseen. "It was a little jewel," Marylou lamented to a magazine writer, "but not big enough for all of us."[11] The Whitneys continued to visit Palm Beach regularly as status houseguests, and finally, in 1988, when Whitney had begun to find the more northerly winters a little too harsh, they purchased their own place, an elegant estate called Elephant Walk on fashionable Jungle Road. The massive new house, "designed with no budget in mind,"[12] in the words of one reporter, was all done up in peach and cream, had huge formal columns in the living room and boasted a pristine glassed-in white loggia overlooking a turquoise pool.

For about fifteen years, they also owned a condo in Lake Placid called Snowshoe Five, which Sonny had purchased for Marylou when they were heavily involved in the Winter Olympics there. A bit smaller than most of their places, it was a lodge-like structure done in Palm Beach whites and animal prints and accented with polar bear rugs from Whitney's grandfather.

A favorite getaway for nearly two decades was their home on the island of Majorca. This was a semitropical spot in the Mediterranean Sea halfway between Spain and Africa with rolling hills and

The New York apartment at 834 5th Avenue was where the Whitneys held parties for Her Majesty Queen Siriki of Thailand — one in 1981 and another in 1985.

Marylou purchased the palace in Trujillo, Spain, with her own money and restored it to its original splendor and beauty.

deep aquamarine seas. They became friendly there with an assortment of luminaries, including artist Channing Hare, who created two portrait studies of Marylou.

For a time they even owned a looming palace in Trujillo, Spain, which Marylou purchased. She had, in the 1960s, been intensely involved in restoring the Spanish settlement in St. Augustine, near Marineland, and had thus become friendly with a variety of Spaniards over the years. The Whitneys made a great many visits to Spain after that, and almost inevitably, there grew a desire to have a

house there as well. The Whitneys bought a crumbling palace in the Extremadura province of Spain, and years of work and hundreds of thousands of dollars went into it. For her efforts at restoration, the Spanish government awarded Marylou the Order of Isabel la Catolica, the highest decoration given a foreigner.

Among his many talents, Whitney was also an accomplished painter. His seductive "Sailor's Warning" was a favorite of many.

CHAPTER TWELVE

THE ART OF RELAXATION

MANY WEALTHY MEN ARE patrons of the arts, and in this, Whitney was not unlike others of his stature. He contributed frequently to groups for the arts, making several contributions of such magnitude that the grateful recipients named buildings or wings in his honor.

When he was in his fifties, however, he did something quite unusual in his circle when he tried his hand at painting. He bought an easel and some oils and began turning out rather impressive paintings of nature.

"I started painting when I read something about Winston Churchill taking it up to escape into some other kind of concentration besides his work," he told a newspaper columnist. "I tried and found it did the same for me."[1]

And as it turned out, he was reasonably good at it. He had always possessed a strong creative urge, which manifested itself in writing, photography, and piano playing. But as a painter, he really shone, and through this he raised hundreds of thousands of dollars for charity.

Whitney was a controlled and fastidious artist with a good eye for the drama of nature. He had studios built on nearly all of his properties, and he spent hours in contemplative pursuit of the craft. After he and Marylou married, she took up painting as well so they could pass the long hours of artistic pursuit together.

"Painting together was wonderful," remembered Marylou. "It really was great fun. We'd lose ourselves in our work, and we never even knew when the other one was in the studio."[2]

His were large oil paintings, usually of dramatic landscapes or wild animals (although Marylou served as his model on several occasions, appearing in his works as a redhead, a brunette, and once, covered by nothing but her hair). Stark and realistic, his paintings conveyed a deep and penetrating sense of solitude. They were works from a man who felt that life was a rather solitary existence.

"The love of my life is the outdoors, so I do outdoor scenes, usually, with dramatic touches, maybe animals or birds," Whitney said.[3]

Marylou's paintings were on the opposite end of the continuum from his. Hers were bright and cheerful acrylics and oils, mostly of smiling children and happy cats and dogs.

The first display of their work occurred in 1966 at the Palm Beach Galleries, where Sonny's sister Barbara Headley and his first cousin

---

Marylou's genuine gold "Evening Purse," on loan to the Headley-Whitney Museum, is a work of art. The upper portion is set with diamonds, and a black pearl surrounded by diamonds sits at its top. *(Photo courtesy the Headley-Whitney Museum.)*

Mrs. Charles L. Payson were on the board. It was billed as a Vanderbilt-Whitney showing, featuring Sonny and Marylou; his cousin Gloria Vanderbilt; his sister Barbara and her husband, George Headley; Barbara's daughter Gerta; and G. MacCullouch Miller, his sister Flora's husband. After the death of Sonny's mother, Flora had assumed the mantle of leader and fundraiser for the Whitney Museum in New York.

Proceeds from the February event were to go to the Whitney Museum, a Marcel Breuer–designed edifice on Madison Avenue in New York that would triple the space of the previous museum on 54th Street. Thus there was much hubbub surrounding the event, not only because it was regarded as a worthwhile cause but because of the names that appeared in the corners of the paintings.

By October of that year, the couple had finished nearly forty more pieces to hang in the Wally Findlay Galleries in Manhattan. The fundraiser of choice this time was the Edward R. Murrow Fund for the Overseas Press Club. The Syracuse University Museum bought one each of their works, and the sellout event was covered by none less than the *New York Times.* The Whitneys celebrated at a midnight supper at El Morocco with high-roller pals like Ann Ford, ex-wife of Henry Ford II; Mr. and Mrs. Gardner Cowles of publishing fame; and actress Irene Dunne.

The Whitneys featured additional showings in subsequent years — all of them sellouts and all of the proceeds devoted to charity. They were applauded not only for their skill with paints and canvases but for their total lack of ego or stuffi-

The Whitneys received a lot of press for their painting endeavors. Their works were displayed in galleries across the country, and the proceeds of these events always went to charity.

This page: Sonny is hard at work in his rustic Lexington studio (left) and poses with his painting "The Fisherman" at a fundraising event (right).

Opposite page: Sonny and Marylou enjoyed their time spent painting together, but their interest in art went beyond their own work. At far right, the Whitneys lounge in front of the statue of Buffalo Bill in Cody, Wyoming, which was created by his mother.

ness about their work. They worked hard at their paintings, and they were pleased to use them as a means of raising funds for causes in which they had an interest, but they did not kid themselves into believing their work would be in huge demand were it not for the Whitney name. As one reporter noted, "It would be easy for them to take themselves seriously as so many of their boring peers do, but they're too secure for that silliness."[4]

Many other arts organizations received the benefit of Whitney's interest and money. For many years, he was on the boards of the Natural History Museum and the Whitney Museum in New York. And in 1968 he was elected to the board of directors for the New York Philharmonic. He also founded the Whitney Gallery of Western Art at the Buffalo Bill Historical Center in Cody, Wyoming, to which he donated $500,000 to build an edifice near the site of his mother's famous Buffalo Bill sculpture. He continued donating large amounts every year for the rest of his life. The Whitneys also were founders and contributors over the years to the Saratoga Performing Arts Center, the National Museum of Dance, and the National Museum of Racing.

Moreover, they were frequently in attendance at arts charity events, contributing thousands of dollars for seats to events aimed at helping various arts groups. One of the most lavish was the supremely chic Venice Ball to benefit Venetian artisans. Their fellow revelers that evening included Princess Grace of Monaco, Elizabeth Taylor (when she was still Mrs. Burton), Mr. and Mrs. Joseph Kennedy, and the Orsini princes, Raimundo and Filippo.

Throughout their marriage, the Whitneys entertained a number of celebrities. Guests at this 1980s Derby party included (clockwise from left) Kathleen Sullivan, Gary Collins, interior designer Stephen Stempler, Mary Ann Mobley, Dr. Craig Foster, Arlene Francis, Budd Calisch, and seated beside Whitney, Jean Taylor.

CHAPTER THIRTEEN

THE RICH AND FAMOUS

THE ORBITS OF THE VERY RICH regularly find confluence with the orbits of others who are very rich or very famous or both. This is the way of the wealthy, a reality born of similar resources, similar interests, and similar lifestyles.

C.V. Whitney was no exception to this. Through his work, his wealth, and his birth into America's highest stratum, Whitney became friends with Hollywood movie stars, leaders in government, notable horsemen, socialites, and international luminaries.

He was on speaking and lunching terms with all the U.S. presidents from Truman through Reagan. He was a regular at White House functions during virtually all administrations from the 1950s through the 1980s, and like many industrialists, he did not let party affiliation stand in the way of developing political friendships. He attended lunches with Lyndon Johnson, visited with Jimmy and Rosalynn Carter, and had tea at the White House with Betty Ford. Whitney and Marylou were particularly close to Nancy and Ronald Reagan, who were guests at the Whitney Farm for over a week, and Gerald and Betty Ford, who invited the Whitneys to several White House functions.

The president with whom Whitney felt the closest affiliation, however, was Harry Truman, who appointed him to his two undersecretary positions. Whitney's friend Ted Bassett recalled that one time Truman, after he had left the presidency, was to be in Louisville for a speaking engagement and contacted Whitney to see if he would like to attend. Whitney made the trip with Bassett, and "When we got there, there was a crowd around Harry Truman, a big crowd who wanted to see him and shake his hand. Somehow in the mess he looked over and saw us. 'Well, hello, Sonny,' he said. 'How are you? You come up here.' And he motioned the people away so he could make way for Sonny. And I remember he paid Sonny a great compliment during his speech about Sonny having put service above self and that he was a credit to his administration. He made the point that Sonny didn't really have to serve in Washington; he had accomplished enough that he didn't need to. But he chose to."[1]

The Whitneys were also friendly with many of the nation's governors, largely because they had homes in many states and had an interest in the

---

The Whitneys' circle of famous friends included government leaders as well. This note from First Lady Rosalynn Carter thanks Marylou for sending her cookbook of goober recipes.

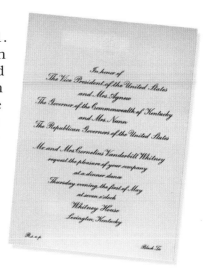

ernor from 1967 to 1971. "Aristocracy never stood in the way of humility and kindness and consideration for other people."[2] At one point in Nunn's career, the Whitneys held a fundraising party for him, and he later learned he had to report the cost of the party as a campaign contribution. "Well, you can imagine how embarrassing and humiliating it was to have to go out and ask how much their party cost. But Sonny said, 'Oh, absolutely, no problem at all. We keep a complete list of everything.' He was just glad to share the information."[3]

In 1969, the Whitneys added to their list of gubernatorial acquaintances when they, along with Nunn as chairman of the Republican Governors Conference, hosted a formal dinner dance in Lexington for twenty-six governors, President Nixon, and Vice President Spiro Agnew. "Only a few people in the world could have thrown a party like it," effused *Town & Country*.[4]

Media stars such as Walter Cronkite and Kathleen Sullivan were included in the Whitney circle, as were a variety of world leaders, including Ferdinand and Imelda Marcos of the

politics of those states, but also because they found the state leaders during those years quite interesting. Kentucky Governor John Y. Brown and his then wife, the former Miss America Phyllis George, were regulars at the Whitney race-season galas in Lexington and Saratoga Springs.

"He was gracious and hospitable," remembered Louie Nunn, who served as Kentucky's gov-

From top: The Whitneys with Governor Ronald Reagan and wife Nancy during the formal dinner dance the Whitneys hosted for the Republican Governors Conference in 1969; Sonny and Marylou with Richard Nixon; Marylou dancing with Gerald Ford; and Marylou with Walter Cronkite, who was a regular guest of the Whitneys for years.

Philippines. In 1976 the Whitneys had taken a whirlwind tour of Asia, during which they were guests of the president and Mrs. Marcos in Manila. Traveling with them were Sanidh Rangsit, the prince of Thailand, and his wife, Princess Christine. The three couples had been on a luxurious cruising trip to Java and Sumatra, and the Marcoses had invited the Whitneys to join them

Clockwise from top: In Palm Beach, Marylou presents the Whitney Cup in polo to Prince Charles; Marylou with Gregory Peck, a guest of the Whitneys at the races; and John Wayne and Marylou ringing a bell to celebrate the bicentennial in Wyoming.

in Manila. The president and his wife gave the Whitneys a delicate shell chandelier that was installed above the heated pool at Cady Hill. And Ferdinand, when he seemed certain to be deposed, offered the Whitneys the sumptuous presidential yacht. They politely declined.

The Whitneys also had constant encounters with the British royals. Princess Margaret stayed at the Whitney Farm, and Prince Charles regularly sought them out at social events. They were also friendly with the Duke of

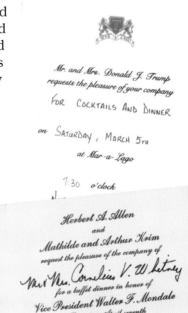

Above: Marylou with Julio Iglesias, Placido Domingo, and Oscar de la Renta, one of her favorite designers for decades, at the Plaza Hotel Supper Dance in New York in 1984.

Right: Whitney's cousin Gloria Vanderbilt. *(Photo courtesy Anderson Cooper.)*

Below: Marylou with Liz Whitney Tippett at the races. Tippett, the ex-wife of Sonny's cousin Jock, was a famed horsewoman.

Windsor, who played golf with Sonny, and Prince Philip, who lunched with them.

They socialized with Hollywood types such as Gregory Peck, John Wayne, Kirk Douglas, Rock Hudson, Merv Griffin, Grace Kelly, Clark Gable, Doris Duke, Eva Gabor, Zsa Zsa Gabor, Esther Williams, and Liza Minnelli. Some of their famous friends were cut from the same birthright cloth as Whitney, such as the du Ponts, the Mellons, the Rockefellers, and Listerine heiress Sue Whitmore. Other celebrities the Whitneys socialized with included the legendary horse-woman Liz Whitney Tippett, the reigning belle of Saratoga for many years; Mary Sanford, long the reigning queen of Palm Beach society; and Mollie Wilmot, of New York and Florida, who received a great deal of media attention when an oil tanker washed up on the shore at her Palm Beach estate.

And there were names-in-the-news people such as Estee Lauder; Dina Merrill, the actress who was the daughter of cereal heiress Marjorie Merriweather Post; and designers Gloria Vanderbilt (Whitney's cousin), Bill Blass, Arnold Scassi, and Oscar de la Renta.

Whitney's relationship with many luminaries was polished and ephemeral, formed like glistening yachts passing in the evening. Others were nurtured with all the care and attention of a prized possession. Television personalities Gary Collins and his wife, former Miss America Mary Ann Mobley, were in frequent contact with the Whitneys for years. Fred Astaire, whom Whitney met in Hollywood and later (along with his cousin Jock) backed for his first show on Broadway, was a close friend for decades, as was Ginger Rogers, who wrote in her autobiography that Whitney was one of the most able dance partners she had ever known.[5]

To Whitney, they were all special, not because they were luminaries but because they were people. "Their fame or wealth meant nothing to my father," said Whitney's stepdaughter Heather Mabee.[6]

Left: Marylou with artist Andy Warhol in 1986.

Below: The Whitneys with Ginger Rogers and the Count and Countess Chandon de Briailles, of Moët-Chandon champagne fame.

Sonny signing his new book, *Live a Year With a Millionaire.* He autographed the picture for Marylou for her birthday in 1985.

CHAPTER FOURTEEN

A LIFE WELL LED

AS THE CENTURY ENTERED its eighties — and Whitney did the same — it was, in Whitney's case at least, with much the same style and verve that had characterized his earlier years. If his footsteps were a bit more tentative, this did not prevent him from taking to the dance floor at every opportunity and outdancing everyone in the place. And if his attention was not as razor sharp as it once had been, this did not impact his ability to tell a fine story or share one of the thousands of jokes he kept on mental file.

"I think one of the worst things we have in the United States is the retirement age of sixty-five," he had told a newspaper reporter when he was approaching the age of eighty. "Men dream about that day when they'll be able to sit on the front porch and be happy. Well, it doesn't work that way."[1]

Not for Whitney, in any event. He had no interest in sliding quietly toward an idle life whose only excitement was a half-remembered snippet of an event gone by. Budd Calisch remembered attending a Whitney dinner party at the Whitneys' New York two-story apartment on 5th Avenue when Whitney called him out to the terrace. "The man was eighty-five years old, and he wanted to talk to me about his five-year plan," said Calisch. "If there hadn't been a railing, I would have landed right down in Central Park. Three years later, he

called and said, 'Budd, remember the five-year plan that I told you about on the terrace? Well, it went through. Just thought you'd like to know.'"[2]

Though Whitney was withdrawing from his earlier business endeavors, he still traveled extensively and maintained a calendar jammed with social and professional appearances. He also continued painting and writing.

In 1981, he published a spirited little ninety-four-page volume called *Live a Year With a Millionaire,* which he sent to 626 of his closest friends during the holiday season. A homey recitation of his various activities and events of 1979, slathered with a liberal helping of his personal philosophy, it was sufficiently amusing and spicy to warrant stories in *Newsweek* and the *New York Times.* The journalists were more intrigued by his numerous references to lunches in Howard Johnson and evenings of cribbage play with his wife than by the intense schedule of arrivals and leave-takings as he jetted about to his various homes. This, of course, pleased Whitney mightily, for it was just what he

---

The Whitneys were very involved in the 1980 Olympics at Lake Placid, contributing large sums of money. Marylou was on the Olympic committee, and Whitney bought her a house in Lake Placid for a gift.

had hoped to do — lay to rest some of the societal presumptions about the daily lives of the very rich and famous.

Whitney credited his wife in this tome with much of his cheery outlook. And then he pointed out that, for him, and presumably for all persons, there are four things required for a contented marriage: "1. good sex relationship, of course … 2. mutual friends … 3. similar way of life pattern … and 4. sense of humor."

He went on to outline a wife's role in a marriage, or at least his wife's role in their marriage: "She always dresses beautifully for whatever scenario we are in…. She decorates and furnishes all our homes in ways that please me, and … she invites the guests [and] sets the tables…. She is a truly good cook."

That holiday season in 1981, as friends and acquaintances were beginning to receive the Whitney Christmas missives, the Whitneys themselves spent the first part of December in their New York apartment, where they held a little dinner gathering to honor Queen Siriki of Thailand. Guests included CBS owner William Paley and the ambassador from Spain to the United Nations, Jaime de Pinies. After this the Whitneys had a traditional friends-and-family celebration in Kentucky and a post-Christmas outing to the Adirondacks.

The Whitneys' social swirl that year and for several subsequent years was quite phenomenal, not only because of the intensity of their schedules but also because of the breadth of their range.

They were still much in demand as a society couple, and they continued to appear with regularity in the New York and Palm Beach columns for attending this party or that, this benefit or that. In 1981 they traveled to the British Isles to explore the Whitney family history and in 1982 to the Netherlands to search out the Vanderbilt family history. They made regular visits to their home in Majorca and an annual trip or two to an exotic faraway land, such as Egypt or Thailand.

Their own parties continued unabated in Kentucky and New York with all the drama and

flair of years past. The Whitneys could always be counted on to have an interesting prince or political figure or international luminary of some note at their gatherings. At the end of 1982, for example, first lady Nancy Reagan was a surprise guest at the Whitneys' New York apartment during a little soiree that included Douglas Fairbanks, designer Bill Blass, Laurence Rockefeller, Mrs. Alfred Bloomingdale, Broadway producer Joshua Logan, Walter Hoving (of Tiffany's fame), and perennial Whitney guest Maggi Newhouse, a former television personality.

A few months later, at the Whitneys' Victorian garden–themed Kentucky Derby party, Henry Kissinger and his wife and Beverly Sills and her husband were house guests at the Kentucky farm. That fall, Sonny and Marylou had a luncheon gathering at Cady Hill to introduce New York's first lady, Matilda Cuomo, to Saratoga society. And they held a dinner for Mr. and Mrs. Douglas Auffm-Ordt (she being the Princess Antoinette von Croy), who were neighbors of the Whitneys in Majorca. Also in the crowd that evening were socialites Pat Buckley and Anne Slater, Whitney's niece Gerta Conner, and her husband, MacCauley Conner.

The glitter and glamour were counterbalanced by some decidedly rural accents. During the first part of the 1980s, Whitney received many honors from several eastern Kentucky mountain communities where he had fished and contributed money. He was given the ceremonial keys to many little towns. The one where the Whitneys had the greatest and most lasting presence, Pineville, held a huge event of gratitude for the Whitneys during which a letter was read from President Ronald Reagan commending the couple for their efforts.

"Sonny became a friend of almost everyone in Pineville," wrote Marylou. "They gave dinners in his honor constantly, and they made him an honorary citizen of Pineville. He had more honors from that mountain area than anyone could ever imagine!"[3]

They still attended an assortment of simple gatherings with friends and acquaintances, where Whitney was able to be just another guest who balanced a plate on his lap and dove into huge slabs of meat. "He loved backyard barbecues. He used to rave about the simplest dinners," said

Opposite: Sonny and Marylou were regulars at all the most important functions.

Linda Toohey. "We had this small house, and we would invite Marylou and Sonny over to dinner. He used to just talk forever afterward about how he had the best time sitting on our mosquito-ridden back deck, eating swordfish or steaks that we'd cook out on the grill."[4]

Whitney loved chatting with ordinary folks. And in some situations, he would go to some trouble to camouflage his identity or stature. He was distressed on more than one occasion when his identity was revealed in situations when he would have preferred it had not been.

The Whitneys, said Toohey, "were as happy and cordial with a groundskeeper who worked for them as they were with someone who worked for the public service department in the city or an elected official. It didn't matter. People could come from any walk of life, and the Whitneys were comfortable with them."[5]

Whitney's comfort with blue-collar people was equaled only by his comfort with royalty. There was, in the 1980s, frequent shoulder-rubbing with queens and princes and others of title.

In 1984, for example, right after the Whitneys held their traditional Kentucky Derby party, they hosted a gala for Olympic contenders who were in Lexington for the Rolex Kentucky International Three-Day Event. World-class competitive riders from the world over who had converged upon the Bluegrass, including Mark Phillips, then husband of Princess Anne of Great Britain, were in attendance. Phillips was a guest at the Whitney Farm for the four days he was in the commonwealth,

Left and below: The Whitneys' Derby parties were among the most prized invitations in Kentucky during the all-important Derby Week. The themes for the party changed from year to year, but guests could always count on something fun and flamboyant.

and he and his team stayed with the Whitneys in Lexington on many other occasions as well.

Not quite five months later, the Whitneys jetted from New York to Kentucky to have lunch at Keeneland race track with the Queen of England and later that day were guests at a small party given in her honor by fellow horseman Will Farrish. Six months after that, Prince Philip was a lunch guest at their Kentucky farm.

Whitney, his voice still vibrant, his eyes still sparkling with the mischief of an adolescent boy, was a courtly presence through it all. It was Marylou who organized and Marylou who took center stage, but Whitney was the manor lord

Left: The Whitneys' public relations consultant, Budd Calisch, was a good friend of both the Whitneys.

Below: Sonny and Marylou conduct an interview in their atrium pool house in Kentucky before they dress for their party guests.

who smiled and presented each guest with that laser-like interest that made everyone feel very special. People who saw him often commented that he seemed the one person in their crowd who appeared very little affected by age.

But if they did not fully appreciate the impact of older age upon him, he did. In the summer of 1984, from his office in Saratoga, he made an announcement that everyone knew was inevitable and yet somehow imagined could never take place. Whitney would retire from thoroughbred racing.

"At my age I just don't have the energy and the time to do it as closely and thoroughly as you should in the game," he said.[6]

His awareness of this reality did not, however, make it especially easy to withdraw from the enterprise. Thoroughbred racing had anchored his yearly calendar for half a century, had brought him glory and fame and had provided a professional and social network he found enormously pleasurable. But with his customary pragmatism, once he had concluded it was proper to make his exit, there was no hint of sentimentality.

"It took me six months to make the final decision," he declared. "And when I make a final decision about my business, that's it. I feel this will be the best thing for my stable, for my family, and for me."[7]

When he passed on the Whitney blue and brown — among the oldest registered silks in the United States — to his nephew Leverett Miller, a breeder outside Ocala, Florida, it symbolized the passing of an era. Three generations of top-notch breeding and racing, with all the care and attention the Whitney fortunes could command, had ended.

Lev Miller, Sonny's nephew and the man he passed his Eton blue and brown racing colors to, smiles with Marylou at one of the Whitneys' frequent parties.

The twenty-six thoroughbreds in his stable were sold in November for $6.69 million, and although he no longer owned thoroughbreds, he still attended the Saratoga and Keeneland tracks.

"When he got out of something, he really got out and didn't pay a lot of attention to it after that," Miller observed, though he still liked to go to the races. This surgical-cut approach had been a lifetime pattern for Whitney, a pattern followed when he left polo in his thirties, when he left Pan Am and his other enterprises, when he had left his previous wives, and when he experienced discord with his older children. He walked away, did not look back, and focused his attention elsewhere.

"He always liked a challenge," said Marylou, "and he was always ahead of other people, but that's because he said he never looked back. Perhaps that was his biggest philosophy in life — never look back."[8]

Less than six months after his retirement announcement, he was in the hospital, fighting for his life. Two weeks before Christmas, the Whitneys' personal physician, Dr. Ben Roach, received a call from Marylou. Whitney was complaining that his stomach hurt, and she wondered if she should give him Kaopectate or Pepto Bismol. Roach had frequently dispensed medical advice to the Whitneys over the phone during their many travels — "They carried a nice little arsenal of pills all the time," he said — but he felt this required a closer look. Roach raced to the Whitney Farm, did an examination, and realized that Whitney had an abdominal aneurysm.[9]

"I told him just to lie there, and I called the ambulance," said Roach. "I called the university and got my best vascular surgeon and told him that Mr. Whitney had an aneurysm that was close to rupturing and I would like for him just to come straight in, go straight to the operating room, and begin surgery."[10]

The surgeon found that the aneurysm was perilously close to rupture, which, in those days, meant almost certain death. Whitney survived the four-hour surgery, but because he was eighty-six years old, there was no real assurance that he would survive much longer.

So Marylou executed what, for the Whitneys, was an extraordinary act. She contacted all the

Always a patron of the arts, Whitney founded the National Museum of Dance in Saratoga Springs in 1986.

children, now scattered throughout the country with various family and work responsibilities of their own, and declared she was flying them to Kentucky for Christmas.

She made no mention of Whitney's surgery in those conversations. "My parents were always ones that never wanted us to know when they were sick," said Heather. And this was no exception. Marylou simply made it very clear that refusing this journey was not an option. "My mother doesn't normally do that kind of stuff," Heather said, so the children began their obedient treks to Kentucky.[11] It was only upon arriving there and

SPREADING THE WEALTH

WHITNEY GAVE AWAY MILLIONS OF dollars over the years to various groups, institutions, and causes. Most millionaires tend to settle their cash on one or two primary philanthropic arenas — perhaps education or the arts — but the Whitney largesse was spread about to a broad variety of recipients.

Sonny would often ask Marylou what she wanted for Christmas or birthday presents, and most often it would be a substantial donation to a charity. Mostly, they donated money to benefit efforts in the various communities in which the Whitneys maintained homes. In Lexington, for example, Whitney gave more than $125,000 to Sayre School, a private school where his daughter and two stepdaughters attended classes, to construct a gym and auditorium, which was named the C.V. Whitney Gymnasium-Auditorium. Later, another part of the building was named the Marie Louise Whitney Lower School building in Marylou's honor. Whitney also contributed $100,000 to Lexington's Headley Museum, which was built by his brother-in-law, jewelry-designer George Headley, to house his collection of jewels and bibelots. The Whitney wing of what was renamed the Headley-Whitney Museum housed, for a time, the two-ton dollhouse, the exact replica of the Whitney House in Kentucky which had toured nationwide and raised more than half a million dollars for charity, mostly for children's museums. Also in Lexington, Whitney contributed substantial amounts to the Cardinal Hill Hospital.

In Saratoga, Marylou raised money to buy the Steinway piano at the Saratoga Performing Arts Center, and the center itself was the beneficiary of much Whitney check writing over the years, including money given to buy the facility air conditioning. The National Museum of Dance there owes its very existence to the Whitneys, as does the National Museum of

Racing, which was founded by Walter Jeffords and Sonny Whitney.

And Marylou was the world's biggest contributor to the 1980 Winter Olympics in Lake Placid. "Sonny had given Marylou a check for $100,000 for Christmas for the charity of her choice," said Ed Lewi. "She had heard that the Olympic Committee was hurting for money, so she called me up and asked who she should make the $100,000 check out to. That check came at a critical time in the financial affairs of the Olympic Games."[1]

Opposite, top: Marylou with Roni the Raccoon at the Whitney party for the Lake Placid 1980 Olympics.

Opposite, bottom: Whitney and Marylou with Lieutenant Governor of Kentucky Wilson Wyatt at the formal dedication of Sayre's C.V. Whitney Gymnasium-Auditorium in 1963.

Below: Marylou and Sonny raise money for the Cardinal Hill Hospital's telethon. Years after Whitney's death, Marylou continued to donate her time and money to this event.

To promote the Olympics, the Whitneys also held a Winter Wonderland–themed party in Lake Placid for over twenty heads of state.

But while the Whitneys were not at all reluctant to write checks of huge sums to various causes that drew their attention at any given time — to the U.K. Cancer Hospital, for example — they also gave smaller amounts to smaller groups. One year, when Whitney and Marylou were attending the Pine Mountain Laurel Festival in little Pineville, Kentucky, they were distressed when the band marched out wearing, not uniforms, but T-shirts and jeans. A massive flood a few weeks earlier had whisked the uniforms away, and the school district was too poor to afford more. Marylou immediately yanked out her checkbook and wrote a check for $5,000. Such gestures were repeated with some regularity. Whenever the couple happened to be in a situation where money would help, they made a spontaneous donation.

Checks were sent out with great regularity to various arts groups, animal protection causes, hospitals, and senior citizens groups who contacted Whitney for help.

Some of Whitney's friends in Kentucky included the famous horseman Leslie Combs (left), of the world renowned Spendthrift Farm, and Albert Clay, whose family went back generations in Kentucky history.

being taken to the hospital where Whitney lay weak, tired, connected to many tubes, but surviving, that they came to understand the gravity of the situation and the importance of their having made the trip.

"It was difficult, but we made the best of it," said Heather.[12]

It was not, however, an episode that anyone in the family dwelled upon or even mentioned again once Whitney left the hospital. They did not even speak of it when he died several years later. "Dad would not want to be remembered for his illnesses and his sicknesses," said Heather.[13]

Amazingly, for a man of his age, Whitney was released on December 30. His patterns resumed much the same as they had been. The Whitneys

spent some time in Spain after the operation and traveled to Los Angeles for several days, where Whitney received a rare and prestigious Eclipse Special Award for his involvement in the thoroughbred industry. Horsemen from all over the country gathered to honor Whitney's fifty-five years of sportsmanship and contributions to the quality of racing. Famed turf writer Joe Hirsch, in writing about the event, noted that Whitney "conducted his racing stable by such high standards of quality and sportsmanship that his name has become synonymous with those achievements."[14] Indeed, the New York Turf Writers named an award after him, the C.V. Whitney Achievement Award, which was given annually to outstanding achievers in the racing business.

Whitney, the reluctant horseman, was deeply touched by the homage. "I think the presentation was the most moving event of my life," he told *Women's Wear Daily.*[15]

Although the awards dinner was the motivation for journeying to Los Angeles, it was by no means the only event of significance once the Whitneys were there. The couple's arrival on the West Coast generated much excitement among their friends and acquaintances, and there was much party giving and entertaining during the three days they were in town, including an outing to Santa Anita track and a lunch hosted by Mr. and Mrs. Kirk Douglas. And, as the columnists pointed out, because the Whitneys were both sentimental and romantic, they chose to stay at the Bel Air Hotel, where Whitney lived while he was courting Marylou.

Later that fall, Pan American Airways did a fiftieth anniversary reenactment of the original, 1935 *China Clipper* flight, the world's first trans-Pacific airmail flight. And the Whitneys were invited to participate as honored guests.

A few days before Thanksgiving, the Pan Am 747 jumbo jet called the *China Clipper II* set out on the same course as that which its namesake had followed: Honolulu, Midway Island, Wake Island, and Guam. There were 291 passengers and twenty-one crew members aboard, among them author James Michener and actor John Travolta.

Before takeoff, Whitney was introduced as a pioneer of Pan American Airways and the only surviving member of the team that had opened the Pacific to flight. Also aboard was Charles Trippe, the son of Juan, and four of Charles Lindbergh's grandchildren. Whitney made a brief speech in which he said, "In founding Pan Am it was my privilege to give Trippe and Lindbergh top positions in the company, and they performed their jobs magnificently."

The champagne and caviar flight to Honolulu, with Whitney and Marylou seated in First Class near Ed Acker, who was then chairman of the board of Pan Am, took only about one-third the time of the original flight.

There was an air of great festivity, but Marylou, long Whitney's most ardent supporter and in his later years increasingly determined to see that he received his due, was not at all pleased with how things were going. That afternoon, as Whitney napped in the presidential suite at the Royal Hawaiian Hotel, where Pan Am had placed them, she spoke with Pan Am's Nancy Holmes and told her that it had been their understanding that the

historic trip was to honor Sonny. "So far," Marylou wrote in her diary of the event, "it had been completely a big show for Mr. Acker and his pretty young wife."[16]

She complained to Holmes that "When we landed at the airport, there was a ceremony with no mention of Sonny, and then the unveiling of a statue at the site of the landing of the *China Clipper I*, where Sonny had first landed, with no mention of his name."[17]

But in Manila, things got better. At the palace they were pleased by the reception they were given

---

In the 1980s, the Whitneys were invited by Pan American Airways to reenact the flight Whitney made fifty years earlier when Pan Am opened the Pacific route to passenger travel to the Orient. The reenactment included several stopovers, including ones at Guam (below) and Manila (inset), where Marylou was greeted by Imelda Marcos.

Top: At eighty-seven years old, Whitney was still up for a day of fishing with his old pal Dave Short.

Inset: Whitney in the Adirondacks with his daughter Cornelia and Dave Short.

by the royal family. The Marcoses had not known the Whitneys were to be on the trip, asked them why they were not staying at the palace, and invited them to use the presidential yacht.

While the Whitneys were at the palace, Imelda invited them on a shopping trip the next day, an outing they happily accepted. And when the Whitneys departed Manila that day for their flight home, not aboard a Pan Am plane, they were "treated like royalty," thanks to a call to the airline by Imelda.

They returned to New York in time for the social season, and they continued taking trips to the Adirondacks. Whitney had, however, lost his appetite for killing game. "He did not enjoy shooting deer" in his later years, said Roach. "He'd go hunting with a guide, but he'd take a book and binoculars, and when he got out in the woods, he would read. 'I don't like to kill things anymore,' he'd tell me."[18]

But fishing still brought him pleasure. One time, he and Dave Short, the ramrod-straight part-Indian guide who had been Harry Payne's guide, then Sonny's guide, and ultimately one of Sonny's best friends, were preparing to go out fishing. As Whitney was getting into the boat, he slipped and fell against the boat slip, where a huge rusty nail ripped his leg open, leaving a wound so big and so deep that it exposed the bone. Short was nearly as old as Whitney, much smaller, and he had a heart condition. But he knew he had to get Whitney out of there. Somehow he hauled his boss and friend across the half mile of marshy terrain to their vehicle and transported him to the caretaker's house, where they called Marylou, who called the emergency squad before racing to the scene. He was given stitches at the hospital, where he stayed for over a week, then went back to Saratoga, where Dr. Moore, Sonny's good friend, changed the bandages every day for several more weeks.

"Sonny was in better shape than Dave Short," Marylou recalled. Short was gray in the face and having trouble breathing, and there was some concern he might not survive, although, as it turned out, he did. No one who knew the two men was at all surprised that Short had done what he had. "He cared more for Sonny than he did for his own life," said Marylou. "We always knew that. Everyone knew that."[19]

With time, Whitney lost his interest in anything having to do with the Adirondacks. "At the end of his life, it bothered him to come here [the Adirondacks] when he had to have a nurse and Dave Short to come over and sit with him," said Marylou. "They would go fishing. They would get the caretaker and Dave and get some people to help him down to the boathouse and get him out there in a boat and let him fish, but he said, 'You know, I don't like it here any more.' I said, 'This is your favorite place.' 'Nope,' he said. 'You know, in different times of your life there are different things you like. When I'm here, I want to do the things I always did, and I can't.'"[20]

They went back to their Saratoga estate, Cady Hill, where there was a lot of land and trees and gazebos and benches. Whitney could walk about with his cane and his nurse and sit and watch the birds and trains.

In 1989, Marylou held an American flag–themed ninetieth birthday party for Sonny at the Everglades Club in Palm Beach that commemorated his full and lustrous life.

He still went on outings, but not to the Adirondacks. By now the Whitneys had purchased another home in Palm Beach, where the climate was easier on him and where they still had a great many good friends. Longtime pal and Listerine heiress Sue Whitmore threw a huge party welcoming them back. It was in Palm Beach, in fact, where Marylou threw an enormous American flag–themed birthday bash in 1989 to celebrate Whitney's ninetieth birthday with more than a hundred well-wishers.

Whitney had not lost his appetite for parties. He would often arrive in a wheelchair, pushed by an attendant, and he would tell jokes to anyone who approached. After the aneurysm, he was sometimes not as alert, but he always remembered his jokes. "And he loved to flirt with the women, all in innocence, you know," said Jeannette Jordan.[21]

By then, he had nurses caring for him around the clock. "He did not like that kind of life," Marylou said. "He used to laugh and say to me, 'Go out and have some fun.' But he would tell our friends, 'Now you get her home at 11 o'clock.' But he'd want me to bring some of our

friends home too because he wanted to know what happened at the party. So he was interested in a way. He just didn't want to participate. I'd bring people home, and we'd have chicken sandwiches and talk and tell him about what went on at the party. He loved that. It gave him an extra something in life when he was getting very old."[22]

But even in his final years, he never lost his knack for picking good horseflesh. "He had an amazing eye," said his nephew Lev Miller. When Whitney was ninety, Marylou, now in the horse business herself, took him to Miller's stable in Florida, where she had some mares. "We went up to the barn," Miller remembered, "and we looked at her horses, and he picked one out, just with a few words, and said, 'That's the best one.'" That horse was, by far, the best of the lot. "It was fairly uncanny at that age to be able to say that," Miller said.[23]

But as with most men of high energy and high achievement, being frail was exceedingly difficult on him. "He was a disciple of Gaylord Hauser," said Heather. "You always have to be innovating and constantly active because if you let your mind start dwindling away, then you will no longer be alive. It depressed him a little bit not to be able to be constantly innovating every single day, because physically his body was just deteriorating on him. It frustrated him because he was a man who was always out there doing something new and different, and he couldn't do that anymore."[24]

He was frustrated with the weakened state of his body, but he was most assuredly not afraid of death. "I think he accepted that he was getting older and would die," said Cornelia. "He actually really accepted that in the last couple of years, and he was very much ready to go and had made peace with himself. Right up until the last time I saw him, he was always thankful to God for everything he had and thankful to Mom and to all of us."[25]

It was a cold and icy night in Saratoga on December 12, 1992, when Sonny and Marylou had an early dinner on the north porch of their Cady

Hill house. They had been invited to a Christmas party, which Sonny insisted Marylou attend.

"I made my way through the crowd and slipped out the back door where our driver, Lester, met me," Marylou remembered. "All in all, I was gone forty-five minutes. When I arrived home, Sonny was watching *Columbo* in the TV room and eating chocolates. We cuddled up together on the big sofa until Sonny announced that he was tired and wished to go to bed. I lay in bed with him until he was sound asleep, and I tip-toed out.

"It was about 7:00 the next morning when I was awakened and told that Sonny's pulse was very, very weak and slow. We called 911, and we went to the hospital. He was dead on arrival.

"As he lay on that hospital bed in the emergency room, I could not believe he was dead, for his enormous bright blue eyes were wide open, looking up at me. I kissed him and closed those wonderful eyes of his and said, 'You are with God at last.' And the smile on his face made me know that he was at peace in heaven."[26]

Cornelius Vanderbilt Whitney was laid to rest in Saratoga on a rainy, blustery day in December. A small group, almost entirely family, assembled in the little chapel at Cady Hill and sang "Amazing Grace." It was a simple service, as he had requested, and he was buried in a plain pine box, also as he had requested. Two men from the Air Force came to pay their respects and to present the widow with an American flag.

Father Parke, who spoke the final words, mentioned that not far away, there had been another death and another funeral. That man had been quite poor and had been buried in a plain pine box identical to the one Whitney had chosen.

Sonny would have liked that.

"My father was a very simple person," said Heather. "He was not a man for fanfare. He wanted to be buried in the way he lived his life. He never did what he did for the glory or to get another plaque on the wall or to have his name in the newspaper. He did it because he felt it was something that either was going to entertain people and give them pleasure and enjoyment, or maybe it was something to make people's lives better. But he never looked for the glory of it. And that's why there's very little press about him — because he never looked for the glory."[27]

Opposite: The Whitneys enjoyed a dance at the Empire State College Golf Club Benefit in Saratoga when Whitney was well into his eighties.

From this day on, call it Whitney Way

Whitney's own memory lane

Times Union/PAUL D. KNISKERN SR.

Marylou Whitney gets a hug from granddaughter Kristine Schlachter, 8, on Tuesday during which the Route 50 arterial in Saratoga Springs was renamed the C.V. Whitney Memorial Highway, in honor of Whitney's late husband, Sonny Whitney. Story on B-6.

Times Union/PAUL D. KNISKERN SR.

SURROUNDED BY family members and dignitaries, Marylou Whitney, in hat, cuts a ribbon stretched across Route 50 where it intersects Broadway in Saratoga Springs during a ceremony Tuesday that officially renamed the arterial in honor of her late husband, C.V. "Sonny" Whitney.

Route 50 renamed for philanthropist

BY JULIE CARR
Staff writer

SARATOGA SPRINGS — The Route 50 arterial was named Tuesday for Cornelius Vanderbilt "Sonny" Whitney as members of Whitney's aristocratic clan helped unveil a new highway sign and cut ribbons bearing the colors of the industrialist's thoroughbreds.

"They're Eaton blue and brown. They were Uncle Sonny's colors; now they're my Dad's," said a daughter of Whitney's cousin, Leverett Miller, as she studied two pieces cut from a ribbon that had been placed across Route 50 where it intersects with North Broadway.

So many family members helped in its cutting that the ribbon fell into a dozen pieces.

At the roadside ceremony, Whitney's widow, Marylou, was showered with mementos that included a certificate of the proclamation naming the highway and an American flag recently flown over the U.S. Capitol in her husband's honor.

"I can't think of anything in the world that would have pleased him more than having this highway named for him," she said at the gathering of several dozen onlookers. "His ancestors, the Whitneys and the Vanderbilts, loved this city and to have this here, where Broadway begins, is such an honor." She appeared moved by the dedication in her late husband's name.

Whitney died in 1992 at the age of 93, after a long life as a philanthropist and industrialist. Many of his missions of goodwill were bestowed upon Saratoga Springs, where he was a major benefactor of the Saratoga Performing Arts Center and National Museum of Dance and first president and co-founder of the National Museum of Racing and Hall of Fame of Saratoga Springs.

The section of Route 50 dedicated to Whitney runs between the end of North Broadway to Exit 15 of the Northway. A sign was erected on each end.

Having his name on Route 50 may be Whitney's first link with the nation's highway system, but Richard Maitino, who directs the state Department of Transportation's regional office, noted at Tuesday's ceremony that Whitney and his family have long been connected with transportation. Whitney's great-great-grandfather was the railroad magnate "Commodore" Cornelius Vanderbilt, and Whitney himself was a fighter pilot with American ace Eddie Rickenbacker in World War I, and founded Pan American World Airways in 1927.

If horsepower counts as transportation, Whitney can be counted as a leader in that related field as well. His thoroughbred farm in Lexington, Ky., was home to many of the country's finest horses, and Whitney once directed Churchill Downs in Louisville, home of the Kentucky Derby.

His stepson Frank Hobbs Hosford said Tuesday that a well-used highway is nonetheless an apt tribute to Whitney. "Mr. Whitney genuinely liked people. He knew wealthy people and he knew ordinary people, and he liked them all. I find it very appropriate that we have a very functional highway named for him, not a highway that does nothing." Hosford said. "He always wanted to make things useful to people."

Whitney's stepdaughter Heather Ann Schlacter said the family was pleasantly surprised to find that Assemblyman Robert "Bobby" D'Andrea and state Sens. Joseph Bruno and Ronald Stafford were instrumental in getting the road named for her stepfather.

"I think it's just wonderful. My father's done so much, and we're just so appreciative that they'd dedicate this highway to him," she said. "It's a real tribute to Daddy."

In 1994, the city of Saratoga Springs honored Whitney by naming Route 50 the C.V. Whitney Memorial Highway.

EPILOGUE

WHEN HE DIED, MUCH of the world tipped its hat in solemn appreciation for all he had done and all he had left as his legacy. Cornelius Vanderbilt Whitney had lived his life with a fullness that most men can only dream of, and he had left a lasting mark in broad and far-reaching arenas.

In the city of Saratoga Springs, where Whitney spent a good part of his life and his wealth, the Board of Supervisors dedicated its minutes for all 1992 meetings to his memory. In its proclamation, the board took note of Whitney's "steadfast support of the ambience and culture of Saratoga."[1]

The following summer, during racing season appropriately enough, a plaque commemorating his life and contributions was placed in Congress Park. That same summer a commemorative stamp cancellation of Whitney was offered at the Saratoga Race Course.

The following racing season, a section of Route 50 was renamed Whitney Way. During the ceremony, his widow was presented with the American flag that had been flown over the U.S. Capitol in his honor.

In 1994, Whitney also was inducted into the National Aviation Hall of Fame in Dayton, Ohio, with board of trustees member Betty Mosely noting that he "truly contributed to the development of aviation."[2]

And the little mountain town of Pineville, Kentucky, erected a monument to the man who had unfailingly visited several times a year and also named the town's convention center after him.

The Whitney largesse continued as well. In 1995 Marylou Whitney gave $50,000 in memory of her husband to the Gluck Equine Research Center of the University of Kentucky and $50,000 to the Jockey Club Research Center. Even years after his death, she continues to give away millions of dollars to charity in her husband's name.

But the true measure of a man, Whitney would have said, is not how many plaques or buildings are named for him or how many checks he wrote. It is that he made a contribution to the world and to the people of importance to him. And those people whom Whitney considered friends reaped profound and very personal benefits from their association with him.

"People who are well known often become branded with a shadow that causes everyone they

A memorial plaque honoring C.V. Whitney was placed in Saratoga Springs' Congress Park the summer after he died.

The C.V. Whitney Convention Center, so named before Whitney's death, stands in Pine Mountain Park, near Pineville, Kentucky.

meet to put a preconceived stamp on them before they have a chance to reveal themselves as worthy of respect," said Gloria Vanderbilt, when reflecting on her cousin's life. "But the important thing, really, finally, is how we are remembered by our family and friends and those whose lives we have touched. That is what is important in the end."[3]

And despite the shadow of fame that pursued him, Whitney left such a legacy. At the time of his death, a friend of his daughter Cornelia wrote a card that said, "As time goes by, you'll find that you didn't really lose your parent. He's always there with you." The first few weeks after Whitney's death, this was of no comfort to Cornelia. It seemed the sort of well-meant platitude that is always offered to the grief-stricken but which is of little real substance. "But as the year went by, I realized that she was right. Whenever I get in a difficult situation, I think, 'What would my father say?' And I know exactly what he would say. He's right here with me all the time."[4]

In keeping with Sonny's spirit, Marylou continued seeking new adventures after he died. In 1994, she sponsored a sleddog team and followed the entire 1,049-mile Iditarod race in Alaska. In November 1995, she spent three weeks trying to reach the South Pole with Norman Vaughan, who had been on Admiral Byrd's expedition. They reached the South Pole on December 4, 1995, on Norman's ninetieth birthday. And on April 16, 1996, Marylou and Norman accomplished a first in history when they brought the American flag from the South Pole to the North Pole.

On one of her adventures in Alaska, in 1993, she met John Hendrickson, a chief aide to Governor Walter J. Hickel and a former Alaskan tennis champion.

"Sonny told me so many times that he hoped I would meet and marry again someone of whom he would have approved," said Marylou. "I did what he requested and in 1997 married John [Hendrickson], who had such respect for the accomplishments of

C.V. Whitney that he commissioned this book to be written. If Sonny and John had ever met, they would have been good friends."[5]

But even when Marylou was happily remarried, Sonny remained a part of her life, as he did with many others. "Because he was larger than life to so many people, he will always be a major force in the lives he touched," she said. "In many ways, he has never died."[6]

Above: Marylou donated money to help build a senior center in the Adirondacks in honor of Sonny and Dave Short. Whitney's stepdaughter Heather and Marylou were on hand to dedicate the plaque, which now hangs on the side of the senior center building.

Right: After Whitney died, *The Blood-Horse* magazine, one of the thoroughbred industry's most important publications, devoted its cover to him. The cover story noted that he "lived the life of great inherited wealth but he lived it with an underlying urge for achievements and contributions of his own."

SIGNIFICANT EVENTS IN THE

1925

Whitney makes more than a million dollars from an innovative salvage operation called the Flin Flon Mine, which soon becomes the Hudson Bay Mining & Smelting Company, worth $30 million.

1947

Whitney goes to Washington to help organize the new U.S. Air Force as an assistant secretary. He eventually becomes assistant secretary of commerce under President Truman and special envoy to England, Luxembourg, Italy, and Spain.

1899

C.V. Whitney, also known as Sonny, is born in Roslyn, Long Island, into both the Vanderbilt and Whitney families.

1927

Whitney cofounds Pan American Airways and becomes the company's president.

| 1890 | 1900 | 1910 | 1920 | 1930 | 1940 |

1918

During WWI, Sonny becomes a second lieutenant in the Air Corps and begins training other men in piloting. He also serves in WWII, doing intelligence work in North Africa and earning several Pentagon positions.

1931

Whitney cofounds Selznick International, which makes such classics as *Rebecca, A Star Is Born,* and *Gone With the Wind.*

1937

Whitney founds Marineland, the world's first public oceanarium. The park quickly becomes a major Florida tourist attraction.

1939

After breeding and racing horses for several years, Whitney buys a stallion named Mahmoud, which begins siring a series of outstanding racers and brood mares.

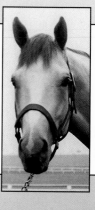

LIFE OF C.V. "SONNY" WHITNEY

1950

Whitney cofounds the National Museum of Racing and Hall of Fame (below). Over the years, he founds several other institutions including the Buffalo Bill Gallery of Western Art (right) in 1959 and the National Museum of Dance in 1986.

1966

Whitney receives the Distinguished Horseman tribute from the Thoroughbred Club of America. That same year, his oil paintings go on display for charity at the Palm Beach Galleries.

1966–1992

Over the years, Sonny and his wife Marylou are behind many social and cultural causes, giving time, energy, and cash to such events as the Olympics in Lake Placid and the Saratoga Performing Arts Center.

1950	1960	1970	1980	1990	2000

1956

C.V. Whitney Pictures releases the critically acclaimed movie *The Searchers,* starring John Wayne and Natalie Wood.

1988

Whitney publishes *The Owl Hoots Again*, a collection of short stories. Over the years he published several other books, including *Lone and Level Sands* in 1951, *First Flight* and *High Peaks* in 1977, and *Live a Year With a Millionaire* in 1981.

1992

Whitney dies on December 13, 1992, at age 93.

1958

Whitney marries Mary Louise Schroeder Hosford, also known as Marylou.

1960

The thirty-four horses Whitney races that year accumulate winnings that exceed $1 million.

NOTES TO SOURCES

Chapter One

1. "Family Values: The Vanderbilt Whitneys," by Brook Peters, *Quest*, Feb. 1994.
2. "A Legend Passes," *Saratogian*, Dec. 14, 1992, p. A-1; "Multibusiness Magnate Started Out as Mucker," by Mitch McKenney, *Palm Beach Post*, Dec. 14, 1992, p. 1A; "C.V. Whitney, Pillar of the Turf, Dead," by Steve Haskin, *Daily Racing Form*, Dec. 16, 1992, p. 1; "Horseman, Man for All Seasons, C.V. Whitney Dies," *Lexington Herald-Leader*, Dec. 14, 1992, p. A-1.
3. "Family Values: The Vanderbilt Whitneys," by Brook Peters, *Quest*, Feb. 1994.
4. Marylou Whitney, interviewed by Jeffrey L. Rodengen, July 15, 1999, transcript p. 132.
5. Gloria Vanderbilt, interviewed by Jeffrey L. Rodengen, Nov. 11, 1999, transcript pp. 1–2.
6. Jouett Redmon, interviewed by Sharon Peters, June 11, 1999, transcript p. 2.
7. Cornelia Vanderbilt Whitney Tobey, interviewed by Jeffrey L. Rodengen, Oct. 6, 1999, transcript p. 6.
8. Pamela LeBoutillier, interviewed by Jeffrey L. Rodengen, Aug. 24, 1999, transcript p. 10.
9. Linda Toohey, interviewed by Melody Maysonet, Oct. 21, 1999, transcript p. 13.
10. Information provided by Marylou Whitney, Dec. 1999.

Chapter Two

1. C.V. Whitney, *High Peaks* (Lexington, Ky.: University Press of Kentucky, 1977) p. 2.
2. C.V. Whitney, *High Peaks* (Lexington, Ky.: University Press of Kentucky, 1977) p. 3.
3. Edwin P. Hoyt, *The Whitneys, An Informal Portrait, 1635–1975* (New York: Weybright & Talley. 1976) p. 189.
4. Edwin P. Hoyt, *The Whitneys, An Informal Portrait, 1635–1975* (New York: Weybright & Talley, 1976) p. 192.
5. B.H. Friedman, *Gertrude Vanderbilt Whitney* (Doubleday, 1978) p. 207.
6. C.V. Whitney, *High Peaks* (Lexington, Ky.: University Press of Kentucky, 1977) p. 1.
7. Ibid.
8. Ibid.
9. Information provided by Marylou Whitney, Dec. 1999.
10. "The Whitneys: A World of the Never-Idle Rich," by Patricia Linden, *Town & Country*, Feb. 1981, p. 99.
11. Ibid.
12. Ibid.
13. E.J. Kahn, Jr., *Jock: The Life and Times of John Hay Whitney* (Doubleday, 1981) p. 35.
14. Edwin P. Hoyt, *The Whitneys, An Informal Portrait, 1635–1975* (New York: Weybright & Talley, 1976) p. 198.
15. "The Whitneys: A World of the Never-Idle Rich," by Patricia Linden, *Town & Country*, Feb. 1981, p. 99.
16. Ibid.
17. Ibid.
18. C.V. Whitney, *High Peaks* (Lexington, Ky.: University Press of Kentucky, 1977) p. 4.
19. Ibid.
20. "The Whitneys: A World of the Never-Idle Rich," by Patricia Linden, *Town & Country*, Feb. 1981, p. 99.

21. Edwin P. Hoyt, *The Whitneys, An Informal Portrait, 1635–1975* (New York: Weybright & Talley, 1976) p. 226.
22. Information provided by Marylou Whitney, Dec. 1999.
23. B.H Friedman, *Gertrude Vanderbilt Whitney* (Doubleday & Company, 1978) pp. 329–330.
24. C.V. Whitney, *High Peaks* (Lexington, Ky.: University Press of Kentucky, 1977) p. 4.

Sidebar Chapter Two, The Whitney Family Tree

1. Edwin P. Hoyt, *The Whitneys, An Informal Portrait, 1635–1975* (New York: Weybright & Talley, 1976) p. 126.
2. Edwin P. Hoyt, *The Whitneys, An Informal Portrait, 1635–1975* (New York: Weybright & Talley, 1976) p. 187.

Sidebar Chapter Two, The Vanderbilt Family

1. B.H. Friedman, *Gertrude Vanderbilt Whitney* (Doubleday & Company, 1978) p. 11.
2. B.H. Friedman, *Gertrude Vanderbilt Whitney* (Doubleday & Company, 1978) p. 15.

Chapter Three

1. C.V. Whitney, *High Peaks* (Lexington, Ky.: University Press of Kentucky, 1977) p. 4.
2. Ibid.
3. C.V. Whitney, *High Peaks* (Lexington, Ky.: University Press of Kentucky, 1977) p. 8.
4. Ibid.
5. C.V. Whitney, *First Flight* (Wayside Studio, 1989).
6. Ibid.
7. Ibid.
8. Ibid.
9. Ibid.
10. Ibid.
11. Ibid.
12. Ibid.
13. C.V. Whitney, *The Owl Hoots Again* (Sunstone Press, 1988) p. 11.
14. Letter to C.V. Whitney from Edward P. Wells, April 12, 1977.
15. Ibid.
16. C.V. Whitney, *High Peaks* (Lexington, Ky.: University Press of Kentucky, 1977) p. 8.
17. Edwin P. Hoyt, *The Whitneys, An Informal Portrait, 1635–1975* (New York: Weybright & Talley, 1976) p. 226.
18. "The Whitneys: A World of the Never-Idle Rich," by Patricia Linden, *Town & Country,* Feb. 1981, p. 108.

19. C.V. Whitney, *High Peaks* (Lexington, Ky.: University Press of Kentucky, 1977) p. 9.
20. B.H. Friedman, *Gertrude Vanderbilt Whitney* (Doubleday, 1978) p. 448.
21. B.H. Friedman, *Gertrude Vanderbilt Whitney,* (Doubleday, 1978) p. 449.
22. C.V. Whitney, *High Peaks* (Lexington, Ky.: University Press of Kentucky, 1977) p. 9.
23. Ibid.
24. C.V. Whitney, *High Peaks* (Lexington, Ky.: University Press of Kentucky, 1977) p. 10.
25. C.V. Whitney, *High Peaks* (Lexington, Ky.: University Press of Kentucky, 1977) p. 11.
26. C.V. Whitney, *High Peaks* (Lexington, Ky.: University Press of Kentucky, 1977) p. 14
27. B.H. Friedman, *Gertrude Vanderbilt Whitney* (Doubleday, 1978) p. 455.
28. Edwin P. Hoyt, *The Whitneys, An Informal Portrait, 1635–1975* (New York: Weybright & Talley, 1976) p. 228.

**Sidebar Chapter Three,
A Gift of Prose**

1. Sue Wylie, interviewed by Sharon Peters, June 10, 1999.

Chapter Four

1. Edwin P. Hoyt, *The Whitneys, An Informal Portrait, 1635–1975* (New York: Weybright & Talley, 1976) p. 225.
2. "Family Values: The Vanderbilt Whitneys," *Quest,* Feb. 1994.
3. Peter Duchin, *Ghost of a Chance, A Memoir* (Random House, 1996) p. 64.
4. Ibid.
5. Ibid.
6. Peter Duchin, *Ghost of a Chance, A Memoir* (Random House, 1996) p. 66.
7. C.V. Whitney, *High Peaks* (Lexington, Ky.: University Press of Kentucky, 1977) p. 18.
8. Ibid.
9. C.V. Whitney, *High Peaks* (Lexington, Ky.: University Press of Kentucky, 1977) p. 19.
10. C.V. Whitney, *High Peaks* (Lexington, Ky.: University Press of Kentucky, 1977) p. 20.
11. C.V. Whitney, *High Peaks* (Lexington, Ky.: University Press of

Kentucky, 1977) p. 24.
12. "C.V. Whitney; Scion of Two Noted Families," *Los Angeles Times,* Dec. 14, 1992, p. A32.
13. Peter Duchin, *Ghost of a Chance, A Memoir* (Random House, 1996) p. 70.

Chapter Five

1. Robert Daley, *An American Saga: Juan Trippe and His Pan Am Empire* (New York: Random House, 1980) p. 14.
2. Ibid.
3. "The 9 lives of the Cornelius Vanderbilt Whitneys," *Venture,* Oct. 1969, p. 47.
4. Robert Daley, *An American Saga: Juan Trippe and His Pan Am Empire* (New York, Random House, 1980) p. 27.
5. C.V. Whitney, *The Owl Hoots Again* (Santa Fe, N.M.: Sunstone Press, 1988) pp. 22, 23.
6. C.V. Whitney, *The Owl Hoots Again* (Santa Fe, N.M.: Sunstone Press, 1988) p. 35.
7. C.V. Whitney, *The Owl Hoots Again* (Santa Fe: N.M.: Sunstone Press, 1988) p. 45.
8. C.V. Whitney, *The Owl Hoots Again* (Santa Fe, N.M.: Sunstone Press, 1988) p. 45.

9. C.V. Whitney, *High Peaks* (Lexington, Ky.: University Press of Kentucky, 1977) p. 53.
10. C.V. Whitney, *High Peaks* (Lexington, Ky.: University Press of Kentucky, 1977) p. 54.
11. C.V. Whitney, *High Peaks* (Lexington, Ky.: University Press of Kentucky, 1977) p. 56.
12. C.V. Whitney, *High Peaks* (Lexington, Ky.: University Press of Kentucky, 1977) p. 57.
13. Robert Daley, *An American Saga: Juan Trippe and His Pan Am Empire* (New York: Random House, 1980) p. 231.
14. Merylin Bender and Selig Altschul, *The Chosen Instrument: Juan Trippe and Pan Am; The Rise and Fall of an American Entrepreneur* (New York: Simon and Schuster, 1982) p. 152.
15. "The Sportsman Pilot," by C.V. Whitney, July 1929.
16. Robert Daley, *An American Saga: Juan Trippe and His Pan Am Empire* (New York: Random House, 1980) p. 236.
17. Robert Daley, *An American Saga:*

Juan Trippe and His Pan Am Empire (New York: Random House, 1980) p. 238.

18. Merylin Bender and Selig Altschul, *The Chosen Instrument: Juan Trippe and Pan Am; The Rise and Fall of an American Entrepreneur* (New York: Simon and Schuster, 1982) p. 298.

19. Robert Daley, *An American Saga: Juan Trippe and His Pan Am Empire* (New York: Random House, 1980) p. 238.

20. Merylin Bender and Selig Altschul, *The Chosen Instrument: Juan Trippe and Pan Am; The Rise and Fall of an American Entrepreneur* (New York: Simon and Schuster, 1982) p. 298.

21. Robert Daley, *An American Saga: Juan Trippe and His Pan Am Empire* (New York: Random House, 1980) p. 239.

22. Robert Daley, *An America Saga: Juan Trippe and His Pan Am Empire* (New York: Random House, 1980) p. 247.

23. Merylin Bender and Selig Altschul, *The Chosen Instrument: Juan Trippe and Pan Am; The Rise and Fall of an American Entrepreneur* (New York: Simon and Schuster, 1982) p. 152.

Chapter Six

1. Edwin P. Hoyt, *The Whitneys, An Informal Portrait, 1635–1975* (New York: Weybright & Talley, 1976) p. 233.

2. "The Whitneys: A World of the Never-Idle Rich," by Patricia Linden, *Town & Country*, Feb. 1981, p. 108.

3. Edwin P. Hoyt, *The Whitneys, An Informal Portrait, 1635–1975* (New York: Weybright & Talley, 1976) p. 216.

4. Edwin P. Hoyt, *The Whitneys, An Informal Portrait, 1635–1975* (New York: Weybright & Talley, 1976) p. 225.

5. Edwin P. Hoyt, *The Whitneys*, An Informal Portrait, *1635–1975* (New York: Weybright & Talley, 1976) pp. 224, 225.

6. Marylou Whitney, interviewed by Jeffrey L. Rodengen, July 15, 1999, transcript p. 130.

7. Marylou Whitney, interviewed by Jeffrey L. Rodengen, July 15, 1999, transcript p. 131.

8. Edwin P. Hoyt, *The Whitneys, An Informal Portrait, 1635–1975* (New York: Weybright & Talley, 1976) p. 234.

9. "The Whitneys: A World of the Never-Idle Rich," by Patricia Linden, *Town & Country*, Feb. 1981, p. 107.

10. C.V. Whitney, *High Peaks* (Lexington, Ky.: University Press of Kentucky, 1977) p. 40.

11. C.V. Whitney, *High Peaks* (Lexington, Ky.: University Press of Kentucky, 1977) p. 41.

12. E.J. Kahn Jr., *The Life and Times of John Hay Whitney* (New York: Doubleday, 1981) p. 116.

13. Ibid.

14. Ibid.

15. C.V. Whitney, *High Peaks* (Lexington Ky.: University Press of Kentucky, 1977) p. 43.

16. Ibid.

17. C.V. Whitney, *High Peaks* (Lexington Ky.: University Press of Kentucky, 1977), p. 44.

18. C.V. Whitney, *High Peaks* (Lexington Ky.: University Press of Kentucky, 1977) pp. 45, 46.

19. "The Whitneys: A World of the Never-Idle Rich," by Patricia Linden, *Town & Country*, Feb. 1981, p. 109.

20. C.V. Whitney, *High Peaks* (Lexington Ky.: University Press of Kentucky, 1977) pp. 110, 111.

Sidebar Chapter Six, The Old Westbury Champs

1. C.V. Whitney, *High Peaks* (Lexington, Ky.:

University Press of
Kentucky, 1977)
p. 47.
2. Ibid.
3. C.V. Whitney, *High
Peaks,* (Lexington, Ky.:
University Press of
Kentucky, 1977)
p. 52.

**Sidebar Chapter Six,
The Politics of Prominence**

1. "What the Neighbors Say
of Candidate Sonny,"
Daily Mirror, Sept. 11,
1932.
2. "Long Island Social Circles
All Astir Over Whitney-
Bacon Race," *Auburn,
N.Y. Citizen Advertiser,*
Sept. 23, 1932.
3. "Whitney Picks Hardest
Way to Congress Seat,"
New York Herald Tribune,
Sept. 16, 1932, p. 4.
4. "Cornelius Vanderbilt
Whitney, New Candidate
for Congress, Says He Is
in Politics to Stay,"
Allentown [PA] *Chronicle
News,* Sept. 22, 1932.

Chapter Seven

1. Merylin Bender and
Selig Altschul, *The
Chosen Instrument*
(New York: Simon and
Schuster,1982) p. 299.
2. C.V. Whitney, Notes on
Mrs. Whitney's Suit for
Separation in the State
of New York, Dec. 11,
1957, p. 1.

3. C.V. Whitney, *Lone and
Level Sands* (New York:
Farrar, Straus and
Young, 1951) p. 9.
4. C.V. Whitney, *Lone and
Level Sands* (New York:
Farrar, Straus and
Young, 1951) p. 33.
5. C.V. Whitney, *Lone and
Level Sands* (New York:
Farrar, Straus and
Young, 1951) p. 34.
6. C.V. Whitney, *Lone and
Level Sands* (New York:
Farrar, Straus and
Young, 1951) pp. 40–41.
7. C.V. Whitney, *Lone and
Level Sands* (New York:
Farrar, Straus and
Young, 1951) p. 69.
8. C.V. Whitney, *Lone and
Level Sands* (New York:
Farrar, Straus and
Young, 1951) p. 70.
9. C.V. Whitney, *Lone and
Level Sands* (New York:
Farrar, Straus and
Young, 1951) p. 98.
10. C.V. Whitney, *Lone and
Level Sands* (New York:
Farrar, Straus and
Young, 1951) p. 132.
11. C.V. Whitney, *High
Peaks* (Lexington, Ky.:
University Press of
Kentucky, 1977)
p. 63.
12. C.V. Whitney, *High
Peaks* (Lexington, Ky.:
University Press of
Kentucky, 1977)
p. 64.
13. Ibid.
14. C.V. Whitney, *Lone and
Level Sands* (New York:

Farrar, Straus and
Young, 1951) p. 203.
15. C.V. Whitney, *High
Peaks* (Lexington, Ky.:
University Press of
Kentucky, 1977)
p. 70.
16. Ibid.
17. Ibid.
18. C.V. Whitney, *High
Peaks* (Lexington, Ky.:
University Press of
Kentucky, 1977)
p 72.
19. C.V. Whitney, *Lone and
Level Sands* (New York:
Farrar, Straus and
Young, 1951) p. 267.
20. C.V. Whitney, *Lone and
Level Sands* (New York:
Farrar, Straus and
Young, 1951) p. 275.
21. C.V. Whitney, *High
Peaks* (Lexington, Ky.:
University Press of
Kentucky, 1977)
p. 74.
22. C.V. Whitney, *Lone and
Level Sands* (New York:
Farrar, Straus and
Young, 1951) p. 298.
23. C.V. Whitney, *Lone and
Level Sands* (New York:
Farrar, Straus and
Young, 1951) p. 300.
24. Eleanor Searle Whitney,
Invitation to Joy (New
York: Harper & Row,
1971) p. 58.
25. Eleanor Searle Whitney,
Invitation to Joy (New
York: Harper & Row,
1971) p. 70.
26. Eleanor Searle Whitney,
Invitation to Joy (New

York: Harper & Row, 1971) p. 73.

27. "C.V. Whitney Is Named to Commerce Dept. Post," *New York Times,* Feb. 25, 1949, p. 10.

28. C.V. Whitney, Notes on Mrs. Whitney's Suit for Separation in the State of New York, Dec. 11, 1957, p. 2.

29. Ibid.

30. Ibid.

Chapter Eight

1. "Sonny Whitney: A Success in Spite of His Money," by Alfred Wright, *Sports Illustrated,* Sept. 4, 1961, p. 50.

2. Joe Hirsch, interviewed by David Patten, July 29, 1999, transcript pp. 9–10.

3. "C.V. Whitney: A Heritage, A Legend," by Bob Stokhaug, *Thoroughbred Record,* Dec. 6, 1975, p. 1890.

4. "C.V. Whitney, A Heritage, A Legend," by Bob Stokhaug, *Thoroughbred Record,* Dec. 6, 1975, p. 1891.

5. C.V. Whitney, *High Peaks* (Lexington, Ky.: University Press of Kentucky. 1977) p. 26.

6. Ibid.

7. "The Whitneys: A World of the Never-Idle Rich," by Patricia Linden,

Town & Country, Feb. 1981, p. 108.

8. C.V. Whitney, *High Peaks* (Lexington, Ky.: University Press of Kentucky, 1977) p. 33.

9. Ibid.

10. C.V. Whitney, *High Peaks* (Lexington, Ky.: University Press of Kentucky, 1977) p. 35.

11. C.V. Whitney, *High Peaks* (Lexington, Ky.: University Press of Kentucky, 1977) p. 36.

12. C.V. Whitney, *High Peaks* (Lexington, Ky.: University Press of Kentucky, 1977) p. 37.

13. C.V. Whitney, *High Peaks* (Lexington, Ky.: University Press of Kentucky, 1977) p. 38.

14. C.V. Whitney, *High Peaks* (Lexington, Ky.: University Press of Kentucky, 1977) p. 38.

15. "Sonny Whitney: A Success in Spite of His Money," by Alfred Wright, *Sports Illustrated,* Sept. 4, 1961, p. 53.

16. Ibid.

17. Joe Hirsch, interviewed by David Patten, July 29, 1999, transcript p. 2.

18. Joe Hirsch, interviewed by David

Patten, July 29, 1999, transcript p. 3.

19. Joe Hirsch, interviewed by David Patten, July 29, 1999, transcript p. 9.

20. Joe Hirsch, interviewed by David Patten, July 29, 1999, transcript p. 11.

21. C.V. Whitney, *High Peaks* (Lexington, Ky.: University Press of Kentucky, 1977) p. 77.

22. Maureen Lewi, interviewed by Melody Maysonet, Nov. 2, 1999, transcript p. 34.

23. Abram S. Hewitt, *The Great Breeders and Their Methods,* p. 93.

24. Ibid.

25. Leverett Miller, interviewed by Melody Maysonet, Oct. 26, 1999, transcript p. 10.

26. Leverett Miller, interviewed by Melody Maysonet, Oct. 26, 1999, transcript p. 15.

Sidebar Chapter Eight, From the Horse Breeder's Mouth

1. "C.V. Whitney: A Heritage, A Legend," by Bob Stokhaug, *Thoroughbred Record,* Dec. 6, 1975, p. 1889.

2. Ibid.

3. Information obtained from Hobbs Hosford, Dec. 1999.

4. "A Pretty Lady Beats the Boys," by James Murray,

Sports Illustrated, March 16, 1969, p. 21.
5. "C.V. Whitney: A Heritage, A Legend," by Bob Stokhaug, *Thoroughbred Record,* Dec. 6, 1975, p. 1916.

Sidebar Chapter Eight, The Gift Horse That Kept on Giving

1. Dr. Benjamin Roach, interviewed by Melody Maysonet, Sept. 7, 1999, transcript p. 1.

Sidebar Chapter Eight, Angus Pride

1. Jouett Redmon, interviewed by Sharon Peters, June 11, 1999, transcript p. 2.
2. Ibid.
3. Ibid.
4. Ibid.
5. Ted Bassett, interviewed by Sharon Peters, Aug. 31, 1999, transcript p. 1.
6. Ibid.

Chapter Nine

1. Eleanor Searle Whitney, *Invitation to Joy* (New York: Harper & Row, 1971) p. 94.
2. C.V. Whitney, Notes on Mrs. Whitney's Suit for Separation in the State of New York, Dec. 11, 1957, p. 3.

3. *The Missouri Traveler* publicity booklet, p. 2.
4. "Hollywood Newcomer," *New York Times,* April 1, 1956.
5. *The Missouri Traveler* publicity booklet, p. 5.
6. Eleanor Searle Whitney, *Invitation to Joy* (New York: Harper & Row, 1971) p. 2.
7. Eleanor Searle Whitney, *Invitation to Joy* (New York: Harper & Row, 1971) p. 121.
8. Mrs. Cornelius Vanderbilt Whitney, *One Cook's Tour,* p. 5.
9. Ibid.
10. Mrs. Cornelius Vanderbilt Whitney, *One Cook's Tour,* p. 6.
11. Mrs. Cornelius Vanderbilt Whitney, *One Cook's Tour,* p. 24.
12. Mrs. Cornelius Vanderbilt Whitney, *One Cook's Tour,* p. 56.
13. Mrs. Cornelius Vanderbilt Whitney, *One Cook's Tour,* p. 57.
14. Mrs. Cornelius Vanderbilt Whitney, *One Cook's Tour,* p. 80.
15. Marylou Whitney, interviewed by Jeffrey L. Rodengen, Nov. 23, 1999, transcript p. 11.
16. Marylou Whitney, interviewed by Jeffrey L. Rodengen, July 15, 1999, transcript p. 87.
17. C.V. Whitney, *High Peaks* (Lexington, Ky.: University Press of

Kentucky, 1977) p. 85.
18. Marylou Whitney, interviewed by Jeffrey L. Rodengen, July 15, 1999, transcript p. 88.
19. Ibid.
20. Marylou Whitney, interviewed by Jeffrey L. Rodengen, July 15, 1999, transcript p. 89.
21. Marylou Whitney, interviewed by Jeffrey L. Rodengen, July 15, 1999, transcript p. 91.
22. Ibid.
23. Marylou Whitney, interviewed by Jeffrey L. Rodengen, July 15, 1999, transcript p. 90.
24. *The Missouri Traveler* publicity booklet, p. 4.
25. Ibid.
26. Eleanor Searle Whitney, *Invitation to Joy* (New York: Harper & Row, 1971) p. 123.
27. Marylou Whitney, interviewed by Jeffrey L. Rodengen, July 15, 1999, transcript p. 94.
28. Ibid.
29. Information obtained from Marylou Whitney, Dec. 1999.
30. Marylou Whitney, interviewed by Jeffrey L. Rodengen, Nov. 23, 1999, transcript p. 13.

Chapter Ten

1. Mrs. Cornelius Vanderbilt Whitney, *One Cook's Tour,* p. 192.

2. C.V. Whitney, *High Peaks*, (Lexington, Ky.: University Press of Kentucky, 1977) p. 90.
3. Marylou Whitney, *Cornelia Vanderbilt Whitney's Dollhouse* (Farrar, Straus & Giroux, 1975) p. 17.
4. Information provided by Marylou Whitney, Dec. 1999.
5. Marylou Whitney, *Cornelia Vanderbilt Whitney's Dollhouse* (Farrar, Straus & Giroux, 1975) p. 18.
6. Marylou Whitney, interviewed by Jeffrey L. Rodengen, July 15, 1999, transcript pp. 100–101, 104.
7. Budd Calisch, interviewed by Melody Maysonet, Nov. 5, 1999, transcript p. 5.
8. Marylou Whitney, interviewed by Jeffrey L. Rodengen, July 15, 1999, transcript p. 102.
9 "Reveries of Camp Deerlands," by Maria Bucciferro, *Adirondack Life*, Aug. 1988, pp. 122, 123.
10. Gerta Conner, interviewed by Jeffrey L. Rodengen, Oct. 19, 1999, transcript pp. 4, 10.
11. Gerta Conner, interviewed by Jeffrey L. Rodengen, Oct. 19, 1999, transcript p. 2.
12. Gerta Conner, interviewed by Jeffrey

L. Rodengen, Oct. 19, 1999, transcript pp. 4, 5.
13. Information provided by Hank Hosford, Jan. 7, 2000.
14. Marylou Whitney, interviewed by Jeffrey L. Rodengen, July 15, 1999, transcript pp. 99–100.
15. "Hello Marylou," *W*, Sept. 7–14, 1984, p. 18.
16. "Reveries of Camp Deerlands," by Maria Bucciferro, *Adirondack Life*, Aug. 1988, p. 68.
17. Budd Calisch, interviewed by Melody Maysonet, Nov. 5, 1999, transcript pp. 13–14.
18. Heather Mabee, interviewed by Jeffrey L. Rodengen, Sept. 23, 1999, transcript p. 21.
19. Information provided by M'lou Llewellyn, Dec. 1999.
20. Hobbs Hosford, interviewed by Jeffrey L. Rodengen, Sept. 21, 1999, transcript p. 3.
21. Information provided by M'lou Llewellyn, Dec. 1999.
22. Cornelia Vanderbilt Whitney Tobey, interviewed by Jeffrey L. Rodengen, Oct. 6, 1999, transcript p. 2.
23. Information provided by M'lou Llewellyn, Dec. 1999.
24. Heather Mabee, interviewed by Jeffrey

L. Rodengen, Sept. 23, 1999, transcript p. 14.
25. Information provided by M'lou Llewellyn, Dec. 1999.
26. Heather Mabee, interviewed by Jeffrey L. Rodengen, Sept. 23, 1999, transcript p. 13.
27. Jouett Redmon, interviewed by Sharon Peters, June 11, 1999, transcript p. 2.
28. Louie B. Nunn, interviewed by Melody Maysonet, Nov. 2, 1999, transcript pp. 3–4.
29. Louie B. Nunn, interviewed by Melody Maysonet, Nov. 2, 1999, transcript p. 12.
30. Information provided by Marylou Whitney, Jan. 2000.
31. Robert Mason Combs, interviewed by Melody Maysonet, Jan. 6, 2000, transcript p. 10.
32. Hobbs Hosford, interviewed by Jeffrey L. Rodengen, Oct. 6, 1999, transcript p. 12.
33. "Weddings, Parties and People," by Earl Blackwell, *Town & Country*, April 1965, p. 20.
34. Dr. Benjamin Roach, interviewed by Melody Maysonet, Sept. 7, 1999, transcript p. 7.
35. "Parties Are Part of My Job," by Enid Nemy, *Good Housekeeping*, Aug. 1982, p. NY3.

36. Gerta Conner, interviewed by Jeffrey L. Rodengen, Oct. 19, 1999, transcript p. 14.

37. Linda Toohey, interviewed by Melody Maysonet, Oct. 21, 1999, transcript p. 8.

38. "How Christmas Makes Scents," *Town & Country*, Christmas 1969, p. 162.

39. "The Woman Who Lost $780,000 in Jewels but Still Has Everything," by Gael Greene, *Ladies' Home Journal*, Nov. 1968, p. 109.

40. Ibid.

41. "Kentucky's Far-Famed Derby Hostesses," *Town & Country*, April 1970, p. 87.

42. Interview, *Louisville* magazine, April 1976, p. 90.

43. Dr. Benjamin Roach, interviewed by Melody Maysonet, Sept. 3, 1999, transcript p. 19.

44. C.V. Whitney, *High Peaks* (Lexington, Ky.: University Press of Kentucky, 1977, p. 103.

45. Ibid.

46. C.V. Whitney, *High Peaks* (Lexington, Ky.: University Press of Kentucky, 1977) p. 105.

47. Dr. Benjamin Roach, interviewed by Melody Maysonet, Sept. 3, 1999, transcript p. 2.

48. Heather Mabee, interviewed by Jeffrey L. Rodengen, Sept. 23, 1999, transcript p. 6.

49. Information provided by M'lou Llewellyn, Dec. 1999.

50. Heather Mabee, interviewed by Jeffrey L. Rodengen, Sept. 23, 1999, transcript p. 8.

51. Heather Mabee, interviewed by Jeffrey L. Rodengen, Sept. 23, 1999, transcript p. 7.

52. Cornelia Vanderbilt Whitney Tobey, interviewed by Jeffrey L. Rodengen, Oct. 6, 1999, transcript p. 4.

53. Heather Mabee, interviewed by Jeffrey L. Rodengen, Sept. 23, 1999, transcript p. 9.

54. Jouett Redmon, interviewed by Sharon Peters, June 11, 1999, transcript p. 3.

55. Marylou Whitney, interviewed by Jeffrey L. Rodengen, July 15, 1999, transcript p. 134.

56. Ibid.

57. Ibid.

58. Cornelia Vanderbilt Whitney Tobey, interviewed by Jeffrey L. Rodengen, Oct. 6, 1999, transcript p. 7.

59. Heather Mabee, interviewed by Jeffrey L. Rodengen, Sept. 23, 1999, transcript p. 1.

60. Cornelia Vanderbilt Whitney Tobey, interviewed by Jeffrey L. Rodengen, Oct. 6, 1999, transcript p. 6.

61. Linda Toohey, interviewed by Melody Maysonet, Sept. 21, 1999, transcript p. 10.

62. Jeannette Jordan, interviewed by Melody Maysonet, Sept. 15, 1999, transcript p. 4.

63. Dr. Benjamin Roach, interviewed by Melody Maysonet, Sept. 7, 1999, transcript p. 13.

64. Cornelia Vanderbilt Whitney Tobey, interviewed by Jeffrey L. Rodengen, Oct. 6, 1999, transcript p. 12.

65. Hobbs Hosford, interviewed by Jeffrey L. Rodengen, Oct. 6, 1999, transcript p. 8.

66. Flora Biddle, interviewed by Jeffrey L. Rodengen, Sept. 23, 1999, transcript pp. 2–3.

67. Flora Biddle, interviewed by Jeffrey L. Rodengen, Sept. 23, 1999, transcript p. 3.

68. Dr. Benjamin Roach, interviewed by Melody Maysonet, Sept. 3, 1999, transcript p. 6.

69. C.V. Whitney, *High Peaks* (Lexington, Ky.: University Press of Kentucky, 1977) p. 114.

70. C.V. Whitney, *High Peaks* (Lexington, Ky.: University Press of Kentucky, 1977) p. 118.

71. Maureen Lewi, interviewed by Melody Maysonet, Nov. 2, 1999, transcript p. 15.

72. Dr. Benjamin Roach, interviewed by Melody Maysonet, Sept. 7, 1999, transcript p. 4.

73. Dr. Benjamin Roach, interviewed by Melody Maysonet, Sept. 7, 1999, transcript pp. 5–6.

**Sidebar Chapter Ten,
In Touch with Tranquility**

1. Marylou Whitney, interviewed by Jeffrey L. Rodengen, July 15, 1999, transcript p. 103.

2. Information provided by Marylou Whitney, Dec. 1999.

3. "Final Flight: A Tribute to C.V. Whitney," by Robert Mason Combs, *Pineville Sun,* May 27, 1993.

4. Robert Mason Combs, interviewed by Melody Maysonet, Jan. 6, 2000, transcript pp. 11–12.

5. Dr. Benjamin Roach, interviewed by Melody Maysonet, Sept. 3, 1999, transcript p. 26.

6. Dr. Benjamin Roach, interviewed by Melody Maysonet, Sept. 3, 1999, transcript p. 25.

7. Hobbs Hosford, interviewed by Jeffrey L. Rodengen, Sept. 21, 1999, transcript pp. 4–5.

8. Cornelia Vanderbilt Whitney Tobey, interviewed by Jeffrey L. Rodengen, Oct. 6, 1999, transcript p. 7.

9. Information provided by M'lou Llewellyn, Dec. 1999.

10. Jouett Redmon, interviewed by Sharon Peters, June 11, 1999, transcript p. 3.

11. Marylou Whitney, interviewed by Jeffrey L. Rodengen, Nov. 23, 1999, transcript p. 22.

**Sidebar Chapter Ten,
A Boost for Saratoga**

1. Jeannette Jordan, interviewed by Melody Maysonet, Sept. 15, 1999, transcript p. 2.

2. Maureen Lewi, interviewed by Melody Maysonet, Nov. 2, 1999, transcript p. 39.

Chapter Eleven

1. Heather Mabee, interviewed by Jeffrey L. Rodengen, Nov. 9, 1999, transcript p. 1.

2. "For the Whitneys It's Homes Sweet Homes," *Lexington Herald-Leader,* April 27, 1985, p. D-1.

3. Ibid.

4. Marylou Whitney, interviewed by Jeffrey L. Rodengen, Nov. 23, 1999, transcript p. 17.

5. Linda Toohey, interviewed by Melody

Maysonet, Oct. 21, 1999, transcript p. 6.

6. "In the Adirondacks: The Last of the Great Camps," *M,* Dec. 1984, p. 47.

7. Ed Lewi, interviewed by Melody Maysonet, Nov. 2, 1999, transcript p. 31.

8. "The Brook Trout of Little Tupper Lake — Treasure or Tragedy?" Essay by John E. Adamski.

9. Maureen Lewi, interviewed by Melody Maysonet, Nov. 2, 1999, transcript p. 31.

10. "The Brook Trout of Little Tupper Lake — Treasure or Tragedy?" Essay by John E. Adamski.

11. "The Woman Who Lost $780,000 in Jewels but Still Has Everything," by Gael Greene, *Ladies' Home Journal,* Nov. 1968, p. 188.

12. "Society's Dramatic Dynamo," *Kansas City Star,* March 28, 1990, p. F-1.

**Sidebar Chapter Eleven,
Cornelia's Dollhouse**

1. Budd Calisch, interviewed by Melody Maysonet, Nov. 5, 1999, transcript p. 21.

2. Marylou Whitney, interviewed by Jeffrey L. Rodengen, Nov. 23, 1999, transcript pp. 7–8.

3. Budd Calisch, interviewed by Melody Maysonet, Nov. 5, 1999, transcript p. 22.

Chapter Twelve

1. "Inside Fashion," *New York Post,* June 14, 1977, p. 27.
2. Marylou Whitney, interviewed by Jeffrey L. Rodengen, Nov. 23, 1999, transcript p. 22.
3. "The Cornelius Vanderbilt Whitneys," *Daily Palm Beacher,* March 4 and 5, 1978.
4. "Suzy Knickerbocker," *World Journal Tribune,* Oct. 2, 1966.

Chapter Thirteen

1. Ted Bassett, interviewed by Sharon Peters, Aug. 31, 1999, transcript pp. 1–2.
2. Louie B. Nunn, interviewed by Melody Maysonet, Nov. 5, 1999, transcript p. 3.
3. Louie B. Nunn, interviewed by Melody Maysonet, Nov. 5, 1999, transcript p. 9.
4. "Splendor: The Great Whitney Way," *Town & Country,* Sept. 1969.
5. Ginger Rogers, *Ginger, My Story* (HarperCollins Publishers, 1991) p. 79.
6. Heather Mabee, interviewed by Jeffrey

L. Rodengen, Nov. 9, 1999, transcript p. 3.

Chapter Fourteen

1. "Whitneys Find Relaxation At Their Easels," *Sun Sentinel,* March 3, 1978, p. 1C.
2. Budd Calisch, interviewed by Melody Maysonet, Nov. 5, 1999, transcript pp. 8–9.
3. Information provided by Marylou Whitney, Dec. 1999.
4. Linda Toohey, interviewed by Melody Maysonet, Oct. 21, 1999, transcript p. 13.
5. Linda Toohey, interviewed by Melody Maysonet, Oct. 21, 1999, transcript p. 14.
6. "C.V. Whitney Has Emergency Surgery on Weakened Artery," *Louisville Courier-Journal,* Dec. 13, 1984.
7. "Whitney's Decision to Retire," *Saratogian,* Aug. 26, 1984, p. 1.
8. Marylou Whitney, interviewed by Jeffrey Rodengen, Nov. 23, 1999, transcript pp. 15, 16.
9. Dr. Benjamin Roach, interviewed by Melody Maysonet, Sept. 3, 1999, transcript p. 11.
10. Ibid.
11. Heather Mabee, interviewed by Jeffrey L. Rodengen,

Sept. 23, 1999, transcript p. 17.
12. Ibid.
13. Heather Mabee, interviewed by Jeffrey L. Rodengen, Sept. 23, 1999 p. 18.
14. "Whitney's First Obligation: Sportsmanship," by Joe Hirsch, *Daily Racing Form,* Jan. 9, 1985, p. 13.
15. "Eye Is Everywhere," *Women's Wear Daily,* Feb. 21, 1985.
16. Marylou Whitney's diary of the Pan Am commemorative flight.
17. Ibid.
18. Dr. Benjamin Roach, interviewed by Melody Maysonet, Sept. 3, 1999, transcript p. 24.
19. Marylou Whitney, interviewed by Jeffrey L. Rodengen, July 15, 1999, transcript p. 71.
20. Marylou Whitney, interviewed by Jeffrey L. Rodengen, July 15, 1999, transcript p. 105.
21. Jeannette Jordan, interviewed by Melody Maysonet, Sept. 15, 1999, transcript p. 4
22. Marylou Whitney, interviewed by Jeffrey L. Rodengen, Nov. 23, 1999, transcript p. 3.
23. Leverett Miller, interviewed by Melody Maysonet, Oct. 26, 1999, transcript p. 19.

24. Heather Mabee, interviewed by Jeffrey L. Rodengen, Sept. 23, 1999, transcript p. 16.

25. Cornelia Vanderbilt Whitney Tobey, interviewed by Jeffrey L. Rodengen, Oct. 6, 1999, transcript pp. 8–9.

26. Information provided by Marylou Whitney, Jan. 4, 2000.

27. Heather Mabee, interviewed by Jeffrey L. Rodengen, Sept. 23, 1999, transcript p. 22.

Sidebar Chapter Fourteen, Spreading the Wealth

1. Ed Lewi, interviewed by Melody Maysonet, Nov. 2, 1999, transcript pp. 5–6.

Epilogue

1. Letter to Marylou Whitney from Philip W. Kelin, chairman of the board of supervisors, Dec. 23, 1992.

2. Letter to Marylou Whitney from Betty Mosely, Jan. 7, 1993.

3. Gloria Vanderbilt, interviewed by Jeffrey L. Rodengen, Nov. 11, 1999, transcript pp. 10, 11.

4. Cornelia Vanderbilt Whitney Tobey, interviewed by Jeffrey L. Rodengen, Oct. 6, 1999, transcript p. 11.

5. Information provided by Marylou Whitney, Feb. 2000.

6. Ibid.

Index